Working with Specialized Language

'An intelligent and accessible book which meets a real need. Anyone who wants to know what a corpus is and what you can do with one should reach for this book first.'

Raphael Salkie, University of Brighton, UK

Working with Specialized Language: a practical guide to using corpora introduces the principles of using corpora when studying specialized language.

The resources and techniques used to investigate general language cannot be easily adapted for specialized investigations. This book is designed especially for users of language for special purposes (LSP). Providing guidelines and practical advice, it enables LSP users to design, build and exploit corpus resources that meet their specialized language needs. Highly practical and accessible, the book includes exercises, glossary and an appendix describing relevant corpora and corpus analysis software.

Working with Specialized Language is ideal for translators, technical writers and subject specialists who are interested in exploring the potential of a corpus-based approach to teaching and learning LSP.

The accompanying web site can be found at:
www.routledge.com/textbooks/0415236991/

Lynne Bowker is Assistant Professor in Translation at the University of Ottawa, Canada. She is the author of *Computer-Aided Translation Technology* (2002) and, with Jennifer Pearson, one of the editors of *Unity in Diversity? Current Trends in Translation Studies* (1998) and *Bibliography of Translation Studies* (1998, 1999, 2000, 2001). **Jennifer Pearson**, until recently Senior Lecturer in Translation Studies at Dublin City University, Ireland, is Chief of Translation at UNESCO Headquarters, Paris, France. She is the author of *Terms in Context* (1998).

Working with Specialized Language

A practical guide to using corpora

Lynne Bowker and
Jennifer Pearson

London and New York

First published 2002
by Routledge
11 New Fetter Lane, London EC4P 4EE

Simultaneously published in the USA and Canada
by Routledge
29 West 35th Street, New York, NY 10001

Routledge is an imprint of the Taylor & Francis Group

© 2002 Lynne Bowker and Jennifer Pearson

Typeset in Sabon by
Florence Production Ltd, Stoodleigh, Devon
Printed and bound in Great Britain by
St Edmundsbury Press, Bury St Edmunds, Suffolk

British Library Cataloguing in Publication Data
A catalogue record for this book is available from the
British Library

Library of Congress Cataloging in Publication Data
Bowker, Lynne.
  Working with specialized language: a practical guide to using
  corpora / Lynne Bowker and Jennifer Pearson.
    p. cm.
  Includes bibliographical references and index.
  ISBN 0–415–23698–3 — ISBN 0–415–23699–1 (pbk.)
  1. Sublanguage—Data processing. I. Pearson, Jennifer. II. Title.
P120.S9 B69 2002
418'.00285—dc21   2002069960

ISBN 0–415–23698–3 (hbk)
ISBN 0–415–23699–1 (pbk)

Contents

Figures

Acknowledgements

Completion of this book would not have been possible without the assistance of several individuals and institutions. The authors would like to thank the reviewers who gave feedback on an early draft of part of this book. They are also deeply indebted to Françoise Blin, Maggie Gibbon and Dorothy Kenny at Dublin City University for their willingness to read and comment on the work in progress.

Concordances from *Scientific American* are used with permission from Scientific American, Inc. All rights are reserved. Concordances from *Pour la Science* are used with permission from Pour la Science.

Screen shots from WordSmith Tools, MultiConcord and ParaConc are used with the kind permission of Michael Scott, David Wools and Michael Barlow respectively.

Jennifer Pearson would like to thank Dublin City University and her colleagues in the School of Applied Language and Intercultural Studies for giving her the time to complete this project. She would also like to thank Daniel for his moral support, patience and enduring good humour.

Lynne Bowker would like to acknowledge the support of the Social Sciences and Humanities Research Council of Canada and the University of Ottawa. On a more personal note, she would also like to thank Peter, Lisa, Joyce and Keith, who were a constant source of encouragement and support.

Introduction

If you have picked up this book, you may be looking for answers to questions such as 'What exactly are **corpora**?' and 'How can I use corpora to help me learn a specialized language?' The aim of this book is to answer such questions.

Corpora are essentially large collections of text in electronic form. They are stored on computers and can be manipulated with the help of software known as corpus analysis tools. Corpora are a wonderful resource for people interested in studying language, but the way that people interact with corpora is different from the way they interact with printed texts. Typically, you interact with printed texts by consulting them one at a time and reading them sequentially from beginning to end. In contrast, when you investigate a **corpus**, you usually look at small fragments of a text (e.g. individual words or single lines of text), and you can look at multiple fragments simultaneously. Does this sound confusing? Do not worry; it is actually quite straightforward.

Corpora are becoming a very popular resource for people who want to learn more about language use. Most of the corpora that are currently used by language students contain texts written in language for general purposes (**LGP**) – the kind of everyday language that you find in newspapers, for example. If you are interested in learning more about using corpora for LGP investigations, you can consult a number of publications, including Sinclair (1991), Barnbrook (1996), McEnery and Wilson (1996), Stubbs (1996), Aston and Burnard (1998), Biber et al. (1998), Kennedy (1998), Partington (1998) and Tognini-Bonelli (2001).

More recently, however, teachers and students of language for special purposes (**LSP**) have begun to wonder whether corpora could also be used for LSP investigations. The answer is a resounding 'yes'! Corpora have a lot to offer to you as an LSP user, but sometimes it is hard to know where to begin. There are very few publications available that provide guidance on using corpora to study LSP, so that is why we have written this book. Whether you are a student, a language teacher or a practitioner (e.g. a translator or technical writer), our aim is to show you how to go about using corpora and corpus analysis tools in your own LSP investigations.

How to use this book

This book is designed to give you all the information you need to begin working with corpora that contain specialized language. There are a number of different ways in which you can consult this book, depending on the nature of your LSP needs and on the level of experience that you have. If you are new to the world of corpora, you might like to start at the beginning of the book, where you will learn the basic concepts and principles of working with corpora. You can then move on to the chapters on designing and compiling corpora, followed by the chapters on how to use corpus analysis tools, and finally you can consult some of the chapters that outline specific applications. In contrast, if you have already worked with corpora (e.g. in an LGP context), you may choose to go directly to the chapters that describe LSP applications. Then, once you have some ideas about how LSP corpora can be used, you may decide to go back and consult the chapters that tell you how to go about building your own LSP corpora. We encourage all readers to begin by reading Chapters 1 and 2, which introduce corpora and LSP respectively. Where you go from there is up to you. The following outline of the contents may be useful for helping you decide where to begin.

Outline

The book is divided into three main parts. The first part (Introduction to Chapter 2) provides an introduction to the book, to corpora and to LSP. It presents the basic concepts, principles and practices underlying the creation and use of language corpora and, most importantly, it explains why you might want to consider using corpora to help you investigate LSP. The second part (Chapters 3 to 7) provides a practical introduction to corpus-based studies. It explains how to design and compile monolingual and multilingual corpora for special purposes, how and why to tag and align texts to aid LSP studies, and how to interact with corpora using specially designed corpus analysis tools. The final part (Chapters 8 to 12) looks at some specific applications of special purpose corpora. It explains how to exploit corpora for applications such as terminology extraction, glossary building, technical writing and translation. It also looks at the ways in which corpus analysis tools are being customized for use in LSP investigations. In addition, the book contains a glossary explaining relevant concepts and terms, as well as an appendix listing a variety of corpus-related tools and resources.

Part I: Setting the scene

Following the Introduction, Chapter 1 introduces corpora and corpus analysis tools. Here you will learn the basic terminology of the field (e.g. corpus, **general reference corpora**, special purpose corpora, **parallel and comparable corpora, concordance, types, tokens**). You will also find out why and how corpora are useful for investigating language, particularly as compared to more conventional resources such as dictionaries or printed texts.

Chapter 2 introduces the notion of language for special purposes (LSP) by explaining how this is different from language for general purposes (LGP). In this chapter, you will learn about different types of LSP users and different levels of LSP communication. Most importantly, you will find out why it is important to learn a specialized language and how learning a specialized language is different from learning specialized subject matter (i.e. how learning the language of chemistry is different from learning chemistry). Of course, you will also find out how corpora can help with LSP acquisition.

Part II: Corpus design, compilation and processing

Chapter 3 explores issues relating to corpus design by outlining the criteria that are typically applied in the compilation of general purpose corpora and considering which of these are relevant for the design of special purpose corpora. These criteria include size, text extracts vs full texts, number of texts, medium, subject, text type, authorship, language and publication date. To help you understand how these criteria come into play during the corpus design stage, this chapter also presents a case study that culminates in the creation of a 'wish list' of texts to include in a corpus.

Chapter 4 moves beyond design issues to address techniques for corpus compilation. This chapter takes you through the various stages of text collection and corpus compilation, explaining where to find texts, how to obtain permission to use them, and how to retrieve and store them. In particular, you will discover the potential of the World Wide Web and CD-ROMs as resources for building corpora and you will continue to follow the case study as it examines practical problems that may hinder the construction of your 'ideal' corpus.

In Chapter 5, you will be introduced to the concepts of markup and annotation. Here, you will take a look at different types of **markup** and **annotation** systems and their uses in corpus-based investigations. First, you will learn about markup systems that determine the appearance of documents, as well as those that represent the structure of documents. Next, you will find out about different types of annotation systems, particularly those used for **part-of-speech tagging** (**POS**). A number of examples are used to show you how corpus tagging can allow you to refine your queries. For instance, with a tagged corpus, you can specify the grammatical category of the lexical items that you wish to investigate (e.g. noun + noun combinations).

Chapter 6 begins by considering two different types of bilingual and multilingual corpora – namely parallel and comparable corpora – and then goes on to focus on parallel corpora alone. Here you will get a brief overview of the applications of parallel corpora, as well as an introduction to issues surrounding the collection and selection of texts to be included in a parallel corpus. Since you will probably find it useful to align your corpora in order to optimize your investigations, you are shown how to pre-process and align your texts. Practical examples are provided to give you some indication of how parallel corpora can help with language learning and translation.

In Chapter 7, you will find out about the basic processing tools used in **corpus linguistics**: word listers and concordancers. By following practical examples, you will learn how to produce and interpret **word lists** and concordances. For instance, you will discover how to read concordances to identify **knowledge-rich contexts** (i.e. contexts that reveal something about the meaning or usage of terms), and how to use concordances in order to identify domain-specific linguistic patterns.

Part III: Corpus-based applications in LSP

Chapter 8 shows you how to use corpora and corpus processing tools to produce **glossaries**. It starts by considering what glossaries are and why they might be necessary. Then, using examples, issues such as **term** selection, formulation of definitions, content and layout of glossaries are discussed. Particular attention is paid to phraseology and the building of conceptual frameworks within special subject domains. It shows you how to compile and maintain useful glossaries of the terminology and phraseology of specialized disciplines. Such glossaries will be useful if you are doing tasks such as translation or technical writing.

Chapter 9 outlines the approaches used in term recognition and extraction and explains how you can adapt some of these techniques for use in LSP studies. Using these tools, you can get a head start on glossary compilation by searching through corpora and extracting lists of potential terms that you might like to include in a glossary. Different tools use different techniques in order to try to identify potential terms. Some of these techniques, along with their strengths and weaknesses, are described in this chapter.

Chapter 10 explores the potential of LSP corpora as a resource for technical writing. By following the examples provided here, you will find out how small specialized corpora containing texts of a particular style can be a useful resource for helping you to write in a particular style or to produce a particular text type.

Chapter 11 provides numerous examples to illustrate how both bilingual and monolingual corpora can be used as translation resources to help you with tasks such as finding suitable equivalents, choosing between synonyms, determining appropriate style and verifying conceptual information.

Finally, Chapter 12 briefly outlines some additional ways in which you can use corpora to investigate specialized language. This includes creating and consulting learner corpora, investigating **neologisms** and studying **metaphor**. The chapter concludes with a look at some of the ways in which corpus analysis tools are being customized for LSP investigations.

Part I
Setting the scene

1 Introducing corpora and corpus analysis tools

Simply speaking, corpus linguistics is an approach or a methodology for studying language use. It is an empirical approach that involves studying examples of what people have actually said, rather than hypothesizing about what they might or should say. As we will see, corpus linguistics also makes extensive use of computer technology, which means that data can be manipulated in ways that are simply not possible when dealing with printed matter. In this chapter, you will learn what a corpus is and you will read about some different types of corpora that can be used for various investigations. You will also get a brief introduction to some of the basic tools that can be used to analyse corpora. Finally, you will find out why corpora can be useful for investigating language, particularly LSP.

What is a corpus?

As you may have guessed, corpus linguistics requires the use of a corpus. Strictly speaking, a corpus is simply a body of text; however, in the context of corpus linguistics, the definition of a corpus has taken on a more specialized meaning. A corpus can be described as a large collection of authentic texts that have been gathered in electronic form according to a specific set of criteria. There are four important characteristics to note here: 'authentic', 'electronic', 'large' and 'specific criteria'. These characteristics are what make corpora different from other types of text collections and we will examine each of them in turn.

If a text is authentic, that means that it is an example of real 'live' language and consists of a genuine communication between people going about their normal business. In other words, the text is naturally occurring and has not been created for the express purpose of being included in a corpus in order to demonstrate a particular point of grammar, etc.

A text in electronic form is one that can be processed by a computer. It could be an essay that you typed into a word processor, an article that you scanned from a magazine, or a text that you found on the World Wide Web. By compiling a corpus in electronic form, you not only save trees, you can also use special software packages known as corpus analysis tools to help you manipulate the data. These tools allow you to access and display the information contained within the corpus in a variety of useful ways, which will be described throughout this book. Essentially, when you consult a printed text, you have to read it from beginning to end, perhaps marking relevant sections with a highlighter or red pen so that you can go back and study them more closely at a later date. In contrast, when you consult a corpus, you do not have to read the whole text. You can use corpus analysis tools to help you find those specific sections of text that are of interest – such as single words or individual lines of text – and this can be done much more quickly than if you were working with printed text. It is very important to note, however, that these tools do not interpret the data – it is still your responsibility, as a linguist, to analyse the information found in the corpus.

Electronic texts can often be gathered and consulted more quickly than printed texts. To gather a printed corpus, you would probably have to make a trip to the library and then spend some time at the photocopier before heading home to sit down and read through your stack of paper from beginning to end. In contrast, with electronic resources such as the Web at your disposal, you can search for and download texts in a matter of seconds and, with the help of corpus analysis tools, you can consult them in an efficient manner, focusing in on the relevant parts of the text and ignoring those parts that are not of interest. Because technology makes it easier for us to compile and consult corpora, electronic corpora are typically much larger than printed corpora, but exactly how large depends on the purpose of your study. There are no hard and fast rules about how large a corpus needs to be, but we will come back to this issue when discussing corpus design in more detail in Chapter 3. Basically though, 'large' means a greater number of texts than you would be able to easily collect and read in printed form.

Finally, it is important to note that a corpus is not simply a random collection of texts, which means that you cannot just start downloading texts haphazardly from the Web and then call your collection a 'corpus'. Rather, the texts in a corpus are selected according to explicit criteria in order to be used as a representative sample of a particular language or subset of that language. For example, you might be interested in creating a corpus that represents the language of a particular subject field, such as business, or you might be interested in narrowing your corpus down even further to look at a particular type of text written in the field of business, such as company annual reports. As we will see, the criteria that you use to design your corpus will depend on the purpose of your study, and may include things like whether the data consists of general or specialized language or written or spoken language, whether it was produced during a narrow time frame or spread over a long period of time, whether it was produced by men or women, children or adults, Canadians or Irish people, etc.

Who uses corpora?

Corpora can be used by anyone who wants to study authentic examples of language use. Therefore, it is not surprising that they have been applied in a wide range of disciplines and have been used to investigate a broad range of linguistic issues. One of the earliest, and still one of the most common, applications of corpora was in the discipline of **lexicography**, where corpora can be used to help dictionary makers to spot new words entering a language and to identify contexts for new meanings that have been assigned to existing words. Another popular application is in the field of language learning, where learners can see many examples of words in context and can thus learn more about what these words mean and how they can be used. Corpora have also been used in different types of sociolinguistic studies, such as studies that examine how men and women speak differently, or studies comparing different language varieties. Historical linguists use corpora to study how language has evolved over time and, within the discipline of linguistics proper, corpora have been used to develop corpus-based grammars. Meanwhile, in the field of computational linguistics, example-based machine translation systems and other natural language processing tools also use corpus-based resources. Throughout the remainder of this book, you will learn about other applications of corpora, specifically LSP corpora, in disciplines such as terminology, translation and technical writing.

Are there different types of corpora?

There are almost as many different types of corpora as there are types of investigations. Language is so diverse and dynamic that it would be hard to imagine a single corpus that could be used as a representative sample of all language. At the very least, you would need to have different corpora for different natural languages, such as English, French, Spanish, etc., but even here we run into problems because the variety of English spoken in England is not the same as that spoken in America, Canada, Ireland, Australia, New Zealand, Jamaica, etc. And within each of these language varieties, you will find that people speak to their friends differently from the way they speak to their friends' parents, and that people in the 1800s spoke differently from the way they do nowadays, etc. Having said this, it is still possible to identify some broad categories of corpora that can be compiled on the basis of different criteria in order to meet different aims. The following list of different types of corpora is not exhaustive, but it does provide an idea of some of the different types of corpora that can be compiled. Suggestions for how you can go about designing and compiling your own corpora that will meet your specific needs will be presented in Chapters 3 and 4.

General reference corpus vs special purpose corpus: A general reference corpus is one that can be taken as representative of a given language as a whole and can therefore be used to make general observations about that particular language. This type of corpus typically contains written and spoken material, a broad cross-section of text types (e.g. a mixture of newspapers, fiction, reports, radio and television broadcasts, debates, etc.) and focuses on language for general purposes (i.e. the language used by ordinary people in everyday situations). In contrast, a special purpose corpus is one that focuses on a particular aspect of a language. It could be restricted to the LSP of a particular subject field, to a specific text type, to a particular language variety or to the language used by members of a certain demographic group (e.g. teenagers). Because of its specialized nature, such a corpus cannot be used to make observations about language in general. However, general reference corpora and special purpose corpora can be used in a comparative fashion to identify those features of a specialized language that differ from general language. This book will focus on special purpose corpora that have been designed to help LSP learners, hence we often refer to the corpora in this book as *LSP corpora*. If you would like to find out more about general reference corpora, look at resources such as Aston and Burnard (1998) and Kennedy (1998).

Written vs spoken corpus: A written corpus is a corpus that contains texts that have been written, while a spoken corpus is one that consists of transcripts of spoken material (e.g. conversations, broadcasts, lectures, etc.). Some corpora, such as the British National Corpus, contain a mixture of both written and spoken texts. The focus in this book will be on written corpora, but if you would like to know more about spoken corpora and the challenges involved in transcribing texts, please refer to Leech et al. (1995).

Monolingual vs multilingual corpus: A monolingual corpus is one that contains texts in a single language, while multilingual corpora contain texts in two or more languages. Multilingual corpora can be further subdivided into **parallel** and **comparable** corpora. Parallel corpora contain texts in language A alongside their translations into language B, C, etc. These are described in detail in Chapter 6. Comparable corpora, on the other hand, do not contain translated texts. The texts in a comparable corpus were originally written in language A, B, C, etc., but they all have the same communicative function. In other words, they are all on the same subject, all the same type of text (e.g. instruction manual, technical report, etc.), all from the same time frame, etc.

Synchronic vs diachronic corpus: A synchronic corpus presents a snapshot of language use during a limited time frame, whereas a diachronic corpus can be used to study how a language has evolved over a long period of time. The work discussed in this book will be largely synchronic in nature, but more information on diachronic corpora can be found in Kytö et al. (1994).

Open vs closed corpus: An open corpus, also known as a monitor corpus, is one that is constantly being expanded. This type of corpus is commonly used in lexicography because dictionary makers need to be able to find out about new words or changes in meaning. In contrast, a closed or finite corpus is one that does not get augmented once it has been compiled. Given the dynamic nature of LSP and the importance of staying abreast of current developments in the subject field, open corpora are likely to be of more interest for LSP users.

Learner corpus: A **learner corpus** is one that contains texts written by learners of a foreign language. Such corpora can be usefully compared with corpora of texts written by native speakers. In this way, teachers, students or researchers can identify the types of errors made by language learners. Granger (1998) provides more details about learner corpora.

Are there tools for investigating corpora?

Once a corpus has been compiled, you can use corpus analysis tools to help with your investigations. Most corpus analysis tools come with two main features: a feature for generating word lists and a feature for generating concordances. We will introduce these tools here briefly so that you have some idea what they can do, but they will be examined in greater detail in Chapter 7.

A word lister basically allows you to perform some simple statistical analyses on your corpus. For instance, it will calculate the total number of words in your corpus, which is referred to as the total number of 'tokens'. It will also count how many times each individual word form appears; each different word in your corpus is known as a 'type'. The words in the list can be sorted in different ways (e.g. in alphabetical order, in order of frequency) to help you find information more easily. Figure 1.1 shows two extracts from a word frequency list taken from a 5000-word corpus of newspaper articles about fast foods. The list on the left is sorted alphabetically while the one on the right is sorted in order of frequency.

A concordancer allows the user to see all the occurrences of a particular word in its immediate contexts. This information is typically displayed using a format known as keyword in context (KWIC), as illustrated in Figure 1.2. In a KWIC display, all the occurrences of the search pattern are lined up in the centre of the screen with a certain amount of context showing on either side. As with word lists, it is possible to sort concordances so that it becomes easier to identify patterns.

Why use corpora to investigate language?

Now that we understand what corpus linguistics is and how we can generally go about it, let us explore some of the reasons why we might want to use corpora to investigate language use. There are, of course, other types of resources that you can use to help you learn more about LSPs.

a	104	the	224
abdomen	2	and	132
abdominal	1	of	129
about	12	to	112
absolutely	1	a	104
academy	1	in	80
accelerating	1	food	71
accommodated	1	is	58
according	4	for	54
acid	1	far	51
acids	1	fast	50
across	3	that	47
action	1	are	42
actively	1	you	41
activists	1	MG	40
activity	1	more	39
adapt	1	than	39
add	2	calories	38
added	5	with	37
adding	1	at	35

Figure 1.1 Extracts from a word frequency list sorted alphabetically and in order of frequency

For example, you have no doubt consulted numerous dictionaries, and you may also have consulted printed texts, or asked a subject field expert for help. You may even have relied on your intuition to guide you when choosing a term or putting together a sentence. All of these types of resources may provide you with some information, but as you will see, corpora can offer a number of benefits over other types of resources. This is not to say, of course, that corpora are perfect or that they contain all the answers. Nevertheless, we think you will find that a corpus can be a valuable resource and a useful complement to other types of resources, such as dictionaries, printed texts, subject field experts and intuition. In the following sections, we will outline some of the shortcomings of these resources for LSP learners and then look at some of the ways in which corpora can help to overcome these drawbacks.

```
sser, who believes promoting fast food to kids should be ba

ys Eric Schlosser, author of Fast Food Nation, out this mon

he inexpensive appearance of fast food is an illusion." Sti

The simple answer is, yes, a fast food meal can be okay. Th

s, you pull into the nearest fast food restaurant for a qui

u or your kids are eating at fast food restaurants more tha

d to the commercial kitchen, fast food was born, and with I

althy diet. To help you make fast food choices and be an in

  said is not new. Though the fast-food giant has been sayin

  time before consumers force fast-food chains to tame their
```

Figure 1.2 A concordance for 'fast'

Dictionaries

One of the main types of resource used by LSP learners is a printed dictionary, and although dictionaries can be invaluable for solving some types of language learning problems, they are not always sophisticated enough to meet all the needs of an LSP learner.

One of the biggest problems associated with dictionaries is their inherent incompleteness. The world around us and the language used to describe it are evolving all the time, which means that printed dictionaries go out of date very quickly. It takes a long time to compile and publish a dictionary, and fields such as science and technology, for example, frequently evolve so quickly that by the time a dictionary is printed, it no longer reflects the current state of knowledge or language.

Another problem with dictionaries is their size. Although it is possible to compile large, multi-volume dictionaries that attempt to cover a specialized subject field in its entirety, not many people will be able to afford such dictionaries, and they certainly would not want to carry them around! Most users would prefer to have a dictionary that will fit in their rucksack, which means that the lexicographers who create the dictionaries have to choose which information to include and which to leave out. Unfortunately, their choices do not always correspond with the needs of LSP users. For example, acronyms and other abbreviated forms (e.g. 'ISP' for 'Internet Service Provider') are a common feature in many LSPs, but these are frequently omitted from dictionaries. We saw above that some new terms do not make it into the dictionary, but a related problem is that out-of-date terms are not always taken out. Dictionaries often contain 'linguistic deadwood' – terms that remain in the dictionary even though they have dropped out of current usage. This means that an LSP learner who consults a dictionary for help may find and use terms that are no longer appropriate.

Another of the most common criticisms of dictionaries is that they do not provide enough in the way of contextual or usage information. LSP learners must pay attention to how terms are used, which means that in addition to information about what a term means, they also need information about how to use that term in a sentence (e.g. what other words 'go with' the term in question). This information can be provided by presenting terms in context instead of in isolation. Although most lexicographers and users alike would agree that the inclusion of contextual fragments in a dictionary can go some way towards meeting these needs, most dictionaries still do not provide this type of information. As we have seen, one reason for this is because people do not want to have large dictionaries. Given the space restrictions imposed on printed dictionaries, even those dictionaries which do contain usage examples only have room for a few per entry.

An additional point of interest with regard to the limitations of most dictionaries is that they cannot easily provide information about how frequently a given term is used. Texts are better guides to naturalness, as determined by frequency or lexical variety, than either dictionaries or intuition. Of course, for LSP users, decisions regarding the appropriateness of a given lexical choice will be made on the basis of more than just frequency; nevertheless, frequency data can help you to make informed decisions.

Finally, even if the relevant information is contained in the dictionary, users sometimes have trouble knowing where to find it. For example, in a single dictionary, users may find that the entries for some terms are listed under the acronym (e.g. under 'ISP' instead of 'Internet service provider'; under '**HTML**' instead of 'hypertext markup language'), whereas the entries for other terms are listed under the expanded term, even though such terms might be better known by the acronym (e.g. under 'random access memory' instead of 'RAM'; under 'central processing unit' instead of 'CPU').

Printed texts

Given some of the shortcomings of dictionaries described above, many LSP users turn to printed texts to find up-to-date details about the meaning and use of specialized terms. You may have done this yourself, for instance. You may have read books or articles that have been written about the specialized field in question, and such material has probably provided you with a number of examples of the terminology and style that are appropriate to the LSP you are studying.

Nevertheless, consulting texts in their conventional printed form presents a number of pitfalls. As previously mentioned, in order to physically gather together a printed corpus, you may need to spend hours at the library and/or photocopier. Once the printed corpus is gathered, further hours must be spent consulting the texts, which often means reading lots of irrelevant material before stumbling upon a discussion of a pertinent point. Furthermore, in order to find a variety of examples and to make sure that the style or terms you choose are generally accepted by experts in the field and not simply the idiosyncratic usage of a single author, it is necessary to consult a selection of texts, not just one or two. Unfortunately, it can sometimes be difficult to detect patterns of linguistic and stylistic generality when they are spread over several documents. Therefore, acquiring and consulting texts in printed form has two major disadvantages. The first is that you typically cannot gather and consult a wide enough range of documents to ensure that all relevant concepts, terms and linguistic patterns will be present. Second, the analysis of printed texts is inherently error-prone: the unaided human mind simply cannot discover all the significant patterns, let alone organize them in meaningful ways.

Subject field experts

As noted above, one of the first things that users learn about dictionaries is that even the best ones do not contain the answers to all their questions. With luck and good research skills, users may be able to find the necessary answers in printed texts, but failing that, they may eventually decide to turn to a subject field expert for help. Subject field experts are people who have received training in and/or work in a specialized subject field, and who are therefore familiar with the LSP used to communicate in that field. Subject field experts can be extremely valuable resources; however, they are typically very busy people, and they may not be able to drop everything to answer your questions in time for you to meet your deadlines.

Even when experts do make themselves available, LSP learners are then faced with the delicate task of eliciting the necessary information from these experts. On the one hand, LSP learners are looking for expert advice because they themselves are not specialists in the subject field, but on the other hand, if the LSP learners do not formulate their questions well, then the experts may unintentionally give advice that is inappropriate to the text in question. When consulting experts, LSP learners must be very careful not to ask leading questions or they risk getting distorted information. Sometimes experts may find it very difficult to spontaneously suggest terms or expressions; however, they are often able to confidently verify or reject suggestions that are put to them.

One final difficulty that LSP learners face when consulting a subject field expert is that they are only getting one person's opinion. Different experts may give conflicting advice on concepts and terms (e.g. they may subscribe to different schools of thought on a subject). Therefore, ideally,

LSP learners would benefit from consulting multiple experts in a given subject field, though in practice, this is not always a realistic aim.

Intuition

An additional resource that you may use as an LSP learner is your own intuition, particularly with regard to language and style. However, this can sometimes lead to problems. As we will see in Chapter 2, some people are learning an LSP in a foreign language, and they may experience some **interference** from their native language. For example, a native French speaker who is learning the LSP of optical scanning technology in English may know that the term for '*tête*' is 'head' and the term for '*numériseur*' is 'scanner', but when it comes to putting a sentence together, s/he may rely on intuition to come up with a structure that uses English words but is based on French syntax (e.g. '*tête de numériseur*' translated as 'head of the scanner' instead of 'scan head'). Even people who are learning an LSP in their native language may experience interference because the structures used in an LSP may not be the same as those used in general language. For example, in legal documents, such as wills or contracts, ideas are often expressed using structures that are longer and more complex than those used in general language. Whereas in general language you might say, 'When I die, I would like my children to inherit my house', this same idea might be expressed in legal LSP in the following way: 'I give my entire interest in the real property which was my residence at the time of my death, together with any insurance on such real property, but subject to any encumbrances on said real property, equally to my two children.' In short, relying on intuition that may be useful in another language or in LGP may lead to errors when attempting to communicate in the LSP in question.

Corpora

We will now look at how corpora can help to overcome some of the drawbacks of the resources mentioned above. The first thing to note is that the physical constraint imposed on printed media does not apply to electronic media such as corpora: hundreds of thousands of words of running text can be stored on a diskette and millions can fit easily on to a hard drive or optical disk. Therefore, corpora have the potential to be more extensive than other resources. In addition, their electronic form means that they are easier to update than printed resources, and they are also easier to consult. As we will see in Chapter 7, using specially designed software, data can be searched much more comprehensively in electronic form than in printed form. Searching for a word or phrase in a printed text is a labour-intensive and time-consuming task. In contrast, conducting a full-text search of a corpus can be done in seconds. Moreover, features such as wildcard searches (e.g. using the search string *print** to retrieve *print, printed, printer, printers, printing, prints*, etc.) make it possible to conduct exhaustive searches without exhausting the researcher.

Another strength of corpora is that they contain a wealth of authentic usage information. Since corpora are comprised of texts that have been written by subject field experts, LSP learners have before them a body of evidence pertaining to the function and usage of words and expressions in the LSP of the field. Moreover, with the help of corpus analysis tools, you can sort these contexts so that meaningful patterns are revealed. In addition, a corpus can give an LSP learner a good idea of how a term or expression *cannot* be used. The discovery that certain words or uses of words do not occur in a corpus of authentic texts written by subject field experts can be invaluable for helping learners to establish that even though words may appear in dictionaries, they cannot be used in certain contexts, and that even if a sentence is grammatical, it may not be idiomatic in the LSP in question.

Frequency information is another type of data that is much more easily obtainable when using an electronic corpus and corpus analysis tool. Knowledge about frequency allows you to analyse the lexical patterns associated with words in a more objective and consistent way, but such observations are difficult to make when working with printed documents since the human eye may simply not notice a pattern when its occurrences are spread over several pages or documents. As we saw on page 14, the word lister feature of a corpus analysis tool makes it possible to calculate how many times a given word appears in a corpus.

An LSP corpus basically contains thousands of words that have been written by subject field experts and, as such, it can be seen to represent distilled expert knowledge. Obviously, actual subject field experts cannot make themselves constantly available for consultation; however, once compiled, a corpus is constantly available to the LSP learners, and they can consult it as often as they like. The unrestricted availability of the corpus is important because language learning goes on all the time. In addition, the fact that a corpus contains articles written by many subject field experts means that LSP learners have access to more than one expert opinion, which means they are better able to judge whether terms or expressions are generally accepted in the subject field, or whether they are simply the preference of one particular expert. Finally, LSP learners do not need to worry about asking leading questions since all the evidence contained in the corpus is available to the user.

As an LSP learner, you will probably always use your intuition to a certain extent; however, a corpus can provide you with a means of backing up this intuition. One common reason that LSP learners turn to external resources is for reassurance. A corpus can be seen as a testbed that you can use to verify or reject your hypotheses about the LSP that you are learning. This approach is more reliable than assuming that LGP or native-language norms can be transferred directly into the LSP. Unlike judgements based on intuition, naturally occurring data has the principal benefit of being observable and verifiable by all who examine it. This means that a corpus can act as an objective frame of reference.

An additional advantage of the corpus-based approach is that it is more efficient to consult a single corpus-based resource than multiple types of conventional resources. As a busy LSP learner who is probably working to tight deadlines, you may not have the luxury of being able to spend hours and hours searching for material that will help you with your task. Therefore, the fewer resources that you are required to consult, the better. A corpus is a single yet broad-ranging resource that can meet the majority of your LSP needs: because a corpus consists of naturally occurring running text, you can retrieve information about both lexical and non-lexical (e.g. style, punctuation, grammar, register) elements of language. In other words, a corpus is a 'one-stop shop'. With the help of an LSP corpus, you can spend less time looking for reference material and more time studying it.

Using a corpus can be an enjoyable as well as an informative experience. In our experience, we have found that learners often find it tiresome and frustrating to consult conventional resources and are excited by the possibility of using electronic resources. Corpus-based resources are not only more interesting for learners to use, but they can also be effectively employed to teach research skills and to improve LSP proficiency. Corpora can be used not only to find answers to questions, but also to prompt discussions about students' work or other interesting issues. Corpora have been frequently known to reveal aspects of language that neither the teacher not the students would ever have thought of investigating!

In conclusion, we should repeat that corpora may not provide the answers to all your questions, and they should not necessarily be seen as a replacement for all other types of resources. Instead, they can be viewed as a complementary resource that can be used in conjunction with other types of resources. For example, intuition or dictionary use might lead you to come up with a hypothesis that can be further investigated in a corpus, or an investigation in a corpus might provide you with information that helps you to formulate some questions for a subject field expert.

Key points

- Corpus linguistics is an approach or a methodology for studying language use.
- A corpus is a large collection of authentic texts that have been gathered in electronic form according to a specific set of criteria. These criteria depend on the nature and purpose of the project at hand.
- Corpora have been used in a wide range of disciplines, including lexicography, language teaching and learning, and sociolinguistics.

- Many different types of corpora have been developed for different applications, including written and spoken corpora, general reference corpora, special purpose corpora, monolingual and multilingual corpora, synchronic and diachronic corpora, open and closed corpora, and learner corpora.
- Corpora can be manipulated and analysed with the help of corpus analysis tools, such as word listers and concordancers.
- Corpora offer a number of advantages over other types of resources (e.g. dictionaries, printed texts, subject field experts, intuition) and can therefore be used as useful complements to such resources.

  — Their electronic form means that corpora can be larger and more up-to-date than printed resources, and they can be searched more easily.
  — Corpora consist of authentic texts that can be used to find out what people do and do not say, as well as how often they say it.
  — Corpora can be used to conduct new investigations or to test existing hypotheses.
  — Corpora can be fun and interesting to explore!

Further reading

Barnbrook, Geoff (1996) *Language and Computers*, Edinburgh: Edinburgh University Press.
Biber, Douglas, Conrad, Susan and Reppen, Randi (1998) *Corpus Linguistics: Investigating Language Structure and Use*, Cambridge: Cambridge University Press.
Kennedy, Graeme (1998) *An Introduction to Corpus Linguistics*, London/New York: Longman.
McEnery, Tony and Wilson, Andrew (1996) *Corpus Linguistics*, Edinburgh: Edinburgh University Press.
Tognini-Bonelli, Elena (2001) *Corpus Linguistics at Work*, Amsterdam/Philadelphia: John Benjamins.

Exercises

Exercise 1

Write down three sentences containing the word 'umbrella'. Ask a classmate or friend to do the same. Compare your sentences with those of your classmate. Did you both think of exactly the same sentences? Now compare your sentences to those shown in Figure 1.3, which were taken from the British National Corpus Online (http://sara.natcorp.ox.ac.uk/).

The sentences that you thought up are probably not the same as the ones thought up by your classmate, and there is a good chance that none

Anglo-Amalgamated company under the EMI umbrella brought to the company under

time afterwards making a special metal umbrella.

from the DES (under whose departmental umbrella the group currently resides)

ple who take up prescriptions under the umbrella of the NHS are exempt from ch

And fancy borrowing her ghastly old umbrella, when you could have have had

Do I have an umbrella?

rella, but it was a very old and ragged umbrella (selflessly, she'd left behin

nd forcing the attacker to back off; an umbrella is excellent for this.

learned to relish shade and arranged my umbrella continually in order to be un

ce the 'l' in 'elephant' or the 'm' in 'umbrella'?

was made boss of the party's powerless umbrella body, the Patriotic People's

eakfast one of the men returned with an umbrella; everyone else worked with sc

Square where I'd been waiting under an umbrella watching a group of Czech sol

reatly on just what to assess under the umbrella word 'science' - and how to a

ovely girl ran out of the house with an umbrella and held it over my head.

on book-collecting, since the ephemera umbrella seems to cover an extraordina

lank walls and tapped the handle of his umbrella against his chin.

The fact that "I'll return your umbrella" is in the future tense does

poked the leaves with the point of his umbrella, a wrinkle of pain on his for

ifold capabilities which fall under the umbrella term 'learning' are not suffi

Gothic pew, a rusty suit of armour, an umbrella stand in the form of a bear.

with the rain falling on trees, on the umbrella, the only sounds.

iding his female companion with a large umbrella, they moved off toward the ho

shadow cone much like rain falls off an umbrella, as shown in Fig. 1.

te spats, a gangster's hat and a rolled umbrella, Gallacher projected the imag

is to spread the top growth over a wire umbrella to get the hanging stems well

branches on the principle of an opening umbrella; Santa Claus masks, red and w

locating the briefcase, hat and furled umbrella, and the front door made a cl

rm forward, the hand clutching a furled umbrella by its ferrule, the crook of

The Doctor hooked the handle of his umbrella over his top pocket and pulle

Figure 1.3 Concordance for 'umbrella'

of these sentences are the same as the ones that are shown in the concordance. The point of this exercise is to demonstrate that a corpus can be a rich source of data that may provide you with information that you would not have arrived at through introspection alone.

Exercise 2

Now compare the concordance in Figure 1.3 against this dictionary entry for the term 'umbrella' taken from the Oxford Paperback Dictionary (1988 edition):

> **umbrella** n. **1.** a portable protection against rain, consisting of a circular piece of fabric mounted on a foldable frame of spokes attached to a central stick that serves as a handle. **2.** any kind of general protecting force or influence.

What information do you learn from the corpus that was not present in the dictionary, and vice versa? These two types of resource may offer complementary information.

2 Introducing LSP

This chapter sets out to introduce language for special purposes (LSP) and to describe some of the ways in which it is different from language for general purposes (LGP). In addition to discovering why it is useful to learn about LSP, you will find out about different types of LSP users and their particular needs. You will also be introduced to ways in which a corpus can help you to identify the features of an LSP and to acquire the knowledge you need in order to be able to communicate effectively in an LSP.

What is LSP?

LSP stands for *language for special purposes*. Perhaps the easiest way to describe LSP is to put it in opposition to LGP, which refers to *language for general purposes*. LGP is the language that we use every day to talk about ordinary things in a variety of common situations. In contrast, LSP is the language that is used to discuss specialized fields of knowledge. It is actually more accurate to talk about LSP in the plural (i.e. languages for special purposes) since different LSPs are used to describe different areas of specialized knowledge.

Every language (e.g. English, French, Spanish, etc.) has both LGP and LSP. A native speaker of a given language is usually quite an expert in the LGP of that language. We are not suggesting that native speakers are 'walking dictionaries' who know every single word and grammatical rule of the language, but they do typically have a reasonably broad vocabulary base, and they know how to put these words together to form sentences that sound natural and can be understood by other speakers of that language. In many cases, people who study a foreign language also begin by learning the LGP of that language. Being conversant in the LGP of a language allows you to function in that language by doing things such as asking for directions, ordering a meal in a restaurant, chatting with a friend about the film you saw last night, or talking about the weather. All of these subjects can be discussed in a very general way using LGP, and they can also be discussed at a different, more specialized level using LSP. Fields of knowledge such as orienteering, gastronomy, cinematography and meteorology are discussed by experts using the LSPs appropriate to these fields. As an LGP speaker, you might feel a little out of your element if you overheard two meteorologists discussing the weather using terms like 'advection', 'helicity' and 'radiational cooling'!

Of course, there is some degree of overlap between LGP and LSP. LSP typically contains a number of specialized terms, and may also combine these words in a special way; however, a lot of general language words show up in LSP conversations. It would be very difficult to have a conversation about anything – even the most specialized subject – without using a few everyday words such as 'the', 'it', 'very', or 'is'. Similarly, some specialized words do make their way into general language through a process known as **de-terminologization** (Meyer and Mackintosh 2000). This usually happens when terms that once belonged exclusively to a specialized domain make their way into the everyday lives of ordinary people, either through the mass media or through direct impact. For instance, medical terms such as 'Ebola', 'AIDS', 'diabetes', 'BSE' and 'anorexia' were once used only by doctors and other health professionals, but now they are recognized and used by many ordinary people who may read these terms in the newspaper, hear them on television, or know someone who has one of these conditions. Similarly, a large number of terms relating to computers, such as 'byte', 'modem' or 'email', are now familiar to many non-computer specialists. Of course, a lay person's understanding of such terms may not be as deep as an expert's understanding, which means that the terms may be used in a slightly different way in LGP from in LSP.

Specialized vocabulary is clearly an important feature of an LSP, and there is a discipline known as terminology that is concerned with collecting and describing the vocabulary (generally known as terms) of specialized subject fields. The people who work in this discipline are known as **terminologists**, and their primary job is to compile glossaries for specialized fields. Chapter 8 provides more information about glossaries and about how corpora can be used to help with glossary compilation.

Although the specialized vocabulary of an LSP is often its most striking feature, it is important to note that LSP is not simply LGP with a few terms thrown in. An LSP may also have special ways of combining terms or of arranging information that differ from LGP.

Let us look briefly at the LSP of chemistry as an example. The LSP of chemistry certainly has a great number of specialized terms that are not part of LGP (e.g. sodium chloride, nitroglycerine). An additional feature of this LSP is that these terms can also be expressed using chemical formulas (e.g. $NaCl$, $C_3H_5(NO_3)_3$). Although these terms and formulas may be the most obvious difference between the LSP of chemistry and LGP, they are not the only feature of this LSP.

For example, this LSP also contains collocations, which are words that are typically used together. If you are writing up a chemistry experiment, you may need to know what verbs are generally used with the noun 'experiment'. Based on your knowledge of LGP, you might assume that the verb 'do' can be used (e.g. 'to do an experiment'), but a search in a specialized corpus demonstrates that in the LSP of chemistry, experiments are typically 'conducted' or 'carried out'. This type of search also reveals another interesting feature of the LSP of chemistry – it shows that the use of passive constructions is very common (e.g. 'the experiment was conducted' rather than 'X conducted the experiment').

In addition, you may discover that there are stylistic features that are relevant to a particular LSP. For example, if you are writing up the results of an experiment that you performed in your chemistry class, there is a typical way in which you are expected to present and organize this information, which includes stating the purpose of the experiment, describing the equipment used, outlining the methodology that was followed, presenting and discussing the data that were generated and, finally, formulating some type of conclusion. In most cases, it is not considered logical or acceptable to leave out any of this information nor to present it in a different order.

All of these elements – specialized vocabulary, collocations, stylistic features – contribute to the formation of LSP. Chapters 8 to 11 provide many more examples of these different elements of LSP and explain how you can use a corpus to identify them.

Who uses LSP?

Essentially, we have established that LSP is the language used to talk about a specialized subject field. The purpose of LSP is therefore to facilitate communication between people who wish to discuss a specialized subject, but who are these people? We can identify a number of different types of LSP users, including experts, semi-experts and non-experts.

Experts can be considered to be people who have training or experience in the specialized field in question. Keep in mind that a specialized field does not necessarily have to be one that is highly 'technical', nor do the experts have to be 'professionals'. For instance, if you have a hobby, such as quilting or mountain biking, you have probably noticed that there are some specialized terms associated with this hobby (e.g. 'sashing', 'basting', or 'appliqué' in quilting, or 'barge', 'granny gear' or 'bunny hop' in mountain biking). Any language that is used to discuss a specialized subject can be considered an LSP.

Semi-experts may include students (i.e. people who are in the process of learning about the field in question), or experts from related fields who may be familiar with some of the terms and concepts in question (e.g. a tailor may recognize some of the terms used in quilting).

Non-experts are people who, for one reason or another, find themselves in a situation where they must use an LSP with which they are not familiar.

This may include people such as technical writers or translators, who have training in language or linguistics, but who are not very familiar with the specialized subject matter that is discussed in the texts that they have to write/translate.

Different levels of LSP communication

Because LSP users have different levels of expertise, there are also different levels of LSP communication. When experts communicate (e.g. through publications in research journals), they tend to use a highly specialized language. Because these experts share a common background and specialized language, they understand what is meant by specific terms and phrases in the field and do not provide explanations for their readers.

Another type of communication takes place between experts and semi-experts, such as students or experts from related fields. In such cases, the experts will probably use the same highly specialized terms that they would use when communicating with another expert from their own field, but they will accompany these terms with explanations where necessary (e.g. in text books). In this way, they help the semi-expert to learn the terms and concepts of the subject field.

A third type of communication occurs between experts and non-experts. In this case, the expert will use fewer terms, and may even use general language words to give simplified descriptions of a specialized concept. This is the type of language that can be found in texts such as special interest columns in newspapers. The expert does not expect the non-expert to achieve the same level of understanding of the terms used as long as the general idea is understood. Non-experts such as translators or technical writers often begin learning about a subject field by reading this type of material, although they typically go on to deepen their knowledge as the texts that they are responsible for translating are often texts intended for expert-to-expert or expert-to-semi-expert communication.

Why learn an LSP?

There is a difference between knowing a subject and knowing the LSP used to describe that subject. For instance, you may be able to solve an arithmetic problem, but can you explain the process to someone else? Imagine that a child is having difficulty doing his or her arithmetic homework and has asked you for assistance. One way of helping this child may simply be to work through the arithmetic problem and have him or her watch. In order to do this, you clearly have to understand the mathematical concepts involved and be able to apply them to the problem at hand. Of course, simply watching you work may not be all that helpful to him or her. A better solution might be for you to explain what you are doing as you are working through the problem. To do this effectively,

Explanation given without using the LSP of arithmetic	Explanation given using the LSP of arithmetic
X = 5 * (8 – 2) The answer to this question is the number you get as a result of making another number bigger by multiplying it by another number but not until after you have made this first number smaller by taking yet another number away from it because those are inside the curvy things which means you should do that part first.	X = 5 * (8 – 2) To solve this equation, you need to find the value of the variable X. You need to begin by working out the value of the expression contained in the brackets because the arithmetic order of operations requires that expressions in brackets be calculated first. So begin by subtracting 2 from 8, which leaves a difference of 6. You can now go on to the next part of the equation, in which you take the difference (6) and multiply it by 5 to get a product. 6 times 5 gives you a product of 30. There are no more operations to be done; therefore, the value of the variable X is equal to 30.

Figure 2.1 Explanations that can be given to explain how to solve the arithmetic problem X = 5 * (8 – 2)

you need to be familiar with the LSP of arithmetic. If you do not know the LSP of arithmetic, you may end up confusing the child. Look at the examples shown in Figure 2.1 and determine which explanation would be more helpful.

We hope that you will agree that the explanation given using the LSP of arithmetic is more helpful than the non-LSP explanation. Of course, in order for this explanation to be truly useful to the child, he or she too must have some understanding of the LSP of arithmetic. In other words, he or she must know what you mean when you use terms such as 'variable', 'product' or 'equation'.

The important point to note here is that there is a difference between knowing/learning a subject and knowing/learning the LSP used to discuss that subject. In other words, knowing how to do arithmetic and knowing how to communicate effectively your knowledge of arithmetic are two separate, but complementary, things.

The example given here shows the importance of being able to communicate in an LSP in a teaching context, but this is not the only situation in which it is desirable to be familiar with an LSP. You may be motivated to learn an LSP for a variety of reasons. You may be learning an LSP because you are a student who is working to become an expert in a certain field, in which case you are probably learning an LSP in your native language (e.g. in order to hand in reports for class assignments). You may already be an expert who wishes to communicate with experts who speak a different natural language, in which case you are probably learning an LSP in a foreign language (e.g. in order to read or publish research in a foreign-language journal). Or you may be a non-expert who has to learn a given LSP in both your native language and a foreign language, such as a translator.

As an LSP learner, you will face different challenges depending on your level of subject field expertise and linguistic expertise. For example, if you are a subject field expert who wants to learn how to express your knowledge in a foreign language, you will probably be comfortable with many of the concepts in the field, and will be seeking to increase your linguistic knowledge.

If you are a student learning an LSP in your native language, you will have to work on acquiring both conceptual and linguistic knowledge since some of the concepts in the subject field will be new to you, and so will some terms and structures in the LSP. Just bear in mind that being a native LGP speaker does not automatically make you well versed in a given LSP! Although LSPs have some features in common with LGP, they also have many unique terms and structures.

If you are a non-expert, you will need to familiarize yourself with both the concepts in the subject field and the language used to describe them. The situation is somewhat different for students of a particular domain (e.g. students of engineering) and other types of students (e.g. students of translation or journalism). Students of a particular domain learn the typical terms and structures of the LSP while learning about the specialized subject matter. Thus, engineering students acquire the vocabulary of engineering, science students the vocabulary of science, etc. In contrast, other types of students, such as student journalists or student translators must set about consciously learning the LSP terms and structures through a separate systematic effort using resources such as texts or corpora because they do not receive formal training in any particular LSP. Imagine if translators had to attend classes on all the different subjects they encountered (or might encounter) over the course of their careers – they would spend all their time in class and have no time left to translate!

It is clear that in order to become a proficient user of an LSP, you will need to acquire two broad types of knowledge: linguistic knowledge and conceptual knowledge. Linguistic knowledge consists of specialized terms, collocations (i.e. words that are often used together, such as 'click' and 'link' in the LSP of the Internet), grammatical structures and stylistic features. Conceptual knowledge, as the name suggests, consists of information about the specialized concepts that are described using the LSP. Conceptual knowledge is very important because, in order to communicate effectively in a specialized subject field, you need to be able to do more than just throw out a few key phrases; you need to actually *know* what you are talking about, which means understanding the concepts behind the terms. As explained above, different types of LSP learners will be faced with slightly different challenges and may need to focus their attention on different aspects of the LSP in question, but, eventually, all types of users must be comfortable with both the linguistic and the conceptual elements of an LSP.

How can a corpus help with LSP acquisition?

The aim of this book is to explore the different ways in which corpora can be used to help you learn an LSP. In the following sections, we will give you a brief overview of some basic ways in which you can use corpora to learn more about the linguistic and conceptual aspects of an LSP. Do not worry if you do not fully understand how to create a corpus or how to manipulate it using corpus analysis tools – this will be covered in detail elsewhere in the book. For now, just try to follow these examples in order to get a general picture of some of the different ways in which a corpus can help you to acquire the specialized linguistic and conceptual knowledge that you need to be a proficient LSP user. These simple examples have been taken from the subject field of weather since this is a field with which everyone is at least a little bit familiar. Two different corpora have been used. The first contains three weeks' worth of weather forecasts for the Ottawa region in June 2001, while the second contains a number of introductory texts that explain how different types of precipitation are formed.

Using a corpus to identify specialized terms

One way that you can use a corpus to investigate an LSP is to find out what words are most common in that LSP. You can do this by generating a list that presents all the words in the corpus and indicates how often each appears. This list can be organized in such a way that the most frequently occurring words are presented at the top of the list. Figure 2.2 contains a word frequency list from a small corpus of weather forecasts. As you can see, some of the most common words in this corpus are general language words, such as 'in', 'the', 'and', 'to', 'with', 'of'; however, there are also some terms that are more specific to the LSP of weather forecasts, including 'cloudy', 'highs', 'lows' and 'winds'.

Once you have used a corpus to identify some potentially interesting terms belonging to the LSP, you can look at these terms in context using a concordancer. As you will see in the upcoming sections, looking at the terms in context will help you to learn more about their meaning and behaviour.

in	38
the	38
cloudy	36
partly	29
low	25
and	22
highs	21
lows	21
to	19
mph	12
upper	12
winds	12
near	11
with	10
of	9

Figure 2.2 A word list showing the most frequently occurring words in a small corpus on weather forecasts

Using a corpus to learn about words that 'go together'

Collocation is one type of word behaviour that can be identified with the help of a corpus. Collocations are characteristic co-occurrence patterns of words, and they feature quite prominently in LSP. Simply put, collocations are generally regarded as words that 'go together' or words that are often 'found in each other's company'. For instance, if you want to describe the weather situation where there are some clouds in the sky, but not too many, there are a variety of ways in which you *could* express this situation. You could say 'There are some clouds', 'There are a few clouds', 'It is a bit cloudy', 'It is somewhat cloudy', etc. These are all perfectly valid ways of expressing the situation in question – they are grammatically and semantically correct, but they are not 'normal' or 'idiomatic' in the LSP of weather forecasts. If we generate a concordance for the terms 'cloud/cloudy', as shown in Figure 2.3, we see that there are a number of terms that collocate with cloudy on a regular basis. An examination of these contexts reveals that in the LSP of weather forecasts, the natural way to say that there are a few clouds in the sky is 'partly cloudy'.

Using a corpus to learn about grammar

If you are learning an LSP in a foreign language, you may experience some interference (e.g. putting words in the wrong order) from your native language, just as you would if you were learning LGP in a foreign language.

```
on 30%. Friday: A mix of sun and clouds. High near 78F. Winds S 10 to
F. Winds W 10 to 15 mph. Friday: Cloudy. Skies becoming partly cloudy
tered Showers.  Thursday: Mostly cloudy with isolated thunderstorms.
o 10 mph. Thursday night: Mostly cloudy. High near 66F. Winds W 10 to
NW 5 to 10 mph. Saturday: Mostly cloudy with isolated thunderstorms e
tion 30%. Thursday night: Mostly cloudy with isolated thunderstorms.
ly cloudy. Skies becoming mostly cloudy late. Highs in the low 70s an
in the low 60s. Thursday: Partly cloudy. Highs in the low 80s and low
in the mid 50s. Thursday: Partly cloudy. Highs in the low 70s and low
tion 30%. Thursday night: Partly cloudy. Low around 57F. Winds N to N
ion 30%. Wednesday night: Partly cloudy. High around 68F. Winds W to
n the low 50s. Wednesday: Partly cloudy. Highs in the upper 60s and 1
s in the mid 50s. Sunday: Partly cloudy. Highs in the upper 70s and 1
in the upper 50s. Sunday: Partly cloudy. highs in the low 70s and low
the upper 50s. Wednesday: Partly cloudy. Highs near 70 and lows in th
 to 15 mph. Friday night: Partly cloudy. Low around 58F. Winds S to S
W 10 to 15 mph. Saturday: Partly cloudy. Highs in the low 70s and low
in the upper 40s. Monday: Partly cloudy with scattered showers. Highs
s in the low 50s. Friday: Partly cloudy with scattered showers. Highs
s in the low 50s. Friday: Partly cloudy with scattered showers. Highs
s in the low 60s. Friday: Partly cloudy. Thursday: Variably cloudy wi
y: Cloudy. Skies becoming partly cloudy late. Highs in the mid 60s an
in the low 50s. Thursday: Partly cloudy with scattered showers. Highs
ws around 60F. Wednesday: Partly cloudy with a slight chance of a thu
 NE 10 to 15 mph. Friday: Partly cloudy with a slight chance of a thu
and lows near 60. Monday: Partly cloudy. Highs in the low 80s and low
 in the low 60s. Tuesday: Partly cloudy. Highs in the low 80s and low
iation 30%. Friday night: Partly cloudy. Low near 53F. Winds N to NW
artly cloudy. Thursday: variably cloudy with a slight chance of a thu
```

Figure 2.3 A concordance for 'cloud/cloudy' revealing some common collocations

Prepositions, for instance, are notoriously difficult to learn in foreign languages, and prepositions are just as much a part of LSPs as they are of LGP. For example, when discussing temperature in weather forecasts, you may be unsure of which preposition(s) to use with words such as 'high' and 'low'. In LGP, 'high' and 'low' are primarily used as adjectives, but in the LSP of weather forecasts, they are often used as nouns

```
30%. Wednesday night: Partly cloudy. High around 68F. Winds W to SW 10 to
0%. Friday. A mix of sun and clouds. High near 78F. Winds S 10 to 15 mph.
h a slight chance of a thunderstorm. High near 68F. Winds N to NE 10 to 1
h a slight chance of a thunderstorm. High near 69F. Winds N 15 to 20 mph.
 mph. Thursday night: Mostly cloudy. High near 66F. Winds W 10 to 15 mph.
 cloudy with isolated thunderstorms. High near 76F. Winds SE 5 to 10 mph.
he low 60d. Thursday: Partly cloudy. Highs in the low 80s and lows in the
 to 15 mph. Saturday: Partly cloudy. Highs in the low 70s and lows in the
e low 50s. Wednesday: Partly cloudy. Highs in the upper 60s and lows in t
the low 60s. Tuesday: Partly cloudy. Highs in the low 80s and lows in the
 the mid 50s. Sunday: Partly cloudy. Highs in the upper 70s and lows in t
artly cloudy with scattered showers. Highs in the mid 60s and lows in the
lows near 60. Monday: Partly cloudy. Highs in the low 80s and lows in the
 the mid 50s. Friday. Partly cloudy. Highs in the low 70s and lows in the
artly cloudy with scattered showers. Highs in the upper 60s and lows in t
artly cloudy with scattered showers. Highs in the upper 50s and lows in t
artly cloudy with scattered showers. Highs in the upper 60s and lows in t
. Skies becoming mostly cloudy late. Highs in the low 70s and lows in the
. Skies becoming partly cloudy late. Highs in the mid 60s and lows in the
he upper 40s. Sunday: Partly cloudy. Highs in the upper 60s and lows in t
e upper 50s. Tuesday: Partly cloudy. Highs in the low 70s and lows in the
he mid 50s. Thursday: Partly cloudy. Highs in the low 70s and lows in the
 the mid 50s. Monday: Partly cloudy. Highs in the mid 70s and lows in the
he upper 50s. Sunday: Partly cloudy. Highs in the low 70s and lows in the
e low 60s. Wednesday: Partly cloudy. Highs near 80 and lows in the low 60
 isolated thunderstorms ending late. Highs near 70 and lows in the upper
upper 50s. Wednesday: Partly cloudy. Highs near 70 and lows in the mid 50
```

Figure 2.4 Concordance for 'high/highs' sorted according to following word

and can also appear in the plural. A concordance search can be used to find all the examples of 'high/highs' in the corpus. By sorting the data according to the word that comes after 'high/highs', you can see which prepositions are typically used as shown in Figure 2.4.

In this particular corpus, 'in' is the most commonly used preposition when discussing a range of temperatures (e.g. 'highs in the mid 60s'),

```
cloudy with isolated thunderstorms. Low around 62F. Winds E to SE 5 t
5 mph. Friday night: Partly cloudy. Low around 58F. Winds S to SW 10
to 15 mph. Thursday: Partly cloudy. Low around 50F. Winds W to SW 5 t
30%. Thursday night: Partly cloudy. Low around 57F. Winds N to NE 10
n 30%. Friday night: Partly cloudy. Low near 53F. Winds N to NW 5 to
 a slight chance of a thunderstorm. Low near 56F. Winds SW 5 to 10 mp
d showers. Highs in the mid 60s and lows in the low 50s. Tuesday: Par
y: Partly cloudy. Highs near 70 and lows in the mid 50s. Thursday. Pa
ly cloudy. Highs in the mid 70s and lows in the upper 50s. Tuesday: P
ly cloudy. Highs in the low 70s and lows in the upper 50s. Wednesday:
ly cloudy. Highs in the low 70s and lows in the mid 50s. Monday: Part
orms ending late. Highs near 70 and lows in the upper 40s. Sunday: Pa
 cloudy. Highs in the upper 60s and lows in the upper 40s. Monday: Pa
showers. Highs in the upper 60s and lows in the low 50s. Wednesday: P
ly cloudy. Highs in the low 80s and lows in the low 60s. Friday: Part
 cloudy. Highs in the upper 60s and lows in the low 50s. Thursday: Pa
showers. Highs in the upper 60s and lows in the low 50s. Friday: Part
oudy late. Highs in the mid 60s and lows in the low 50s. Saturday: Pa
showers. Highs in the upper 60s and lows in the low 50s. Saturday: Sc
ly cloudy. Highs in the low 80s and lows in the low 60s. Wednesday: P
oudy late. Highs in the low 70s and lows in the mid 50s. Sunday: Part
y: Partly cloudy. Highs near 80 and lows in the low 60s. Thursday: Pa
ly cloudy. Highs in the low 80s and lows in the low 60s. Tuesday: Par
ly cloudy. Highs in the low 70s and lows in the mid 50s. Friday: Part
ly cloudy. Highs in the low 70s and lows in the upper 50s. Sunday: Pa
ly cloudy. Highs in the low 70s and lows in the upper 50s. Saturday:
 cloudy. Highs in the upper 70s and lows near 60. Monday: Partly clou
```

Figure 2.5 Concordance for 'low/lows' sorted according to following word

while 'near' is the most commonly used preposition when referring to a specific point on the temperature scale (e.g. 'high near 68F'). For non-native speakers, it may also be helpful to note that 'near' can be used with both the plural 'highs' and the singular 'high', whereas 'in' occurs only with the plural 'highs'. As shown in Figure 2.5, a concordance search for the terms 'low/lows' reveals similar uses of prepositions, but this time the preposition 'around' is used slightly more often than the preposition 'near' when referring to 'low' in the singular.

Using a corpus to learn about style

Non-native speakers are not the only ones who may encounter interference when learning an LSP. If you are learning an LSP in the same natural language as your native LGP, you may find that your LGP knowledge interferes with your LSP production – at least in the beginning. Although there is some overlap between LGP and LSP, and while LSPs do sometimes follow the style of LGP, there are also numerous exceptions. This means that LSP learners must be prepared to do the relevant research rather than automatically assume that an LSP will follow the same rules as an LGP. For example, legal texts differ significantly from general language texts, not only with regard to terminology, but also syntactic constructions. Compared to LGP texts, legal texts contain an abnormally large number of passives, conditionals, prepositional phrases, multiple negatives, unusually long sentences and very complex embeddings. If you relied on your LGP instincts to write or translate a legal text, you might be tempted to break up the long and complex sentences into numerous

Extract that uses the terminology and style appropriate to legal LSP	Extract that does **not** use the terminology or style appropriate to legal LSP
In accordance with the Constitution of the People's Republic of China, the Basic Law of the Hong Kong Special Administrative Region of the People's Republic of China is hereby enacted by the National People's Congress to provide for the systems to be practised in the Hong Kong Special Administrative Region, in order to safeguard the implementation of the basic principles and policies of the State towards Hong Kong.	In agreement with constitutional law in China, the National People's Congress is implementing guidelines for interactions between China and the Hong Kong special administrative zone. This is to protect Hong Kong's legal rights.

Figure 2.6 Two versions of the same material written using different vocabulary and style (adapted from Mok 1995)

```
1.   a thunderstorm. High near 68F. Winds N to NE 10 to 15 mph.

2. f a thunderstorm. Low near 56F. Winds SW 5 to 10 mph. Chanc

3.   a thunderstorm. High near 69F. Winds N 15 to 20 mph. Chanc

4.   sun and clouds. High near 78F. Winds S 10 to 15 mph. Frida

5. thunderstorms. Low around 62 F. Winds E to SE 5 to 10 mph.

6. d thunderstorms. High near 76F. Winds SE 5 to 10 mph. Chanc

7. : Mostly cloudy. High near 66F. Winds W 10 to 15 mph. Frida

8. Partly cloudy. High around 68F. Winds W to SW 10 to 15 mph.

9.  : Partly cloudy. Low near 53F. Winds N to NW 5 to 10 mph.

10. Partly cloudy. Low around 57F. Winds N to NE 10 to 15 mph.

11. Partly cloudy. Low around 58F. Winds S to SW 10 to 15 mph.

12. Partly cloudy. Low around 50F. Winds W to SW 5 to 10 mph.
```

Figure 2.7 A concordance for 'wind/winds'

short and simple sentences and to use features such as the active voice instead of the passive and adjectival modifiers instead of prepositional phrases. The resulting text may be grammatically correct according to the rules of the LGP, but it would not be stylistically appropriate in the legal LSP. Figure 2.6 shows sample extracts from a legal text – the extract on the left is written using the vocabulary and style that are appropriate to this LSP, whereas the extract on the right is grammatically correct, but is not terminologically or stylistically appropriate.

Weather forecasts are another example of a type of text that has a style that differs considerably from the normal LGP style. For example, if we look at Figure 2.7, we see a concordance generated for the term 'wind/winds' and, even based on these short extracts, we can make a number of observations about the style of weather forecasts.

First, we notice that the style of weather forecasts is very sparse. Sentences are very short, and there are no unnecessary words such as articles (e.g. 'the' or 'a'), nouns (e.g. 'temperature') or even verbs (e.g. 'blowing'). In this corpus, the term 'winds' is used only in the plural, never in the singular. We can also see that each individual forecast is very formulaic: it begins with a description of cloud cover and precipitation, moves on to temperature and ends with a description of the winds. The order never changes. Even within each of these descriptions, the information is presented in a systematic way: winds are always described first in terms of direction and then in terms of speed.

If we were to take the information contained in line 8 of the concordance and express it according to the norms of LGP, we might say something like:

> It's going to be a bit cloudy outside tomorrow, but the temperature
> will get up somewhere around 68 degrees Fahrenheit. It will be a little
> bit breezy, but should feel warm because the wind will be blowing
> from the west or south-west.

This passage expresses essentially the same information as that contained
in line 8, but it cannot be considered representative of the LSP of weather
forecasts. The sentences are too long and follow the grammatical requirements of LGP (e.g. all sentences have verbs), rather than the LSP. There
are also numerous explicit references that should be left implicit (e.g.
'degrees', 'outside', 'temperature', 'blowing'). An expert reading this text
would certainly be able to understand its meaning; however, it would be
immediately clear that it was written by someone who was not familiar
with the LSP. This may not be a big deal in the case of a weather forecast, but, in other contexts, it is very important to respect the norms of
the LSP in question (e.g. legal contracts).

Using a corpus to learn about concepts

We mentioned previously that in order to be able to communicate comfort-
ably and confidently in an LSP, you have to understand the **concepts**
behind the terms. Although students who are learning about a subject
field may acquire knowledge about these concepts and their relationships
as part of their studies, non-experts, like translators or technical writers,
generally have to take it upon themselves to become 'mini-experts' in the
subject fields in question. Sometimes a word may look familiar because
you have seen it being used as part of LGP, but it is important to realize
that words may have a different, more specialized, meaning in the LSP.
For example, in LGP the word 'bowls' typically refers to dishes that people
eat soup or breakfast cereal from; however, in a sporting context, 'bowls'
are small round wooden balls. Furthermore, just because a word can be
used to refer to two separate concepts in one natural language, does not
mean that both these concepts are designated by the same term in other
languages (e.g. in French, soup bowls = *bols*, but sporting bowls = *boules*).
Therefore, if you are a translator or a foreign-language LSP learner, you
have to be sure that you know which concept is being referred to so that
you can choose the correct equivalent.

A corpus can be useful for providing conceptual information. Sometimes,
the context surrounding a particular term contains a definition, explanation or description of some of the characteristics of the concept designated
by that term. Figure 2.8 shows a concordance for the term 'droplet', and
by reading the contexts surrounding the term, we can learn something
about what a droplet is.

For example, we learn that droplets are very small, with a diameter
between 0.01 and 0.02 millimetres. Because of their small size, they can

```
diameter of a typical cloud droplet is 0.01 to 0.02 mm whereas a typical raind
inds in the clouds blow the droplet around. It hits other drops and joins up w
                    Cloud droplets are so small that you need a magnifying g
f 5 to 8 mm. The tiny cloud droplets float in the air, borne aloft by the wind
as in the size of the cloud droplets and the raindrops. The diameter of a typi
pull of gravity. Tiny cloud droplets are so small that they are kept aloft and
```

Figure 2.8 A concordance for 'droplet' reveals some characteristics of this concept

float in the air and are kept aloft by the wind. Finally, we learn that they can combine with other droplets. And we learn all this from these tiny fragments of text! As we will learn in Chapter 7, it is possible to expand the concordance lines so that we can see an even larger, and potentially more informative, context.

Key points

- LGP is the language we use to discuss ordinary things in everyday situations.
- LSP is the language used to discuss specialized fields of knowledge. These fields of knowledge can include everything from professional activities to hobbies, as long as they treat a restricted subject.
- In addition to having a specialized vocabulary, an LSP may also have specialized collocational or stylistic features that differ from LGP.
- There is a difference between learning a specialized subject and learning the LSP that is used to describe that subject.
- There are different types of LSP users, including experts (e.g. people with training or experience in a given subject), semi-experts (e.g. students or experts from related fields) and non-experts (e.g. translators or technical writers).
- Different types of users learn LSP for different reasons (e.g. to communicate with experts who speak other natural languages, to do assignments for class, to work as a translator).
- Two broad types of knowledge are required in order to become a proficient LSP user: linguistic knowledge and conceptual knowledge.
- A corpus can be a useful resource for learning about the linguistic features of an LSP, such as knowledge about terms, collocations, grammar and style. It can also provide conceptual information, such as knowledge about the characteristics of the concepts behind the terms and about the relationships concepts have with one another.

Further reading

Cabré, M. Teresa (1999) *Terminology: Theory, Methods and Applications*, Amsterdam/Philadelphia: John Benjamins.

Douglas, Dan (1999) *Assessing Language for Specific Purposes*, Cambridge: Cambridge University Press.

Dubuc, Robert (1997) *Terminology: A Practical Approach*, adapted by Elaine Kennedy, Brossard, Quebec: Linguatech.

Dudley-Evans, Tony and St John, Maggie Jo (1998) *Developments in English for Specific Purposes*, Cambridge: Cambridge University Press.

Galinski, Christian and Budin, Gerhard (1996) 'Terminology', in Ronald Cole et al. (eds) *Survey of the State of the Art in Human Language Technology*, http://cslu.cse.ogi.edu/HLTsurvey/ch12node7.html#SECTION125

Kittredge, Richard and Lehberger, John (eds) (1982) *Sublanguage: Studies of Language in Restricted Semantic Domains*, Berlin: Walter de Gruyter.

Meyer, Ingrid and Mackintosh, Kristen (2000) 'When terms move into our everyday lives: an overview of de-terminologization', *Terminology* 6(1): 111–38.

Pearson, Jennifer (1998) *Terms in Context*, Amsterdam/Philadelphia: John Benjamins.

Sager, Juan C. (1990) *A Practical Course in Terminology Processing*, Amsterdam/Philadelphia: John Benjamins.

Sager, Juan C., Dungworth, David and McDonald, Peter F. (1980) *English Special Languages*, Wiesbaden: Oscar Brandstetter Verlag.

Exercise

This exercise uses an LSP that most of you will be familiar with – recipes. Read the following text and, without consulting any reference material, try to rewrite the text in such a way that it conforms to the LSP in question. Once you have finished, look on the Internet for some recipes. Compare your version to the recipes that you find. How did you do? Are the terms, collocations and style that you used in line with those of the recipes that you found?

> To make this recipe for a creamy potato casserole, you will need a package of frozen hash brown potatoes (a 2 pound bag), some green onions, cheddar cheese, cream of potato soup (a 10oz can), butter, sour cream and salt and pepper.
>
> First turn on your oven. Set it to 350 degrees Fahrenheit (or 175 degrees Celsius if it is a metric oven). Get a pan and put it on the stove on a setting that's not too high, then pour in the soup as well as a quarter of a cup of butter and two cups of sour cream. Now chop up one third of a cup of green onions and grate two cups of cheddar cheese. Get a bowl (not too small!) and put in the package of frozen potatoes along with the green onions and one cup of cheddar cheese. Put the soup/butter/sour cream from the pan into the bowl with the potatoes/green onion/cheddar cheese. You can also put in

enough salt and pepper so that it will be to your liking. Now pour everything into a casserole dish that measures nine inches by thirteen inches. Put the rest of the grated cheddar cheese on the top. Now it all goes into the oven for about thirty to forty-five minutes. Eat it before it gets cold!

Part II

Corpus design, compilation and processing

3 Designing a special purpose corpus

The aim of this chapter is to introduce a number of basic guidelines that you can use to help you design special purpose corpora that will meet your own LSP needs. We consider the criteria required to design a useful special purpose corpus, paying particular attention to issues such as size, number of texts, medium, subject, text type, authorship, language and publication date. The main focus of this chapter will be monolingual corpora, though many of the issues raised here are applicable to multi-lingual corpora as well. In addition, Chapters 8, 10 and 11 will give you suggestions for designing LSP corpora to carry out specific tasks such as glossary building, writing and translation.

As we learnt in Chapter 1, corpora are not merely random collections of texts but, rather, they are collections that have been put together according to specific criteria. These criteria are determined by your needs and by the goals of your project. There are many guidelines available for helping users to design corpora that can be used for LGP investigations (e.g. Aston and Burnard 1998; Atkins et al. 1992; Kennedy 1998; Sinclair 1991); however, in Chapter 2, we identified a number of ways in which the needs of LSP users differ from those of LGP users. Therefore, when you set out to design a special purpose corpus, you cannot simply adopt the criteria used to design LGP corpora. Rather, you will need to adapt and possibly expand these criteria to address the specific needs of your LSP investigation, and this will be the focus of the following sections.

Corpus size

One of the criteria to be addressed is the size of a corpus. A corpus is often referred to as a 'large' collection of texts, but the adjective 'large' is rather vague. Unfortunately, there are no hard and fast rules that can be followed to determine the ideal size of a corpus. Instead, you will have to make this decision based on factors such as the needs of your project, the availability of data and the amount of time that you have. It is very important, however, not to assume that bigger is always better. You may find that you can get more useful information from a corpus that is small

```
 1.   stud in place by screwing a nut all the way against the strap,

 2.   g box, and thread the collar nut onto the nipple protruding from

 3.   ll go. Screw the compression nut onto the threads of the valve c

 4.   n the supply riser fastening nut, and then loosen the jamb nut a

 5.   r pipe, and attach its flare nut to the other end of the flare u

 6.   the Union.  Thread the flare nut onto one of the ends of the fla

 7.   ut, and then loosen the jamb nut above it.  Then using a slip-ja

 8.   tened behind it by a knurled nut. in the manual, for removal ins

 9.    states, "Remove the knurled nut behind the instrument cluster".

10.   the basin. Turn the mounting nut counterclockwise (to the left)

11.   unscrew the faucet mounting nut and the washer from the shank u

12.   screw with a screwdriver or nut driver (depending on the head s

13.   le wrench, back the retainer nut from each escutcheon. If the re

14.    escutcheon. If the retainer nut will not move, apply some penet

15.   lues. Choose the SFK Rivet - Nut when a flush mount or countersu

16.           A low profile rivet-nut with superior torque values. Ch

17.   lange on the LF series Rivet-Nut provides the widest bearing sur

18.   a wrench to tighten the slip nut. If you are using a dishwasher,

19.   justable wrench, tighten the nut forcing the compression ring on

20.   it again.    With the wing nut assembly, it allows you to add
```

Figure 3.1 Concordance for 'nut' in an LSP corpus on manufacturing

but well designed than from one that is larger but is not customized to meet your needs.

For example, suppose that you need to learn the vocabulary of the LSP of manufacturing. Now imagine that you can choose one of two corpora to help you. One is a 10,000-word corpus containing catalogues, product descriptions and assembly/installation instructions from companies in the manufacturing industry, while the other is a much larger LGP corpus, such as the 100-million word British National Corpus (BNC). If you were to look for information about 'nuts', what do you think you would find in the two corpora? A concordance search on the term 'nut' in the manufacturing corpus reveals forty-nine occurrences of this term, and a random selection of these are shown in Figure 3.1.

The LSP corpus reveals that there are many different kinds of nuts used in manufacturing (e.g. 'collar nut', 'compression nut', 'flare nut', 'knurled nut', 'wing nut'). The corpus also contains information about what you

```
1.               Mechanical, sliding nut devices never seem to have becom
2.    & Cranberry Dressing; Mixed Nut Salad with Garlic Vinaigrette; S
3.   earer man said, tightening a nut.
4.   was, after all, some kind of nut.
5.   e Willy Hunter, a local hard nut awaiting trial for murder, and a
6.   ng a sledgehammer to crack a nut.
7.   of the teachers' unions, the NUT, who were largely responsible fo
8.   machine and various bolt and nut machines; boiler-makers work on
9.               He who eats the nut must first crack the shell.
10.  ny, giants among the British nut people, and purveyors of nuts to
11.  ther air-blast separates the nut from the hull, which goes to fee
12.               Technically, a nut is a single-seeded fruit, with t
13.    'Maybe she's some kind of nut.'
14.  ates a small spanner for the nut, so only a screwdriver was neede
15.       A beautifully cut bone nut carries the strings over to the
16.  cken and pasta and fruit and nut salad and make borscht and buy b
17.      Although at first united, Nut and Geb were then separated by t
18.  arsh ties, pied flycatchers, nut hatches, redstarts, and tawny ow
19.  anager and former Sunderland nut, he changed allegiance in 1980 w
20.   terminal at Kharg Island, a nut that proved particularly difficu
```

Figure 3.2 Concordance for 'nut' taken from the general language British
        National Corpus

can do with nuts (e.g. you can 'thread', 'screw', 'tighten' or 'loosen' them)
and about the tools you can use (e.g. 'wrench', 'nut driver').

Meanwhile, a search on the same term in the BNC produced 670 occurrences – more than a dozen times the number of occurrences in the
manufacturing corpus. However, as you can see from the randomly selected
concordances shown in Figure 3.2, many of these contexts are not useful
for learning about the LSP of manufacturing.

Although a few of the contexts are describing the type of nuts that are
used in manufacturing, most of the concordance lines show examples of
'nut' being used in other ways, such as the type of nuts that you can eat.
What other uses of the term 'nut' can you identify in the concordance?

We have used this example to demonstrate that even though the BNC
is a bigger corpus and it contains a far greater number of occurrences of
the term in question, not all of these contexts will be useful because they

are not specific to the LSP of manufacturing. In short, bigger is not always better when dealing with corpora!

Early electronic LGP corpora, such as the Brown Corpus and the Lancaster-Oslo-Bergen (LOB) Corpus, contained approximately one million words. Now, with the increasing availability of text in electronic form, it is not unusual to find general language corpora containing hundreds of millions of words (e.g. British National Corpus, Bank of English). It is generally accepted, however, that corpora intended for LSP studies can be smaller than those used for LGP studies, and there are logical reasons for this. First, it is more difficult and time consuming to obtain samples of specialized texts as opposed to general texts, and second because LSP represents a more restricted subset of natural language. As we saw in the example above, a small corpus can be a very useful resource provided it is well designed.

There are, however, some drawbacks associated with small corpora. If your corpus is too small, it may not contain all the concepts, terms or linguistic patterns that are relevant to the LSP you are investigating. In addition, if your corpus is too small, you will not be able to make any valid generalizations. For instance, if you wish to establish that the term 'clock speed' is used more often than its synonym 'clock rate' in the LSP of computing, you need to have more than just two or three occurrences in your corpus in order to validate your hypothesis. Although we saw above that bigger is not necessarily better, it is important to have a substantial corpus if you want to make claims based on statistical frequency. In our experience, well-designed corpora that are anywhere from about ten thousand to several hundreds of thousands of words in size have proved to be exceptionally useful in LSP studies.

Another decision you will have to make that is related to the issue of size is whether the corpus will be closed or open. As described in Chapter 1, a closed corpus is one that is finite – it is of a fixed size and contains a snapshot of the state of a language at a given time. This is in contrast to an open or monitor corpus, which is a more flexible entity to which you can add and remove texts to reflect the changing state of language. Specialized language is typically dynamic – concepts in specialized subject fields are constantly evolving and the terms used to describe these concepts also change. For example, in the mid-1990s a new type of computer storage medium known as the 'digital video disc' was developed; however, it soon became apparent that such discs could be used to hold more than just video, so the name was changed to 'digital versatile disc', which soon became widely known by its acronym 'DVD'. Given the dynamic nature of specialized language, an open corpus that can be updated on a regular basis is likely to be more appropriate for many of your LSP needs.

Text extracts vs full texts

The previous section focused on the issue of the overall size of a corpus, but the size of an individual text in a corpus is also relevant for LSP studies. In a number of LGP corpora, the size of any given text sample may be limited. For example, the LOB (Lancaster-Oslo-Bergen corpus) contains extracts of only 2000 words, while the LLELC (Longman-Lancaster English Language Corpus) consists of extracts of not more than 40,000 words. In LSP studies, however, the concepts, terms, patterns and contexts that interest you might appear in any section of a text. In fact, their location in a text may be highly relevant. For instance, an important concept may be defined only in the opening paragraph, or a complete term, such as 'read-only memory', may be used at the beginning of a text whereas its abbreviation 'ROM' may be introduced at a later stage. If you decide to choose an extract at random, you might accidentally eliminate a part of the text that could be very interesting for your study. Therefore, it is a good idea to use full texts when compiling LSP corpora.

Number of texts

So far, we have been discussing the size of corpora in terms of the total number of words in the corpus and the size of individual texts, with particular reference to whether or not the texts are complete. It is also important to consider how many different texts you are going to include in your corpus, as well as how many of these texts have been written by different authors. For example, there is a big difference between a 20,000-word corpus that is made up of twenty different texts written by twenty different authors and a 20,000-word corpus that is made up of just two long texts written by the same author. In the case of the multi-author corpus, you will be able to get a good idea of what terms and concepts are commonly used in the LSP in question, whereas in the case of the single-author corpus, you will only be exposed to the terms that are preferred by that particular writer. As an LSP learner, you are probably interested in getting an overview of the type of language used throughout the subject field, so in this case it would be a good idea to design your corpus in such a way that it contains a greater number of texts written by a range of different authors, rather than just a few texts written by only one or two different authors.

Medium

Medium refers to whether the text in question was originally prepared as a written text or whether it is a transcription of a spoken text. Some types of LSP users, such as translators or terminologists, typically work with written texts, whereas other LSP users, such as subject field experts, regularly communicate both orally and in writing. The decision about whether you want to compile a written, a spoken or a mixed-medium corpus will again depend on what you want to study, but you should be aware of the fact that it is much easier to build a corpus of written texts. This is because the collection and transcription of spoken language material is extremely labour-intensive. There are also a number of other difficulties associated with the collection of spoken material. For example, if the speakers are aware that you are recording their conversation, they may be intimidated and be careful about what they say. This means that your language sample may not be completely natural. In contrast, if you were to record a conversation without the speakers' knowledge, you would get a more natural sample, but this type of practice raises many ethical questions. This book focuses on building and using corpora that contain written material, but if you want to learn more about the issues involved in collecting and processing spoken texts, refer to Leech et al. (1995).

Subject

Although it may seem too obvious to mention, the texts that you include in your corpus need to be about the specialized subject that you are studying. This is not always as easy as it sounds. Many specialized subjects are multidisciplinary (e.g. biochemistry), which means that it can be difficult to know where one subject field ends and the next begins. For instance, where does biochemistry stop and chemistry begin? In addition, it can be equally difficult to determine the upper boundary. For example, although an operating system is a type of software, should a text giving a general description of software be included in a corpus on operating systems?

If your project sets out to study particular features of specialized language, it may not be necessary for all your texts to be about the same subject. For example, if you want to investigate the use of passive constructions in scientific research articles, your corpus could include texts on a range of subjects in the sciences, as long as all the texts were research articles. Of course, if you want to make statements about texts from any one domain (e.g. texts from physics as opposed to biology), then you will need to be able to identify those texts in the corpus that belong to the domain in question. You can do this by using annotation, which is discussed in Chapter 5.

Text type

Even within very specialized subject fields, a number of different **text types** exist. Texts written by experts for other experts (e.g. research papers) are different in terms of style and vocabulary from those written by experts for non-experts (e.g. popular science magazines, textbooks). For example, an 'oocyte' in a scientific journal is more likely to be called an 'egg' in a popular science magazine or newspaper. Furthermore, even though text-books and advertisements can both be aimed at non-experts, these still represent two very different text types. For example, a text book might explain that acronyms such as 'GB' and 'MHz' stand for 'gigabyte' and 'megahertz', whereas an advertisement, which has limited space, would simply use the acronyms with no explanation.

The types of texts that you include in your corpus will depend on what you wish to study. For example, if you are a translator who has been hired to translate a research paper on treatments for asthma, then you will benefit from a corpus that consists primarily of other research papers on asthma because these will contain examples of the vocabulary and style that are appropriate to this text type. However, if you are a termi-nologist who has been hired to compile a wide-ranging glossary of terms used in the subject field of asthma, then you would benefit more from a different type of corpus. In order to ensure a more complete conceptual and linguistic coverage of the LSP in question, you would need to compile a corpus that includes a variety of text types dealing with the subject 'asthma', such as research papers, text books, informative literature prepared for patients, advertisements or promotional literature for different products or drugs used to treat asthma, instructional texts (e.g. explaining how to use inhalers), newspaper articles or other popularized discussions of asthma, etc.

Authorship

In order to ensure that your corpus contains authentic LSP material, the author of each text should be an acknowledged subject-field expert. This means that the authors must have a suitable educational and/or profes-sional background in the discipline about which they are writing, and they should be recognized by their peers as having the level of expertise required to write about the particular subject. Although it is relatively easy to identify the author of a printed document, this is not always the case when dealing with electronic media, such as the Web. Nevertheless, when compiling your corpus, you should do your best to exercise good judgement with regard to the quality of the text. For example, if a text is posted on someone's personal home page, this text may be less reliable than a text that is posted on the web site of a recognized professional organization.

Language

As we learnt in Chapter 1, corpora can be either monolingual or multi-lingual, but in all cases, the texts must obviously be written in the language(s) that you are investigating. Other things that you might consider if you are compiling a monolingual corpus include whether or not the texts are original language texts (as opposed to translations) and whether or not they have been written by a native speaker. Texts that have been translated or that have been written by non-native speakers may contain some non-idiomatic expressions. If you want to learn how things are expressed naturally in the LSP in question, it may be best to try to exclude non-original or non-native texts from your corpus.

We should mention, however, that it can sometimes be difficult to determine a person's native language merely by looking at a text. For example, an author whose native language is English may have a name that sounds Polish or Spanish because that person's ancestors came from Poland or Spain. Furthermore, a non-native speaker may have engaged the help of a native speaker to edit a text. As always, when building your corpus, you must exercise good judgement in determining whether or not a text is appropriate for inclusion in a given corpus.

If you are constructing a multilingual corpus, it may be important that all the texts in language A are original language texts while all the texts in language B are translations, or it may be acceptable to have a mixture of original and translated texts in each language. The type of study you undertake will determine whether or not to include translations alone, or original texts alone, or a combination of both in each language.

Publication date

The age of the texts that you include in your corpus will depend on what you hope to learn from your corpus. If you are investigating a particular subject field, you probably want to know about the current state of that field, both at the linguistic and conceptual level. In this case, you will want to include mainly up-to-date texts in the corpus. However, older texts can also be valuable. For instance, experts usually provide lots of definitions and explanations when a new concept is developed or a new term is introduced, but these explanations become less frequent as this information becomes part of the experts' general knowledge. If you are a non-expert who is trying to become familiar with an LSP, you will probably benefit from this type of explanatory information and so it may be worth including a selection of older texts in the corpus.

In another example, imagine that you are a translator. It sometimes happens that texts are not translated until several years after they have been written, so in such a case you may need information about older terms and concepts too. Once again it is clear that the specific needs of your project must always be a primary consideration when designing a corpus.

Corpus design: an example

Imagine that you are an avid photographer. A non-native speaker of English, you have just moved abroad to an English-speaking country and have decided to join a photography club in order to meet new friends. Before going along to the club, you decide that it might be useful to learn some of the LSP of photography in English, and you decide to build a corpus to help you with this task. Where should you begin?

Initially, you set a goal of collecting a corpus of about 25,000 words. A corpus of this size is not likely to provide exhaustive coverage of the LSP of photography, but it will probably be enough to provide you with information about the key terms in the LSP. You decide that your corpus will be open, which means that you can expand it over time, eventually increasing the coverage of the field. You intend to look for at least twenty texts written by different authors; if you were to restrict your corpus to only one or two texts/authors, you could not really be sure that the terminology in these texts was representative of the LSP.

Although you eventually plan to use your new LSP knowledge to talk to other people at the photography club, you decide to focus on written texts when compiling your corpus. This is a very practical decision because written texts are easier to collect and process.

With regard to subject matter and text type, you decide to start with the fundamentals. You are interested in learning the terms for the basic concepts in photography (e.g. lighting, composition) as well as the different parts of conventional cameras (i.e. not digital cameras or video cameras). At a later date, you may decide to add more specialized material, such as texts that focus on film development, on wildlife photography or on other types of cameras and equipment, but for the moment, you are interested in introductory material, such as tutorials, text books and introductory articles.

Since you want to be able to communicate effectively with your new friends, you decide that you will try to find texts that have been written by expert authors who are native English speakers. In addition, you plan to identify material that has been published within the past three years since you do not want to learn the terms for techniques or equipment that are no longer used. You summarize all your ideal criteria into a wish list, such as that shown in Figure 3.3.

The criteria summarized in this wish list will act as a useful starting point for identifying texts to include in your corpus. In the next chapter, you will learn how to go about compiling special purpose corpora, and we will refer back to this wish list to see how it can be used to guide your search for suitable texts.

Key points

When designing a corpus, you should determine the precise criteria by analysing the goals of your project. The following guidelines may provide a helpful starting point:

- Size: anywhere from a few thousand to a few hundred thousand words have proved useful for LSP studies.
- Full text or extract: full texts are generally preferable because important information can be found anywhere in a text.
- Number of texts: selecting a number of texts from a variety of authors, rather than one or two texts from a single author, will help you to gain a better understanding of terms and patterns that are typical of the LSP.
- Medium: corpora containing written material are easier to compile and pre-process.
- Subject: to study the LSP of a particular subject field (or subfield), you should include only texts dealing with that subject in your corpus.
- Text type: to make observations about a particular type of text, you should include only texts of that type in your corpus.
- Authorship: texts produced by authors with proven credentials are likely to contain more authentic examples of LSP use than texts by authors who are not proven experts.
- Language: using original language material in a monolingual corpus will provide you with authentic examples of typical LSP use; parallel corpora will, of course, consist of original and translated texts.
- Publication date: many LSP studies are concerned with the current state of the language and subject field, and in this case the majority of texts in your corpus should consist of recent publications.

Size	Initial goal of 25,000 words, but corpus will be open and can be expanded
Number of texts	Minimum of 20 texts by different authors
Medium	Written
Subject	Photography basics, parts of conventional cameras
Text type	Introductory texts (e.g. tutorials, text books, introductory articles)
Authorship	Texts written by experts
Language	Texts written in English by native speakers
Publication date	Recent texts (not more than 3 years old)

Figure 3.3 Wish list for basic photography corpus

Further reading

Atkins, B. T. S., Clear, Jeremy and Ostler, Nicholas (1992) 'Corpus design criteria', *Literary and Linguistic Computing* 7(1), 1–16.

Barnbrook, Geoff (1996) *Language and Computers*, Edinburgh: Edinburgh University Press.

Engwall, Gunnel (1994) 'Not chance but choice: criteria in corpus creation', in B. T. S. Atkins and A. Zampolli (eds) *Computational Approaches to the Lexicon*, Oxford: Oxford University Press, 49–82.

McEnery, Tony and Wilson, Andrew (1996) *Corpus Linguistics*, Edinburgh: Edinburgh University Press.

Exercises

Exercise 1

Imagine that you are required to create a corpus on the ethics of human cloning. A web search using the keyword 'clones' turns up a number of texts. Based on the following extracts, which of these texts would you include in your corpus? Justify your answer.

Text 1: First cloned human embryos created

(http://www.newscientist.com/hottopics/cloning/cloning.jsp?id=ns99991605)

The first cloned human embryos have been created, claims a US bio-technology company, as predicted by *New Scientist* on 13 July. The achievement is a technological feat, but more significantly crosses a major ethical boundary. Advanced Cell Technology (ACT) of Worcester, Massachusetts says its intention is not to produce a cloned baby, but to develop a way of obtaining embryonic stem cells matched to patients.

Text 2: A clone in sheep's clothing

(http://www.sciam.com/explorations/030397clone/030397beards.html)

A sheep cloned from adult cells opens vast scientific possibilities and ethical dilemmas. Photographs of a rather ordinary-looking lamb named Dolly made front pages around the world last week because of her start-ling pedigree: Dolly, unlike any other mammal that has ever lived, is an identical copy of another adult and has no father. She is a clone, the creation of a group of veterinary researchers.

Text 3: The Clones Society Inc.

(http://www.clones.ca/)

The Clones Society Inc. specializes in computing and communication systems. We have been serving Eastern Canada since 1990, building custom computers for a wide array of applications. Meeting your computer needs is our aim. We offer a wide spectrum of products and services, including the sale and installation of complete computer systems, computer peripherals and accessories, network and storage solutions, and much, much more.

Text 4: Scientific and medical aspects of human cloning

(http://www4.nationalacademies.org/pd/cosepup.nsf/web/human_cloning)

The questions surrounding human cloning are controversial and growing more complicated, especially as animal-cloning efforts move forward. The nation needs a clear, unbiased examination of the state of the science in this area as lawmakers and the public grapple with public policy and ethical issues. A joint panel of the National Academies' Committee on Science, Engineering and Public Policy and the Board on Life Sciences has undertaken a study to review the relevant scientific and medical research on human cloning as well as closely related issues regarding scientific and medical ethics.

Text 5: Mavericks claim creation of many cloned human embryos

(http://www.newscientist.com/hottopics/cloning/cloning.jsp?
id=ns99991612)

Mavericks aiming to produce the first cloned person have claimed they are already a step or two ahead of Advanced Cell Technology, the Massachusetts-based company that announced on Sunday it had created cloned human embryos. 'We've created many human embryos,' says Brigitte Boisselier, chief executive officer at Clonaid, a California-based UFO cult that has vowed to produce cloned people. She welcomes news of ACT's cloned embryos: 'I'm not feeling alone any more.'

Exercise 2

For each of the following scenarios, describe what you would consider to be an *ideal* corpus in terms of the criteria outlined in this chapter (e.g. size, publication date, authorship, etc.). Be able to justify your answers and provide one or two specific examples of texts that you would ideally like to include in such a corpus.

Scenario 1

Juan, a third-year undergraduate exchange student from a Spanish-speaking country, is spending a year at a university in an English-speaking country. Juan is studying chemistry and, although he is familiar with many of the concepts in the discipline, he is worried that he will not be able to express himself properly in English when it comes time to write his assignments and exams. Describe the contents of the corpus that you would ideally design to help Juan familiarize himself with the English LSP of chemistry.

Scenario 2

Caught up in the excitement of World Cup fever, a major sports equipment manufacturer has approached you for help in compiling a glossary of soccer terminology to be distributed free of charge to fans around the world. For those of you who are not familiar with the term, a glossary is a list of the most commonly used words in a domain (soccer in this case), together with definitions and equivalents in other languages. Here, the sports equipment manufacturer has decided that, initially, the glossary will be produced in English and will contain definitions of the most frequently used soccer terms. Your job is to compile a corpus from which these terms and definitions will be taken. What should be taken into consideration when designing such a corpus?

Scenario 3

Emily is a trained French-to-English translator. Although she has no formal training in computer science, she specializes in translating texts in the field of computer hardware. She has found that the field is evolving so quickly that many of the dictionaries she consults are out of date. Furthermore, she works on such tight deadlines that she finds it difficult to collect and read recent comparable English documentation on the subject. Emily has asked you to help her compile a corpus that she can use as a type of comparable English document from which she can draw appropriate terminology, usage references (e.g. collocations, syntactic constructions) and subject field knowledge in order to help her produce accurate and idiomatic translations in the specialized subfield of computer hardware. How would you go about designing such a corpus?

4 Compiling a special purpose corpus

Now that you have learnt the basics about designing a special purpose corpus, we will turn our attention to issues relating to corpus compilation. Once you have mapped out the design of your ideal corpus, your next task is to identify and collect suitable texts for inclusion in that corpus. At this point you may find that you run into practical problems that make it difficult for you to actually build your ideal corpus. For example, you may not be able to find all the texts you need in electronic form. You may find the process of identifying and downloading texts from the Web or CD-ROMs more time consuming than expected, or you may not have copyright permission to hold certain texts in your corpus (see discussion on page 59). What this means is that you may have to be willing to make some adjustments to your ideal design. It is important to be realistic and to balance the time and effort required to construct your corpus against the benefits that you will gain by consulting it. For instance, if you are building the corpus to help you with one short assignment for class, then it is probably not a good use of your time to spend a month constructing the corpus, but if you plan to use the corpus over the duration of the academic year, then you can justify spending a longer period of time constructing it. In addition, it is important to remember that a corpus can still be a useful resource, even if it does not perfectly resemble the ideal corpus that you planned during the design stage. The most important thing is for you to be aware of any shortcomings that your corpus may have (e.g. some of the texts are a little bit old; some of the authors' credentials are unclear) and to keep these in mind when interpreting the data.

We should point out that the discussions in this chapter apply primarily to situations where you can gain access to a reasonable amount of electronic data with a minimum of fuss. For widely used languages, such as English, a great number of texts are readily available in electronic form on the Web. In addition, there are numerous commercially available CD-ROMs and online databases, many of which are dedicated to specialized subject fields (e.g. *Computer Select*, *Business Link*). In the appendix, you will find a list of resources that may prove useful as a starting point for compiling corpora in a number of different subject fields. If you plan to work with less widely used languages, or in extremely specialized subject fields, you may find it more difficult to locate suitable material in electronic form. In such cases, it may be possible to convert printed texts into electronic form by either typing in the text or by using technology such as optical character recognition software or dictation software. However, these technologies are not foolproof and the converted texts must be carefully proof-read and edited, which can be very time consuming. For this reason, it may not be worthwhile typing in or converting printed texts. The good news is, however, that with each passing day, more and more machine-readable data is becoming available in all languages and subject fields. Therefore, even if resources in a particular language or domain are not easily accessible at the moment, the situation is likely to be different in the near future.

In the following sections, we will begin by addressing the issue of copyright, which is an important concern relating to corpus compilation. We will then go on to explain how you can identify and acquire electronic texts from two main sources: the Web and CD-ROMs/online databases. The focus here will be on constructing monolingual corpora, but details regarding additional specialized pre-processing that must be carried out on parallel corpora (e.g. **alignment**) will be explored further in Chapter 6.

Copyright and permissions

When you are building a corpus, it is very important for you to consider whether or not the texts that you find can legally or ethically be incorporated. Like printed texts, electronic texts are also subject to copyright, and if you would like to include a text in a corpus, you should first establish the precise details of the ownership and obtain the owner's permission. Because electronic media are a relatively new phenomenon, copyright laws in some countries may pre-date this technology, which means that these laws may be unclear about ownership of electronic texts. However, the question of ownership may be morally obvious, even if it is not legally clear, and many countries are in the process of updating their laws to address this issue.

In order to be safe, you should contact the owner of any text that you want to include in your corpus and obtain his or her permission. Unfortunately, this is not always a straightforward process. Sometimes, it may not be clear who holds the copyright or it may be difficult to track down contact details (e.g. for some web sites). Even if you are able to identify the copyright holders, one of the biggest problems is that such people may not understand what a corpus is or how it is used. For example, an author may be worried that you will make his or her entire text available for people to read and that fewer people will then buy the book or magazine in question. Therefore, when writing to ask for permission to use a text, it is a good idea to explain what you plan to do with the text and to explain how data looks when it is displayed in a concordance. Figure 4.1 contains a sample explanation that you might include as part of a letter or email to copyright holders.

Once copyright holders understand how you plan to use their texts, they may be more willing to give permission for you to hold these texts in your corpus. Another option is to ask for permission to hold just part of a text (rather than the complete text) in your corpus. Nevertheless, this strategy does have implications for LSP investigations as we saw in the section on text extracts (page 49). In spite of your efforts to reassure copyright holders, there may still be some people who choose not to grant

---

To whom it may concern:

I am conducting a linguistic investigation using an approach based on the study of authentic textual data. This approach involves using a type of software known as concordancing software, which is used to show a word in context. If you enter a specific search word, the program will retrieve all the occurrences of that word from a particular text or collection of texts and then display these in a concordance. A sample concordance for the word 'diseases' is illustrated below:

```
and certain other neurological diseases result from the destru
9th century, most debilitating diseases resulted from bacteria
other progressive degenerative diseases of the brain. Gene the
e achieved by attacking inborn diseases at their source. Among
o be useful for intervening in diseases affecting those tissue
the body.  The proof that such diseases did in fact derive fro
al because they cause no known diseases in people. What is mor
e cells of people with genetic diseases or cancer. A technique
heir source. Among the genetic diseases that have been studied
```

As you can see from this example, each concordance line is short and full sentences are not displayed. I am using the concordances to investigate linguistic patterns (e.g. to see which verbs are typically used with which nouns). I do not discuss the subject content of the concordance lines as this is not relevant to my work. Nor do I intend to display the names of the authors of any of the lines produced.

I have identified a number of articles on your web site and I would like to include these in my corpus of texts. I would be very grateful if you would grant me permission to use these texts to produce concordances similar to the one shown above.

Figure 4.1 A sample letter requesting permission to hold a text in your corpus

you permission to use their texts, and you should respect their wishes and look for other material instead.

Electronic resources

Given the difficulties associated with converting printed texts into electronic form, it is often a better option for you to try to identify texts that are already in electronic form, and there are a number of places where you can go to find electronic texts. One option is to contact the publisher of a printed text to see if it is possible to purchase the text in electronic form. Some publishers are more willing to do this than others, but it may be worth asking. Two other ways of finding electronic texts are searching the Web and searching CD-ROMs or online databases.

Working with the World Wide Web

The World Wide Web (Web) contains a wealth of information, and this is one of its greatest strengths but also one of its biggest weaknesses. Although it is possible to find information on almost any subject, it can be a daunting task to know where to begin looking. In addition, once you begin searching for texts, you may be overwhelmed by the number that you find.

Searching for texts on the Web

There are two main tools that you can use to help you locate candidate texts for inclusion in your corpus: **search engines** and **subject directories**. A search engine is a tool that will search the Web for sites containing the words that you enter as search terms. Examples of search engines include Alta Vista, Google, Northern Light and Yahoo, and some web addresses for popular search engines are provided at the end of this chapter. For example, if you are interested in finding texts about mountain climbing, you can simply enter the search term 'mountain climbing' into a search engine. The search engine will display the results in the form of links to those web sites that contain the search term 'mountain climbing'. If you find that you do not retrieve very many interesting texts, you could try broadening your search by using other related search terms, such as 'mountaineering' or 'outdoor adventure activities'. In contrast, if you find that you have retrieved too much information, you could try narrowing down your search to just one particular facet of mountain climbing, such as 'mountain climbing equipment' or try combining multiple search terms using what are known as **boolean operators**. Boolean operators typically include AND, OR, and NOT, and you can use these to search for sites that contain references to both 'mountain climbing' AND 'Everest', or to either 'mountain climbing' OR 'mountaineering', or even to exclude sites that are not of interest, such as 'mountaineering' NOT 'club'. Instructions about how to use boolean operators can be found on most search engine pages.

Publishers of web pages register their site with one or more search engines and the information is stored in indexed databases that are searched by the engines whenever you enter a search term. Not every site is registered with every search engine, which means that if you do not retrieve many interesting sites when searching with one particular search engine, it may be useful to try the same search again using a different search engine. Another alternative is to try using a meta-search engine, such as C4, ProFusion, MetaCrawler or Dogpile. A meta-search engine does not create its own database of information but rather it searches the databases of other search engines. By using a meta-search engine, you can consult a dozen or more search engines at once.

Unlike search engines, which are computerized tools, subject directories (sometimes called web directories) are created and organized by people who choose their own terms and classify web sites according to their own view of a subject field. When using a subject directory, you conduct your searches by selecting a series of progressively narrower search terms. For example, to find information about mountain climbing using a subject directory, you might start out at a high-level category such as 'recreation', which has been further broken down into subcategories that include 'hobbies' and 'outdoors', and 'outdoors' has been further categorized into 'camping', 'fishing', 'mountaineering', etc. Because subject directories have been created by people, each subject directory may be organized in a slightly different way. Many search engine sites also contain subject directories (e.g. Yahoo, AltaVista, Google).

Both search engines and subject directories have strengths and weaknesses. When using a subject directory, you have more direct control over their searching and you are able to browse more selectively; however, there is a fixed vocabulary associated with these directories. In contrast, a search engine is more automated and you can use it to find more specific sites because any term can be used as a search term; however, the downside is that the search engine might retrieve an excessive number of hits and you may have to spend a long time sorting through them in order to find the ones that are most useful to you.

It is beyond the scope of this book to provide a detailed list of tips that can help you search the Web effectively, but there are a number of excellent tutorials available online that can help you to refine your search skills. Some of these are listed at the end of the chapter.

Selecting appropriate texts

Once you have identified web sites of potential interest, you can examine them more closely. At this time, you need to keep in mind the specific criteria that you drew up during the design stage and you should evaluate each text in the light of these criteria. After you have examined the texts that were retrieved during your search, you may decide that further searches are necessary in order to fill in any gaps that may exist or to increase the size of the corpus.

In addition to bearing in mind the design criteria that you established for the project, there are a number of other factors that may be worth considering when working with the Web. The first is that corpus processing is a text-based activity, but the Web is a multimedia resource. Many of the web pages or sites integrate words with pictures, sound, video, etc., and in some cases, these non-text-based elements may be essential to the understanding of the page. When building a textual corpus, it may be a good idea to try to choose web pages that are not dependent on other forms of media. In saying this, we are not trying to suggest that you would not benefit from consulting multimedia documents, merely that multimedia documents may not be the best type to include in a corpus that is going to be processed using text-based corpus analysis tools.

Another potential drawback to working with the Web is that it may be time consuming. Even if you are fortunate enough to have a high-speed connection to the Internet, the very nature of the Web is that it makes use of hyperlinks, which means that although a web site as a whole may contain a lot of information, each individual page may contain relatively little data. Since each page must be downloaded separately, it can be a labour intensive process to piece together the various elements of a text from different hyperlinked pages. Therefore, when evaluating web sites you may find it useful to identify sites that collect the bulk of their information on one or two pages rather than sites where the data is spread over a great number of pages.

A final problem to be considered when working with web resources is the problem of quality control. One of the reasons that so much information is available on the Web is that virtually anyone can post information to the Web. Unlike printed texts, which typically go through some type of editorial process before being published, the Web is a forum where almost anyone can publish their work, even in an unedited form. Therefore, you must take care when selecting texts from the Web for inclusion in your corpus by considering factors such as whether or not the site has been approved by an official organization or whether the author is a subject field expert.

Downloading texts

Once you have identified the texts that you would like to include in your corpus, the next step is to download them from the Web. Texts on the Web are encoded using a special language called HyperText Markup Language (HTML). A text that has been encoded using HTML contains a number of tags (shown between angle brackets) that contain information such as instructions that tell the computer how to display the text. Figure 4.2 shows a sample extract of text that has been encoded using HTML. Figure 4.3 shows the same text as it would appear if viewed through a web browser, such as Netscape's Navigator or Microsoft's Internet Explorer.

```
<html>
<head>
<title>ScienceDirect Web editions – Developmental Brain Research : Differential expression of
S100B and S100A61 in the human fetal and aged cerebral cortex</title>
</head>
<body bgcolor="#ffffff" text="#000000">
<table width="600" cellpadding="0" cellspacing="0" border="0">
<tr width="600">
<td width="340" align="left" valign="middle"><b>
<a href="toc_brain.htm">Volume 119, Issue 2</a></b></td>
</tr>
</table>
<p><img src="line.gif" border="0" alt width="600" height="5"><br>
<font size="-1">PII: S0165-3806(99)00151-0</font><br>
<font size="-1">Copyright © 2000 Elsevier Science B.V. All rights reserved.
</font></p>
<h4>Research report</h4>
<p><strong><big><big>Differential expression of S100B<a name="fnb1">
</a><a href="#fn1"><sup>1</sup></a>
and S100A6<sup>1</sup> in the human fetal and aged cerebral cortex </big></big></p>
<p>S. C. Tiu<a href="#orfa"<sup>a</sup></a>, W. Y. Chan<sup><a href=
"#orfa">a</a>,</sup><a nme="bcor*"></a><a href="#cor*"><sup>*</sup>
</a>, C. W. Heizmann<a href="#orfb"><sup>b</sup></a>, B. W. Schäfer
<a href="#orfb"><sup>b</sup></a>, S. Y. Shu<a href="orfc">
<sup>c</sup></a> and David T. Yew<a href="#orfa"><sup>a</sup></a>
</strong><br>
<br clear="ALL">
<a name="orfa"><sup>a</sup> Department of Anatomy, Faculty of Medicine, The Chinese
University of Hong Kong, Shatin, NT, Hong Kong, China<br clear="ALL">
<a name="orfb"></a><sup>b</sup> Division of Clinical Chemistry and Biochemistry,
Department of Paediatrics, University of Zürich, Zürich, Switzerland<br clear="ALL">
<a name="orfc"></a><sup>c</sup> Institute of Neuroscience, First Military Medical University,
Guangzhou, China<br>
<br clear="ALL">
Accepted 21 September 1999. Available online 14 February 2000. <br clear="ALL">
```

Figure 4.2 An extract from a text that has been encoded using HTML

ScienceDirect Web editions - Developmental Brain Research : Differential expression of S100B an - Microsoft Internet Explorer

File Edit View Favorites Tools Help

Back Forward Stop Refresh Home Search Favorites Media History Mail Print Edit

Address http://www.web-editions.com/brain_summaryplus.htm Go Liens

Go gle Recherche Web Recherche site Infos page Monter

Home Browse Account Help

SCIENCE DIRECT
Web editions

1 of 19 article list previous next

journals

Developmental Brain Research

Volume 119, Issue 2
7 February 2000
Pages 159-168

▸ SummaryPlus
Article
Journal Format-PDF (1954 K)

PII: S0165-3806(99)00151-0
Copyright © 2000 Elsevier Science B.V. All rights reserved.

Research report

Differential expression of S100B[1] and S100A6[1] in the human fetal and aged cerebral cortex

S. C. Tiu[a], W. Y. Chan[a, *], C. W. Heizmann[b], B. W. Schäfer[b], S. Y. Shu[c] and David T. Yew[a]

[a] Department of Anatomy, Faculty of Medicine, The Chinese University of Hong Kong, Shatin, NT, Hong Kong, China
[b] Division of Clinical Chemistry and Biochemistry, Department of Paediatrics, University of Zürich, Zurich, Switzerland
[c] Institute of Neuroscience, First Military Medical University, Guangzhou, China

Accepted 21 September 1999. Available online 14 February 2000.

Done Internet

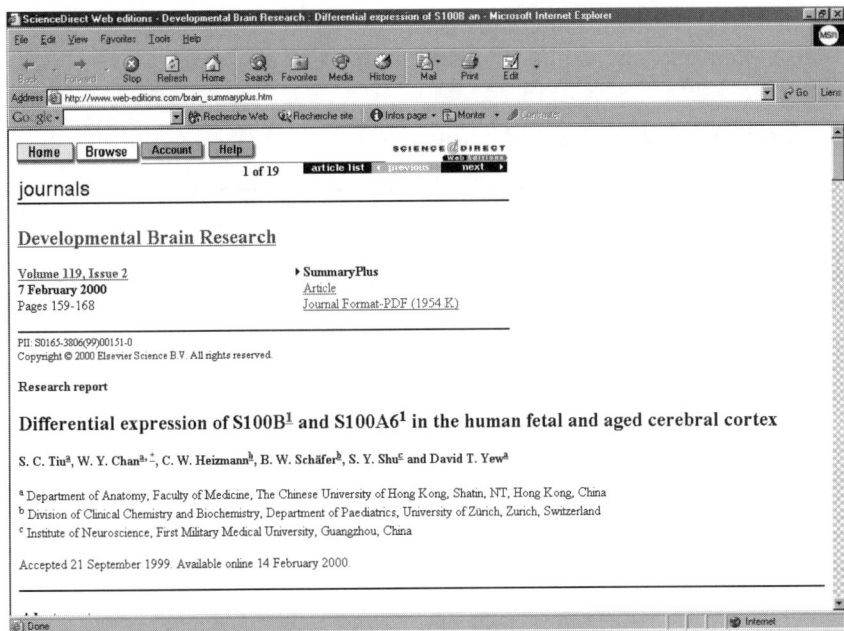

Figure 4.3 A text viewed through a web browser

If a text is downloaded from the Web in HTML format, this may or may not cause problems when you want to process the text using corpus analysis software. Some corpus analysis tools are capable of processing HTML text, and they allow you to hide the tags so that the text appears as if you are simply reading plain text. However, if a text is already encoded in HTML, this may mean that you are not able to annotate the text in other ways that may prove useful (see Chapter 5). Therefore, if you wish to use software that cannot process HTML, or if you plan to annotate the software using a different set of tags, it will be necessary to download the texts from the Web using a different format.

One option is to simply select all the text on screen and then copy and paste it into a word processor (e.g. Notepad, Word, WordPerfect). A drawback of this approach is that, depending on the browser and the word processor in question, the graphics and formatting may be retained. Another option is to use the 'save as' feature of the browser to save the text as a plain text file. In this case, all graphics and formatting will be lost, but the text may contain unwanted line breaks (the same thing can happen when you copy and paste). Depending on the software that you plan to use to process the corpus, it may be necessary to remove these line breaks manually or by using a find and replace feature in a word processor. Of course, it may be the case that some line breaks should be retained (e.g. between paragraphs), so you should think carefully before using *global* find and replace features such as 'replace all'.

Working with CD-ROMs and online databases

In addition to the Web, CD-ROMs and online databases are another source of electronic texts. Many publishers are now making information available in electronic form by publishing it on CD-ROM or in an online database that can be accessed over the Internet. A disadvantage of using CD-ROMs and databases is that it can be costly since many of these services are offered only by subscription. However, if you do not require the most recent edition of a publication, it may be possible to access back issues or archived information at a reduced rate, or even for free.

One advantage of using CD-ROMs or online databases instead of the Web as a resource for finding texts to include in a corpus is that it is generally easier to verify the quality of the information they contain. Most commercially available CD-ROMs and databases contain publications, such as newspapers, encyclopedias, specialized and semi-specialized magazines, or textbooks, which have been edited in a similar fashion to their corresponding print publications. Of course, this raises another issue, which may be considered a drawback to working with CD-ROMs or online databases: only a limited number of text types are likely to be published in this format. It is unlikely, for example, that you will find certain text types, such as tourist brochures or legal contracts, published on CD-ROM. In contrast, there are many sample contracts and electronic brochures published on the Web.

Searching for texts on CD-ROMs and online databases

CD-ROMs and online databases can store vast amounts of data and, therefore, most of them come with specially designed proprietary search-and-retrieval software that allows you to identify and extract relevant texts. Typically, you can do this using a keyword search, but sometimes other types of search criteria can also be used. For example, the *Computer Select* CD-ROM contains thousands of English-language articles that have been published in hundreds of different specialized and semi-specialized computer-related publications. In addition to allowing keyword searches anywhere in the text, the *Computer Select* CD-ROM allows you to search by topic (according to a list of pre-indexed terms), author, date, publication name, product name, company name or article type (e.g. feature, review, column, editorial, buyer's guide, etc.). Other CD-ROMs, such as *New Scientist*, contain multiple issues of a single publication, but you can search in certain sections of the journal (e.g. Features, Review, Columns, Letters, etc.).

Frequently, the different types of search criteria available for use with a given CD-ROM or database can be combined to form complex queries (e.g. searching by keyword AND date AND section). In this way, you can narrow down your searches to meet many of the criteria that were outlined during the design stage. For example, you could construct a search for all *New Scientist* articles containing the term 'pharmaceutical' that were written in the year 2000 and that appeared in the Features section of the journal.

Although the search programs provided by CD-ROMs and databases are largely similar (e.g. they all typically permit keyword searches), the specific ways of formulating a search might differ slightly from program to program. To learn how to conduct effective searches, consult the 'help' feature of the CD-ROM or database that you plan to use.

Selecting appropriate texts

Once the search criteria have been entered, the software will return a list of all the texts on the CD-ROM or in the database that meet those criteria. At this point you generally have the choice of either exporting all these texts or scrolling through them and selecting certain ones for export. It is probably a good idea to scroll through the texts that have been retrieved and to quickly scan through their contents to make sure that they meet the general design criteria that you have outlined for your project. Texts that do meet the criteria can be selected for export while texts that do not meet the criteria can be ignored. Like the Web, CD-ROMs and databases also support multimedia (e.g. text integrated with pictures, sound, video, etc.). Given that corpus processing is primarily a text-based activity, it may be a good idea to select those texts that can be easily understood without relying heavily on other media.

If, during this browsing stage, it becomes clear that you have retrieved too few or too many texts, you should re-examine your search query. Maybe the query was not well formed (e.g. perhaps the range of publication dates should be narrowed down or perhaps a synonym or alternate spelling should be included in the keyword search). It is possible that you will retrieve a more relevant selection of texts if you reformulate or refine your search query.

Exporting texts

Depending on the CD-ROM or database in question, it may be possible to export all the selected texts at once to a single file, or it may be necessary to export each text individually to a separate file. The advantage of keeping the texts in separate files is that it may be easier to manage the corpus (e.g. removing texts that become outdated). However, although some corpus analysis tools allow multiple files to be processed at once, other tools may actually require that all the texts in the corpus be stored in a single file. If the corpus must be stored in a single file, you may have to cut and paste the individual text files into a single large file (e.g. using a word processor).

You may be able to choose the file format you want to use when exporting texts. For example, *Computer Select* gives you the choice of exporting texts as either plain text files (.txt) or in rich text format (.rtf). Your choice may depend on the corpus analysis software that you plan to use to process the corpus. Some corpus analysis tools can only process plain text, while others may require the corpus to be converted into a proprietary format. There are several advantages to saving the texts in plain text format. First, plain text files take up less storage space on the disk than other formats. This might be important as the size and number of corpora that you are working with increase. Second, most applications can process plain text files, and even in those cases where the texts must later be converted to a proprietary format, it is likely that the input format for the conversion process will be plain text. One disadvantage to plain text is that all the formatting information will be lost. In many cases, this is not critical; however, there may be times where it would be useful to retain some types of formatting (e.g. italics or bold could be used to indicate an important term in the LSP). Another disadvantage may be that if structural formatting is lost, you will not be able to search for information in a specific area of the text (e.g. heading, caption).

Clearly, some of the decisions that you need to make (e.g. export format, single vs multiple files) will depend primarily on the tools that you are planning to work with. The best thing to do is to consult the user manual or help files that come with the corpus analysis tool in question and proceed according to these instructions.

Corpus compilation: an example

Looking back to Chapter 3, you will recall that you had constructed a wish list for an ideal corpus to help you familiarize yourself with the basic terms in the LSP of photography, including those used to describe fundamental concepts (e.g. light, composition), as well as those used to discuss basic camera equipment. For your convenience, we have reproduced that wish list in Figure 4.4.

Now that you have your wish list, it is time to begin looking for texts that meet these criteria. You decide that you will use the Web as your principal resource for collecting texts since you have easy access to the Internet. You decide to begin your search using the Yahoo subject directory (http://www.yahoo.com). From here you follow the links *Arts and Humanities > Visual Arts > Photography* and you are presented with the category choices shown in Figure 4.5. The numbers in parentheses indicate the number of web pages linked to each category.

Some of these categories deal with specific techniques (e.g. Zone System, Large Format), specialized equipment (e.g. Digital, Infrared) or particular

Size	Initial goal of 25,000 words, but corpus will be open and can be expanded
Number of texts	Minimum of 20 texts by different authors
Medium	Written
Subject	Photography basics, parts of conventional cameras
Text type	Introductory texts (e.g. tutorials, text books, introductory articles)
Authorship	Texts written by experts
Language	Texts written in English by native speakers
Publication date	Recent texts (not more than 3 years old)

Figure 4.4 Wish list for basic photography corpus

types of photography (e.g. Kirlian Photography, Pinhole Photography, Subminiature and Spy Photography), so you decide to eliminate them from your list. Other categories, such as Contests, Events, and Museums and Galleries, are more related to displaying the finished results, rather than the process and equipment. You decide to begin your search by focusing on the following categories: Cameras and Photographers' Resources.

It is not practical for us to list all the sites linked to these two categories, but both of them lead to a wide variety of potentially useful resources. Why not try investigating some of them yourself by going to the Yahoo subject directory?

Getting back to our example, let us assume that you make note of a number of sites that look as if they might be helpful (e.g. by 'bookmarking' them in your Internet browser). Next, you decide to expand your search with the help of a search engine. In order to retrieve suitable texts using a search engine, you must be careful to formulate an appropriate search query. If you simply type in 'photography' as your search term, you will be overwhelmed by the number of hits, and these will cover all different areas of photography, many of which will not interest you. There are several ways in which you can choose to restrict your search. For example, since you want to restrict your search to English-language texts, you decide to use the Alta Vista search engine (http://www.altavista.com), which allows you to specify English as your search language. Next, you try to refine your search term. Since you are interested in introductory texts about photography, you decide to use terms such as 'introductory', 'introduction' or

3-D (17)	Magazines (87)
Cameras (186)	Medium Format (6)
Chats and Forums (8)	Museums and Galleries (37)
Contests (32)	Organizations (115)
Digital (634)	Panoramic (27)
Education (49)	Photographers (1943)
Events (6)	Photographers' Resources (70)
Exhibits (160)	Pinhole Photography (14)
History (40)	Preservation (5)
Infrared (22)	Subminiature and Spy Photography (5)
Institutes (7)	Thematic (492)
Kirlian Photography (7)	Toy Camera Photography (29)
Large Format (9)	Zone system (3)

Figure 4.5 Subcategories presented as part of a subject directory for
'photography'

'basics' as part of your query, along with the keyword 'photography'. Similarly, to find sites about cameras, you decide to try using a search term such as 'camera parts', rather than just 'camera'. You also use a boolean operator to specify that you want to search for information on cameras that are NOT digital cameras. Can you think of any other ways of narrowing down your search?

If you try these searches yourself (using either a subject directory or a search engine), you will see that there is certainly a lot of information available on photography! Nevertheless, it may not be all that straightforward to build a corpus that matches your specified criteria. As a result, you decide to revisit your ideal wish list and make some changes based on your experience.

For example, although there are definitely enough texts about photography on the Web to meet your goal of 25,000 words from texts written by at least twenty different authors, you have difficulty in obtaining permission from some copyright owners to include their texts in your corpus. In some cases, there were no contact details provided and, in other cases, owners simply were not willing to give permission, even after you had explained how the text would be used. Regrettably, this means that some potentially useful texts will not be included in your corpus.

Another problem that has caused you to rethink the size of your corpus is the fact that it is proving to be time consuming to download individual web pages. You decide to adjust your target goal to 10,000 words for the time being (with a possibility of expanding later on) and to aim for texts written by at least ten different authors, rather than twenty.

With regard to subject, you decide to store the texts in two separate files, thus creating two separate subcorpora – one for basic techniques and one for camera parts. You aim to make the two corpora roughly the same size.

As far as text type is concerned, you discover that there are very few textbooks of any kind available over the Internet, and there are relatively few tutorials on photography. You briefly consider typing or scanning in part of a printed text book, but you quickly decide that this would be too time consuming. This means that you will have to rely mainly on introductory articles to get the type of information that you are looking for, although you are pleased to discover a site for an online encyclopedia of photography that looks very promising – a kind of introductory text that you had not initially thought to look for!

With regard to authorship (whether the author is an acknowledged expert), language (whether the text was written by a native speaker) and publication date (whether the text is recent), the main problem is that these details are not always included on a web page. Nevertheless, there are still some ways in which you attempt to determine the suitability of a text for inclusion in your corpus. For example, if a text comes from the page of a recognized camera manufacturer (e.g. Kodak), you decide that it has probably been composed by a knowledgeable expert. In contrast, if the text in question was found on a personal homepage, such as 'Tom's Guide to Photography' page or 'Carol's Photo Page', you decide not to include this information. Of course, it is entirely possible that Tom and Carol are expert photographers, but unless they indicate their credentials on the web page, you cannot be certain so you decide to play it safe by excluding such texts from your corpus.

With regard to language, as an LSP learner, you do not feel that you are in a position to determine whether or not a text has been written by a native speaker. In some cases, the author's name or address provide some kind of indication, but not always. In unclear cases, you decide to ask one of your friends who is a native speaker to quickly peruse the text and give you his/her opinion with regard to the fluency of the text.

Finally, regarding the publication date, when there is no date listed on the site, there is no way of knowing how current the information is, so you decide to leave undated material out of your corpus. Your revised wish list is shown in Figure 4.6.

The point of this example was simply to demonstrate that while it is useful to carefully analyse the goals of your project and to design a corpus that would ideally meet these requirements, there are often practical constraints that may make it difficult to actually compile your 'ideal' corpus. This does not mean that you should abandon all your corpus-building efforts; it simply means that you should be prepared to be a little bit flexible and to re-examine your ideal criteria in the light of the resources at hand. If you are willing to do this, you will end up with a corpus that,

	Ideal criteria	**Revised criteria**
Size	Initial goal of 25,000 words, but corpus will be open and can be expanded	Reduce to 10,000 words for the initial corpus because it is time consuming to download texts and permission is not always granted by owners (but corpus will remain open)
Number of texts	Minimum of 20 texts by different authors	Reduce to minimum of 10 texts by different authors
Medium	Written	No change
Subject	Photography basics, parts of conventional cameras	Same subject but organized into two separate subcorpora of roughly equal size
Text type	Introductory texts (e.g. tutorials, text books, introductory articles)	Mainly introductory articles plus articles from an online encyclopedia of photography
Authorship	Texts written by acknowledged experts	Texts written by acknowledged experts and texts from professional sites
Language	Texts written in English by native speakers	Texts written in English by native speakers and texts that appear to be fluent based on a native speaker's judgement
Publication date	Recent texts (not more than 3 years old)	No change

Figure 4.6 Revised list of criteria

though not perfect, will still have the potential to provide you with a wealth of valuable information about your chosen LSP. Always keep in mind, however, that critical judgement is essential when interpreting corpus data – any decisions that you make about appropriate LSP use may be corpus-based, but they should not necessarily be corpus-bound!

Key points

- When compiling a corpus, you should obtain permission from copyright holders before including their texts in your corpus.
- Electronic texts can be readily obtained from sources such as the Web or CD-ROMs, though these texts may require some clean up (e.g. removing unwanted line breaks or spaces).
- Given that corpora are text-based resources, it is better to choose documents that do not rely heavily on other media (e.g. graphics, sound, video).
- Remember that even if your corpus does not end up meeting all the requirements you laid out in the design phase (e.g. the corpus is smaller than you would like, some of the authors' qualifications are unclear, some of the texts are not recent), it can still be a useful resource. The most important thing is to be aware of its shortcomings and to take these into account when interpreting the data.

Further reading

Austermühl, Frank (2001) *Electronic Tools for Translators*, Manchester: St Jerome Publishing.
Barnbrook, Geoff (1996) *Language and Computers*, Edinburgh: Edinburgh University Press.

Search engines and meta-search engines

Alta Vista: http://www.altavista.com
C4: http://www.c4.com
Dogpile: http://www.dogpile.com
Google: http://www.google.com
MetaCrawler: http://www.metacrawler.com
Northern Light: http://www.northernlight.com
ProFusion: http://www.profusion.com
Yahoo: http://www.yahoo.com

Tutorials for effective web searching

The Internet Search Tutorial for Translators: http://www.mabercom.com/websearch/index/html

The Complete Planet Guide to Effective Searching of the Internet: http://www.completeplanet.com/Tutorials/Search/index.asp

Finding Information on the Internet: A Tutorial: http://www.lib.berkeley.edu/TeachingLib/Guides/Internet/FindInfo.html

Web Search Strategies: http://home.sprintmail.com/~debflanagan/main.html

Potential LSP resources for corpus building

In the appendix you will find a few suggestions that may serve as starting points for helping you to locate suitable resources in specialized fields. Full access to some of these resources is only available through paid subscription; however, a number are freely available, and most others allow limited access free of charge.

Exercise

Emily is a French-to-English translator who has been commissioned to translate an article on DVDs for publication in a forthcoming issue of a popularized computing magazine. Emily has hired you to help her compile a corpus containing texts that meet the following criteria:

- Complete texts
- Written in English (preferably by native speakers)
- Aimed at the general public (i.e. not too technical)
- Taken from reputable sources (e.g. published by respected authors, organizations or companies)
- Not more than two years old

Using the Web as your principal resource, try to identify ten texts that you would include in the corpus. Use web tools such as search engines and subject directories to help you identify potential texts. Identify the copyright holders of those texts and make note of an address where you could contact them to ask for permission to hold the texts in your corpus. (Note that you do not actually have to contact them; just try to identify who is the copyright holder.) Next, download and clean up the texts in preparation for including them in the corpus. Save the texts in plain text format in a single file. Be prepared to comment on any difficulties that you encountered and to explain how the corpus that you actually compiled differs from the corpus that you would have ideally liked to compile.

5 Markup and annotation

> Corpora are useful only if we can extract knowledge or information from them. The fact is that to extract information from a corpus, we often have to begin by building information in.
>
> (Geoffrey Leech in Garside et al. 1997: 4)

While most of you will work most or all of the time with what is known as 'raw' text, some of you may be interested in working with what are known as 'marked up' and/or 'annotated' texts so that you can carry out more sophisticated linguistic investigations. In this chapter, we will introduce the concepts of markup and annotation and we will take a look at different types of markup and annotation systems and their uses in corpus linguistics. As a starting point, we will look at markup in a word processing environment, as some readers are likely to know something about this already. We will focus initially on markup, which determines the appearance of a document. We will then look at markup systems designed to represent the structure of documents. From there we will move on to a discussion of annotation and different types of annotation systems. We will focus on part-of-speech tagging systems because these are the most readily (and freely) available. As a number of web sites now offer automatic part-of-speech tagging, we will use the output from some of these sites to explain tagging procedures and to show how corpus tagging can allow you to refine your queries.

What is markup?

While we tend nowadays to associate the term with documents generated on computer, the concept of markup goes back a long way, right back to pre-computer days in fact. Marks were put on texts in order to tell typesetters in the printing industry how to lay out texts. The marks were inserted manually with a pen or pencil by the typists or writers of the text. The marks represented specific instructions regarding the physical appearance of a document. Such instructions indicated, for example, which parts of the text were to be displayed as headings and sub-headings, which parts were to be displayed as standard paragraphs, which parts were to be formatted in columns, which parts were to be indented and by how much. The markup scheme used was a type of shorthand language with different symbols representing different instructions. Many of the symbols used to mark up texts in the past are still in use today by proof-readers.

Markup in the word processing environment

When computers replaced typewriters, and word processing programs were developed, the need for manual markup was greatly reduced. This was because word processors (and desktop publishing software) enabled writers of texts to do much of the markup themselves and to format the texts in the manner in which they wished to present them. This type of markup, which involves instructing a computer about how a text is to look on paper, is usually referred to as procedural markup. With procedural markup, writers can centre text, embolden text, put text in italics, create columns and tables, etc. There are different ways of applying procedural markup and we plan to look at them here as a means of introducing you to other types of markup later on in the chapter.

We are assuming that you use word processing packages on a fairly regular basis, and that you are generally required to submit assignments, projects and dissertations in word-processed form. You probably like to use different fonts and different font sizes to mark different sections in your work and to make your work more attractive and easier to read. For example, you may like to put all main headings in Arial 16 bold and all sub-headings in Arial 14 italic. You may like to number your headings and sub-headings. You probably usually achieve the result you want by clicking on the drop down menu for font, font size and by clicking on the embolden feature, the italic feature or whichever other feature you wish to apply. If you number your headings, you probably insert the numbers yourself. An example of the output from this type of manual approach is displayed in Figure 5.1.

Once you have finished your document, you might then decide that you wish to centre all your main headings and to indent your sub-headings slightly. Again, you will probably click on the 'centre' and 'indent' icons respectively as you work your way through the document making the changes to each heading and sub-heading.

Whenever you determine or alter the appearance of any part of your document, you are in fact 'marking up' your document. A note of your changes is made by the system with the result that when you print your document, it will look exactly as you have specified.

The sophisticated word processing users among you may know that there is another more systematic way of applying procedural markup, i.e. of changing the appearance of different types of headings, tables, columns, etc., and that is by using what are known as built-in styles. Built-in styles

1 Main Heading

1.1 Sub-heading

Paragraph text

Figure 5.1 Different text appearance obtained using standard font and manual
numbering options

define the appearance of your document in a systematic way. If you decide
to alter the appearance of a particular style, all sections of a document
already formatted in that particular style will automatically update to
reflect the recent changes.

As you can gather from this brief introduction, if you use a word
processor, you already mark up your texts. The type of markup described
here relates primarily to the appearance of your text, e.g. which part of
the text is to be left aligned, which part indented, etc., and will determine how the text appears on paper or on screen. If you have used
different heading styles for different heading levels, as we have done for
this book, you are not only determining the appearance of the different
heading levels but you are also determining the logical structure of your
document. This makes it possible to generate a table of contents automatically based on the heading levels you have used. Figure 5.2 shows
part of the outline of this chapter, with 5.1 as a level 2 heading, and
5.1.1 and 5.1.2 as level 3 headings, and 5.1.2.1 and 5.1.2.2 as level 4
headings. The numbering is generated automatically based on the different
heading styles that have been applied.

Expanding the notion of markup: introducing SGML

When computerized markup was first introduced, it was usually system
dependent. This meant that if you produced a document using one word
processing program and wished to edit it using a different word processing
program, the chances were that the original procedural markup became
corrupt (i.e. unintelligible) or lost. This meant that not only were changes
in size and type of font likely to be lost but also distinctions between
different style types with the result that editors had to start again from
scratch if they wished to restore the document to its original state. A
further problem was that most markup methods were actually only
computerized versions of the original manual method and centred mainly
round procedural markup. It was gradually recognized that it would be
useful to devise methods which would facilitate the transfer of markup

Figure 5.2 Logical structure of early part of this chapter

from one computer system to another and which would allow for more markup than had previously been envisaged. More especially, there was a desire to develop a markup scheme, which would exploit the capabilities of computing systems and information retrieval systems in particular. The notion of descriptive markup began to emerge. With this markup approach, the different sections of a document (e.g. chapter, section, paragraph, sentence) are named explicitly. In other words, the information that this piece of text is a sentence is made explicit in the system. Gradually, descriptive markup schemes began to emerge as people began to appreciate the potential of explicitly marked-up documents. Yet an underlying problem still remained, the lack of compatibility between different markup schemes. This meant that a document marked up with one descriptive markup scheme could not be read by a system using a different markup scheme. The need for a standardized scheme became increasingly urgent.

In the 1960s, a man called Dr Charles Goldfarb developed just such a standardized scheme. The scheme, which was designed to facilitate exchange of documents between different systems, was known as **SGML** (Standard Generalized Markup Language, ISO8879). SGML is a descriptive encoding scheme. The idea underlying SGML was that if a text were marked up using SGML, all of the SGML tags (as the marks are called) would automatically travel with the document, regardless of the software being used to process the document. In other words, the description of the document would not be lost during transfer and it would be possible to exchange documents between different systems. This was crucial.

SGML is a language that allows users to encode documents so that the documents can be recognized by different pieces of software. The emphasis is on formally encoding the structure and type of a document rather than on simply encoding the appearance of documents, as we saw earlier with procedural markup. Thus, within a document, SGML is concerned with distinguishing explicitly between different components such as headings, sub-headings, paragraphs, footnotes, tables, etc. At document level, it is

```
<heading>Markup in the word processing environment</heading>
<p>When computers replaced typewriters, and word processing programs were developed,
the need for manual markup was greatly reduced.</p>
```

Figure 5.3 SGML tags marking headings and paragraphs

concerned with distinguishing between different types of documents, i.e. distinguishing between reports and novels, to take a rather extreme example, or distinguishing between reports and books perhaps, to take a less extreme example. SGML uses markup or tags to encode different parts of documents. Each tag indicates the beginning (marked by <>) or end (marked by </>) of part of a document. Thus, the tag <p>, for example, will indicate the beginning of a paragraph and the tag </p> will indicate the end of a paragraph. The tag <heading> will indicate the beginning of a heading, the tag </heading> the end of a heading, as you can see in Figure 5.3.

Document type definitions

In addition to specifying tags for the lower-level features of a document (e.g. headings, paragraphs, sentences), SGML is used in the creation of what are known as **document type definitions** (DTDs) to characterize the higher-level components of a document. The aim of a DTD is to define the legal building blocks of a document; in other words, it defines what the structure of a document is going to be and which elements are required. It formally defines the broad components and structure of a particular document type.[1] The document type definition is used by SGML editors to assist writers in the production of documents; writers are given a document structure with which they work by moving from one document component to the next. The document type definition is also used by SGML parsers; in this instance, a document is analysed automatically to check that it complies with a particular DTD. Thus, if a DTD for a poem, for example, specifies that a poem has an author, a title and any number of verses, any document meeting these specifications will be classified as a poem by the SGML parser, and any document not meeting these specifications will not be classified as a poem. Similarly, if a document type definition for a book specifies that it has a title, author, table of contents, any number of chapters and an index, only documents meeting

1 For an excellent introduction to SGML, go to http://etext.virginia.edu/bin/tei-tocs?
 div=DIV1&id=SG

these specifications will be classified as books by the SGML parser. In order for any document to be classified formally as a particular document type, it must meet the specifications of that document type's DTD.

SGML and corpus encoding

The rapidly growing interest in corpus-based research in recent years has given rise to a huge demand for corpora. As corpus compilation is both time-consuming and costly, reusability has always been an important issue. Consequently, one of the objectives of the people involved in large corpus compilation in Europe and the US has been to come up with a system whereby texts and corpora can, if so desired, be exchanged or integrated into larger projects. This has led to the creation of what is known as the Corpus Encoding Standard (CES). The CES is designed to 'serve as a widely accepted set of encoding standards for corpus-based work' (http://www.cs.vassar.edu/CES/). The CES uses SGML to encode those components of texts that are considered to be of interest in corpus-based research. The CES considers that there are three broad categories of information worth encoding for corpus-based research. These are a) documentation, b) primary data and c) linguistic annotation. Documentation refers to information about the text and its content (e.g. bibliographic details, language). Primary data refers to the components of a text, e.g. paragraphs, titles, footnotes, etc., and graphics. Linguistic annotation refers to the addition of explicit linguistic information such as part of speech information, discourse information, etc. (See pages 83–89 for more details.)

The information classified as documentation is generally provided in the form of a header attached to each document. The header is essentially an SGML based declaration. The CES has adopted a TEI header,

`<fileDesc>`	contains a full bibliographic description of an electronic file
`<encodingDesc>`	documents the relationship between an electronic text and the source or sources from which it was derived
`<profileDesc>`	provides a detailed description of non-bibliographic aspects of a text, specifically the languages and sublanguages used, the situation in which it was produced, the participants and their setting
`<revisionDesc>`	summarizes the revision history for a file

Figure 5.4 Four principal components of a TEI header

a header developed by the Text Encoding Initiative. While it is possible, with the TEI header, to provide a very wide variety of information about a document, the CES recommends, for reasons of cost and time, that only necessary information should be included. A TEI header has four principal components, as described in Figure 5.4 (http://etext.virginia/edu/bin/tei-tocs?div=DIV1&id=HD)

Of these, the <fileDesc> element is the only compulsory element in a TEI header; all of the others are optional. A full TEI header would contain the following SGML tags:

<teiHeader>

    <fileDesc> ... </fileDesc>

    <encodingDesc> ... </encodingDesc>

    <profileDesc> ... </profileDesc>

    <revisionDesc> ... </revisionDesc>

</teiHeader>

whereby <teiHeader> signals the beginning of the header and </teiHeader> the end. The appropriate information for each element is provided between the start and end tags of each element. Further elements can be nested within each of the elements above.

The fileDesc element contains three compulsory elements and four optional elements. The three compulsory elements are a) information about the title of a work, b) information concerning the publication or distribution of a work and c) information concerning the source or sources from which a computer file is derived. The file description contains the following, at the very least:

<teiHeader>

    <fileDesc>

        <titleStmt> ... </titleStmt>

        <publicationStmt> ... </publicationStmt>

        <sourceDesc> ... </sourceDesc>

    </fileDesc>

    <!- - remainder of TEI Header here - ->

    </teiHeader>

The basic TEI header for this book would look as follows:

```
<teiHeader>

   <fileDesc>

      <titleStmt>

         <title> 'Working with Specialized Language: a practical
         guide to using corpora</title>

         <author>Lynne Bowker, Jennifer Pearson</author>

      </titleStmt>

      <publicationStmt>

         <publisher>Routledge </publisher>

         <pubPlace>London</pubPlace>

         <date>2002</date>

      </publicationStmt>

      <sourceDesc>

      <bibl>'Working with Specialized Language: a practical guide to
      using corpora by Lynne Bowker and Jennifer Pearson (London:
      Routledge, 2002)</bibl>

      </sourceDesc>

   </teiHeader>
```

The advantages of adopting a standardized approach to the description
of documents and their contents are enormous. If all corpus compilers
were to adopt the Corpus Encoding Standard, the chances of corpus
exchange becoming a viable proposition would be greatly enhanced. As
you can gather from the brief discussion here, encoding is time consuming
and is therefore not for the fainthearted. We would point out, however,
that it is important to consider building in some form of encoding or
descriptive markup even if you are only compiling a very small corpus.
For example, if you have encoded information about document type into
your document header, you will be able to use this as a lever to retrieve
all documents from your corpus belonging to a given document type.
Thus, if you are interested only in investigating the language of reports,
for example, you can use the header information to retrieve and work
exclusively on all reports in your corpus. Similarly, you could retrieve
all texts written in a particular year, or all texts written by a specific
author.

What about HTML and XML?

With the development of the Web, it became necessary to develop a markup system for web documents because these documents differed, in some respects, from standard word-processed documents. For example, they often contained hypertext and multimedia components (music or video). HTML (hypertext markup language) was developed to facilitate the storage of such documents on the Web. HTML is based on SGML but is a great deal less flexible than SGML. With SGML, users can specify their own tags and there is no limit to the size of tagset that can be used whereas HTML only supports a relatively restricted (and fixed) tagset. This means that HTML is ill equipped to handle documents with a complex structure. On the other hand, SGML's flexibility is considered to be a handicap by developers of web browsers because it is not cost effective. Consequently, a new system known as **XML** has been developed in recent years, by a group known as the W3 consortium. XML (extensible markup language) is also based on SGML but uses a much larger tagset than HTML; in particular, users can define their own tags and attributes. XML supports highly complex documents and is specifically designed to facilitate document exchange over the Web.

Summary of discussion

In the preceding sections we have described different ways of marking up texts. Markup can be used to determine the appearance and structure or composition of documents. SGML was designed to facilitate the exchange of documents between different computing systems. SGML forms the basis for most languages used to mark up documents. HTML is used to mark up documents stored on the Web and uses a fairly restricted subset of SGML. XML is an emerging language designed to facilitate the exchange of documents over the Web.

What is annotation?

So far, we have concentrated on markup that encodes information about the appearance and structural components of documents. In this section, we plan to focus on systems that make explicit the linguistic features of a text. This is done by building in information about the linguistic aspects of a text. The process is called **annotation**. A corpus that has been enriched with some form of annotation is called an annotated corpus.

Many different levels of annotation are possible. The first and most common is what is known as part-of-speech (POS) tagging whereby each word in a corpus is assigned a grammatical tag corresponding to the word class to which it belongs. This type of annotation is discussed in some detail in the remaining sections of this chapter. Other levels of annotation include **syntactic annotation** and **semantic annotation**. Syntactic annotation, as the name suggests, involves adding information about the syntactic structure of sentences to a corpus previously tagged with part-of-speech information. Semantic annotation involves assigning semantic field tags to all words in the corpus. The idea behind this is that it facilitates disambiguation (e.g. a word like 'bridge' has a number of different meanings and can belong to ten or eleven different fields) and information retrieval; you can choose to work only with words belonging to a particular semantic field. We do not propose to discuss syntactic and semantic annotation in any great detail here, as they are not directly relevant to the environment in which you are working. If you are interested in reading more about the topic, we recommend that you read Garside et al. (1997); this book has separate chapters devoted to different types of annotation.

POS tagging

POS (part-of-speech) tagging, as the name suggests, involves assigning part-of-speech tags to all words in a corpus. Essentially, this involves taking a text and assigning a label to each word in the text. At the simplest level, if you were to do this yourself, this would mean that you would have to decide whether the words were nouns, verbs, adjectives, adverbs, conjunctions, etc. Then, when assigning a noun label, you would need to specify whether it was singular or plural. When assigning a verb label, you would need to specify the tense and number, etc. Fortunately, you do not have to do this work yourself, as tagging programs have been developed to do this automatically. Many of these tagging programs are available as a service on the Web or can be downloaded. You will find a list of freely available tagging services or tagger programs at the end of this chapter.

How taggers work

Tagging involves a number of different stages which can be broken down into the following main stages: tokenization, tag assignment, disambiguation. (See http://www.comp.lancs.ac.uk/ucrel/bnc2/bnc2postag_manual.htm for a detailed description of these phases.) In the tokenization phase, texts are broken down into sentences and single words. Sentences are generally considered to consist of a string of words followed by a full stop. There are times when the full stop does not signal the end of a sentence (e.g. after Mr., Dr., Prof.) and tagging programs are usually able to handle these (see page 113 for discussion of stop lists). Words are generally deemed to consist of a string of letters surrounded by a white space; as with sentences, there are exceptions (e.g. should 'don't' be considered as one word or two?) which most tagging programs are able to handle.

Once a text or corpus has been tokenized, the tagger then assigns part-of-speech tags to all of the word tokens in the text or corpus. If a word is unambiguous, i.e. belongs to only one part of speech category or word class (e.g. words such as 'many', 'five', 'boat') it will be assigned a single tag. If a word is ambiguous, i.e. can belong to more than one word class (e.g. words such as 'house', 'bridge', 'foot', all of which can be categorized either as nouns or as verbs), it may initially be assigned two or more tags depending on the number of word classes to which it can belong. Tagging programs usually have a built-in lexicon or dictionary. They assign tags on the basis of what they find in the lexicon. If a particular word is not found in the lexicon, and this can happen quite often, it is assigned a tag based on the likelihood of it belonging to one particular class or another. Thus, a word ending in *ly is likely to be classified as an adverb; a word ending in *hood will be classified as a noun, etc. Some tagging programs will assign a tag such as 'unknown word' or 'foreign word' to any words whose part of speech is not readily identifiable.

Once all words have been assigned one or more tags, those words carrying more than one tag (i.e. ambiguous words) are re-examined by the program, and the program attempts to disambiguate. The context in which the word appears is examined and the most likely solution is selected on this basis. If, for example, a word has been assigned both a noun and a verb tag (as might be the case with a word like 'house'), it is less likely to be classed as a verb after the disambiguation phase if it appears in the vicinity of another verb in the text. On the other hand, if it appears in a clause without any other verb, it is more likely to be classed as a verb. As mentioned earlier, it is not our intention to go into this in great detail here but if you wish to find out more about how tagging programs work you can consult the web site mentioned previously or you could try the following one for a description of different types of taggers: http://www.georgetown.edu/cball/ling361/tagging_overview.html.

Deciphering tagged text

When a text has been annotated with part-of-speech tags, the tags are visible in the text. Initially, this can be a bit confusing, especially if one is not familiar with the tagset being used. In this section, we propose to look at the output from three different tagging services, all of which are available free of charge on the Web. These three tagging services were selected because they were easy to find on the Web and easy to work with.

We started by taking the opening paragraph from this chapter and sending it to three different tagging programs. In Figure 5.5, the output from one of these taggers, namely the CLAWS tagger (developed at the University of Lancaster, UK), is displayed in linear form. The text you

While_CS most_DAT of_IO you_PPY will_VM work_VVI most_DAT or_CC all_DB
of_IO the_AT time_NNT1 with_IW what_DDQ is_VBZ known_VVN as_II 'raw'_JJ
text_NN1 ,_, some_DD of_IO you_PPY may_VM be_VBI interested_JJ in_II
working_VVG with_IW what_DDQ are_VBR known_VVN as_II 'marked_JJ up'_NN1
and/or_CC 'annotated'_JJ texts_NN2 so_CS21 that_CS22 you_PPY can_VM
carry_VVI out_RP more_DAR sophisticated_JJ investigations_NN2._.

Figure 5.5 Output from CLAWS tagger for opening sentence of this chapter

see in the figure is the first sentence of the opening paragraph of this chapter.

As you can see, each word in the sentence is assigned a grammatical tag, and the word is connected to the tag by means of an underscore. Each of the tags refers to a particular word class. Thus, JJ is the tag for 'adjective', VM is the tag for 'modal verb', CC is the tag for 'coordinating conjunction', etc. If you would like to find out more about the tagset used by the CLAWS tagger, please consult the web site indicated at the end of this chapter.

In Figure 5.6, we have displayed the tagged output from each of the three taggers for two fairly short sentences from the opening paragraph. We have chosen to display the output in columns so that you can compare the results from the different tagging programs word by word. In each column, the word to be tagged appears first, followed by the tag that has been assigned. As you can see, the tags differ from one tagging program to another. Thus, a noun in singular form is given the tag NN, NN1, or N NOM SG respectively depending on whether it has been tagged by the CLG, CLAWS or EngCG-2 tagger. A noun in plural form is given the tag NNS, NN2, or N NOM PL depending on whether the CLG, CLAWS or EngCG-2 tagger has tagged it. Furthermore, the size of the tagset will vary from one tagger to another. In other words, the taggers will not all have the same number of tags; some will be more detailed than others. Some will distinguish between different types of nouns, though others may not. Some will distinguish between different types of adverbs, whereas others may not. For example, we can see from our tagged output in Figure 5.6 that the words 'a' and 'the' are both classed as DT (determiner) by the CLG tagger but are each assigned different tags by the CLAWS (AT1 and AT) and EngCG-2 (DET SG and DET SG/PL) taggers. Similarly, 'look' and 'represent' are each assigned the same tag by the CLG tagger but are assigned different tags by the other two taggers.

You may have noticed that some of the words in column 1 have been assigned the tag '???'. If the CLG tagger is unable to determine to which word class a word belongs, it will simply assign the tag '???'. Here, for some reason, it has been unable to assign a tag to the words 'document'

CLG tagger, Birmingham	CLAWS tagger, Lancaster	EngCG-2 tagger, Helsinki
We_PP	We_PPIS2	We_PRON PERS NOM PL1
will_MD	will_VM	will_V AUXMOD
focus_NN	focus_VVI	focus_V INF
initially_RB	initially_RR	initially_ADV
on_IN	on_II	on_PREP
markup_NN	markup_NN1	markup_N NOM SG
which_WDT	which_DDQ	which_<Rel>PRON WH NOM SG/PL
determines_VBZ	determines_VVZ	determines_V PRES SG3
the_DT	the_AT	the_DET SG/PL
appearance_NN	appearance_NN1	appearance_N NOM SG
of_IN	of_IO	of_PREP
a_DT	a_AT1	a_DET SG
document_???.	document_NN1.	document_N NOM SG.
We_PP	We_PPIS2	We_PRON PERS NOM PL1
will_MD	will_VM	will_V AUXMOD
then_RB	then_RT	then_ADV
look_VB	look_VV1	look-V INF
at_IN	at_II	at_PREP
markup_NN	markup_NN1	markup_N NOM SG
systems_NNS	systems_NN2	systems_N NOM PL
designed_VBN	designed_VVN	designed_EN
to_TO	to_TO	to_INFMARK>
represent_VB	represent_VV1	represent_V INF
the_DT	the_AT	the_DET SG/PL
structure_NN	structure_NN1	structure_N NOM SG
of_IN	of_IO	of_PREP
documents_???.	documents_NN2.	documents_N NOM PL.

Figure 5.6 Output from three different taggers

and 'documents'. This may be because these words can be classed either as a noun or as a verb, and the tagger does not have sufficient contextual information to opt for one or the other. You may also have noticed that the tagger has assigned an incorrect tag to one of the words in column 1. The word is 'focus'. Here, it has been tagged as a noun when it should of course have been tagged as a verb accompanying the modal 'will'.

While it is inevitable that taggers will sometimes get things wrong, it is also worth mentioning that most tagging programs perform with a very high level of accuracy – developers will generally claim accuracy well in excess of 90 per cent which, though not perfect, is adequate for many purposes. If you would like to find out more about the taggers used in this chapter, please consult the web sites indicated at the end of this chapter.

Why tag a corpus?

There are a number of very good reasons for working with a tagged corpus. First and foremost, when a corpus has been tagged, all of the implicit part of speech information is made explicit and therefore accessible. In other words, the grammatical role of every single word in your corpus is explicitly marked. This means that more detailed searches become feasible. When you start to work with corpus processing tools, as described in Chapter 7, you will begin to appreciate the usefulness of this additional capability. Here, we propose to describe briefly some of the possibilities open to you if you are working with a tagged corpus.

Let us start by looking at part-of-speech homographs. Part-of-speech homographs are words that are spelt the same but belong to different word classes, e.g. words such as 'process', 'result', 'experiment', 'cross' which can be classed as nouns or verbs (or even adjectives, as in the case of 'cross'). If, as described in Chapter 7, you decide to produce a frequency list of all of the words in an untagged corpus, words such as 'process', 'result', 'experiment', 'cross' will appear only once in the frequency list even if they function as both nouns and verbs in your corpus. Thus, if, for example, 'process' is ranked fiftieth (50th) in your **frequency list** with, let us say, a total of three hundred and forty-five occurrences (345), you have no means of telling from the frequency list how frequently 'process' is functioning as a verb, a noun or a mixture of both in your corpus. You can only determine this by producing a concordance and examining each occurrence of 'process' in the corpus. If you are working with a tagged corpus, however, 'process_verb' and 'process_noun' will appear separately in your frequency list. Thus, you will be able to see immediately which of the two, 'process_verb' or 'process_noun', is more prevalent in the corpus, and by how much.

Tagged corpora are also useful if you are interested in looking at particular classes of words. If, for example, you are working with a corpus of economic reports and you are interested in looking at how writers describe an upturn or downturn in the economy, you may wish to see what types of verbs they use to do this. If you were working with an untagged corpus, you would need to be fairly inventive in order to root out this type of information because you would need to identify some means of identifying the verbs indirectly. You could, for example, do this by producing concordances for words like 'economy', 'recession', 'boom', etc. but you could never be sure of having spotted all of the relevant verbs. With a tagged corpus, however, you can do this relatively easily. This is because you can enter grammatical tags rather than actual words or phrases as your **search pattern** (see pages 120–6) for discussion of how to produce concordances). Let us say that you are interested in all verbs in base form in your corpus. You simply enter the appropriate tag for the word class and tagset used for your corpus (VB in the case of the CLG tagger) as your search pattern, add a wildcard before the tag (*VB), and all verbs in base form will be retrieved. If you look at Figure 5.7, you will see the output from a concordance for the grammatical tag VB.

The opening paragraph of this chapter was used for the concordance. As you can see from the concordance, the word associated with the tag VB appears immediately to the left of the tag, and the base form to the right. Thus, you can see that 'look' is the most common verb in the opening paragraph. If you look a little more closely, you will see that 'look' usually forms part of a larger unit, namely either 'take a look at' or 'look at'. You can carry out similar types of studies to ascertain, for example, what the most common adjectives in your corpus are. Or you may be interested in looking at complex nouns, in which case you will carry out a search using the grammatical composition of complex nouns (e.g. adj + noun, noun + noun) as your search pattern.

Concluding remarks

There is no doubt that a tagged corpus can be very beneficial, particularly if you are interested in investigating grammatical features and patterns. You may, however, find that the effort involved in arranging the tagging of an entire corpus is greater than you are prepared to make. We would suggest that you start with an untagged corpus and see you how you get on. If you find that you are more interested in the behaviour of word classes than in the behaviour of words alone, then you should certainly consider tagging your corpus or having your corpus tagged. If you are planning on building a large corpus to be used by multiple users for a range of purposes, you should also seriously consider adopting the CES guidelines.

Key points

- Markup involves inserting tags to make explicit the appearance and structure of a document.
- SGML has been developed to facilitate the exchange of documents.
- HTML and XML, both based on SGML, have been developed to facilitate the storage and exchange of documents on the Web.
- A Corpus Encoding Standard has been developed to facilitate the exchange of corpora.
- Annotation involves inserting tags in order to make explicit the linguistic features (part of speech, syntactic structure) of a text.

```
agging VBG tag can MD can allow VB all you PP you to TO to ref
hat you PP you can MD can carry VB carry out IN out more JJR mor
sites NNS site to TO to explain VB explain tagging VBG tag proce
we PP we will MD will introduce VB introduce you PP you to TO to
 likely JJ likely to TO to know VB know something NN something
D will take VB take a DT a look VB look at IN at different JJ differe
int, we PP we will MD will look VB look at IN at mark-up NN mark
 will MD will then RB then look VB look at IN at mark-up NN mark
llow you PP you to TO to refine VB refine your PPS your queries.
d VBN design to TO to represent VB represent the DT the structure
 and we PP we will MD will take VB take a DT a look VB look at 1
```

Figure 5.7 Concordance for VB

- Taggers have been designed to insert part of speech tags automatically.
- A tagged corpus is useful if you want to look at classes of words (e.g. all adjectives) rather than individual words in your corpus.
- You can use your usual concordancer to process a tagged corpus.

Further reading

Corpus Encoding Standard. http://www.cs.vassar.edu/CES/

Garside, Roger, Leech, Geoffrey and McEnery, Anthony (eds) (1997) *Corpus Annotation: Linguistic Information from Computer Text Corpora*, London/New York: Longman.

Leech, Geoffrey and Smith, Nicholas: The British National Corpus (Version 2) with Improved Word-class Tagging. UCREL, Lancaster University: http://www.comp.lancs.ac.uk/ucrel/bnc2/bnc2postag_manual.htm

SGML: An Introduction. http://www.incontext.com/SGMLinfo.html

TEI Guidelines for Electronic Text Encoding and Interchange: http://www.etext.virginia.edu/bin/tei-tocs?div=DIV1&id=HD

Van Guilder, Linda (1995) Automated Part of Speech Tagging: A Brief Overview. http://www.georgetown.edu/cball/ling361/tagging_overview.html

Wynne, Martin (1996) A Post-Editor's Guide to CLAWS Tagging. http://www.comp.lancs.ac.uk/computing/users/eiamjw/claws/claws7.html#_Toc334868023

Addresses of tagsets discussed in this chapter

CLG tagger: http://clgl.bham.ac.uk/tagger/tagset.html

CLAWS tagger: http://www.comp.lancs.ac.uk/computing/users/eiamjw/claws/claws7.html#_Toc334868023

EngCG-2 tagger: http://www.conexor.fi/engcg2.html#1

Exercises

Exercise 1

Select a text of not less than 300 words. Search the Web for free taggers online. Send your text to three different taggers. Examine output to assess suitability of each of the taggers for your text type.

Exercise 2

Select a text of not less than 1000 words. Identify a tagger that will handle texts of 1000 words or more. You may have to do this by trial and error. Use a concordancer on your output to draw up a list of all adjective + noun and noun + noun combinations in your text. You will need to know the tags used by the tagger to mark adjectives and nouns. This information is usually available on the same web site as the tagger.

6 Bilingual and multilingual corpora: pre-processing, alignment and exploitation

This chapter begins by considering two different types of bilingual and multilingual corpora, parallel and comparable corpora, and then goes on to focus on parallel corpora alone. A brief overview of the applications of parallel corpora is provided. Issues surrounding the collection and selection of texts to be included in a parallel corpus are considered. Next, readers are shown how to pre-process texts in order to prepare them for alignment or bilingual concordancing. A discussion of what is involved in alignment, the procedure used to prepare parallel texts for linguistic analysis, follows. In the final section of the chapter, some practical examples that give some indication of how parallel corpora can help with language learning and translation are provided.

Bilingual and multilingual corpora

As already discussed in Chapter 1 (page 12) there are two types of bilingual and multilingual corpora: parallel corpora and comparable corpora.

Parallel corpora

Parallel corpora contain texts and their translations into one or more languages. A bilingual parallel corpus contains texts and their translations into one language, and a multilingual parallel corpus contains texts and their translations into two or more languages. Thus, a parallel corpus of computer user documentation, for example, will contain the original documents and their translations into one or more language(s). However, while the word 'parallel' is used to indicate that a corpus contains texts and their translations, the text pairs in a parallel corpus are not always translations of each other. They can be translations of a third text. For example, you might have a bilingual parallel corpus containing the French and German translations of computer user documentation produced in English by an American company. In such circumstances, the user is likely to know that both sets of texts are translations. There are, however, situations where the user has no idea in which language a particular set of texts was originally written. This often happens in multilingual environments (in the European Union, for example) where there is more than one official language. In multilingual working environments, it is even possible for different sections of a single text to have been drafted in different languages and then translated into another language at the end. Here, the user may not even suspect that the text is not only not an original source text but is in fact a translation made up of translations from different languages!

Comparable corpora

While parallel corpora contain texts and their translations, comparable corpora consist of sets of texts in different languages that are not translations of each other. We use the word 'comparable' to indicate that the texts in the different languages have been selected because they have some characteristics or features in common; the one and only feature that distinguishes one set of texts from another in a comparable corpus is the language in which the texts are written. The shared features will frequently include subject matter or topic and may also include features such as text type, period in which the texts were written, degree of technicality, etc. An example of a comparable corpus would be a set of research papers (shared text type) in two or more languages dealing with genetic engineering (shared subject field), written in the last twenty years (shared period). It might be a collection of user handbooks (shared text type) produced by car manufacturers (shared subject field) in different languages. Texts from different languages in a comparable corpus are not linked in the way that texts in parallel corpora are (see discussion of alignment later in this chapter). This does cause problems but comparable corpora offer other benefits which parallel corpora are unable to provide, as you will see in the detailed discussion of comparable corpora in Chapter 11.

Why use a parallel corpus?

The main advantage of using a parallel corpus is that it allows you to produce **bilingual concordances**. The user simply enters a keyword or phrase in one language and the bilingual concordancing software will retrieve all of the sentences where this word or phrase appears in one language together with all of the corresponding sentences in the other language and the two sets of retrieved sentences will usually be displayed side by side. An example of a bilingual concordance is shown in Figure 6.1.

The concordance is drawn from the Hansard Corpus, a corpus of parallel texts in Canadian English and French, drawn from official records of the proceedings of the Canadian Parliament. The corpus can be searched online at http://www.tsrali.com/index.cgi?UTLanguage=en (five-day free trial).

1.	Ils veulent que le monde reste tel qu'il est et ils refusent de reconnaître que l'Amérique du Nord et le monde entier connaissent actuellement un grand courant de mondialisation	They want to keep the world the way it is. They refuse to recognise the great currents of **globalization** that are affecting North America and the world.
2.	Ce que nous disons, c'est que l'Accord de libre-échange nord-américain n'est pas nécessairement une panacée, mais que c'est un pas dans la bonne direction pour aider tous les peuples à répondre aux nouvelles exigences de la mondialisation. Cela devrait contribuer à améliorer la prospérité de tous les habitants de notre continent, y compris les Mexicains.	We are saying that North American free trade is not necessarily a panacea for all, but it is a step forward in helping all peoples confront the new demands of **globalization**, thereby raising the prosperity level for all citizens of this continent including Mexico.
3.	Que les ministres conservateurs fassent semblant que la notion de mondialisation des marchés est leur invention me laisse un peu triste et perplexe.	It leaves me somewhat sad and baffled to see the front benches of the Conservative government trying to pretend that they are inventing **globalization**.

Figure 6.1 Extract from a bilingual concordance of 'globalization' retrieved from the Canadian Hansard corpus

Who uses parallel corpora?

There are, broadly speaking, three different groups of people interested in using parallel corpora. These include (a) language teachers/learners, (b) students and teachers of translation and (c) computational linguists.

Language teachers and learners can, as Barlow (1996: 54) points out, treat parallel corpora like an online contextualized dictionary. Thus, teachers and learners can use parallel corpora to show or study how a particular word or phrase is translated and used in another language. Parallel corpora are especially useful when the word or phrase that the teacher or student wishes to examine does not appear in a dictionary, as so often happens with new terminology.

Translators will use parallel corpora either because, like language learners, they want to know how to say something in another language or, more often, because they want to observe what happens in translation. Translators who use parallel corpora to observe what happens in translation are usually interested in discovering how information is conveyed and whether any information is lost, adapted or misrepresented in the process. They are also interested in seeing whether the translations are as 'natural' as comparable texts originally written in the same language.

Computational linguists use parallel corpora as a testbed for developing alignment software. (Alignment involves creating links between pairs of texts and is discussed later in this chapter.) They are not really interested in the usefulness of parallel corpora for language learning or translation purposes. Rather, they are interested in establishing whether features or characteristics of texts can be expressed computationally in order to facilitate the development of alignment programs. Once an alignment program has been developed, it can then be used to create larger parallel corpora that in turn may be used as testbeds for other types of NLP (natural language processing) applications, including example-based machine translation.

Creating your own parallel corpus

Sourcing your texts

If you decide to create your own parallel corpus, you will need to have access to pairs of texts (source texts and their translations) dealing with the topic or subject you wish to study. You will discover that bilingual and multilingual parallel texts are less easy to find than monolingual texts. Consequently, any parallel corpus that you create is bound to be very much smaller than a monolingual corpus created using the same criteria. Ideally, the texts that you source should be in electronic form as this will save you the effort of scanning or entering the texts manually. Fortunately, you will find that a lot of parallel texts are actually available in electronic form, particularly through the Web. The European Union, for example, publishes large quantities of documentation in several languages on the Web. Bilingual or multilingual countries like Canada, for example, which are obliged by law to produce all government documents in all official languages, are other good sources of parallel texts. It is also possible to purchase parallel corpora from organizations such as the Linguistic Data Consortium (LDC) in the US or the European Language Resources Association (ELRA) in Europe (web addresses at the end of the chapter) but these corpora can be rather expensive and may therefore not be an option for you.

In the future, parallel texts may be available via another source thanks to recent developments in the translation industry. Here, we are referring to the creation of translation memories using translation memory software. Until quite recently, translation services did not tend to make use of previously translated material. Each time a translation was commissioned, it was produced from scratch even if the translation service had previously translated something very similar. No attempt was made to re-use previously translated material. Nowadays, companies using translation memory software can store source texts and translations in a database during the translation process. The next time a similar text has to be translated, the previously translated material is automatically integrated into the new version. Translation memory software enables translation companies to create vast repositories of texts that are essentially parallel corpora. While no one has yet done so, it is just possible that companies using translation memory software may one day decide to market their translation memories as parallel corpora. One can certainly imagine that other companies in the same line of business would be very keen to purchase a ready-made translation memory which would save them the effort of creating their own from scratch.

Choosing your texts

Your area of interest will determine which texts you choose. Thus, if you are studying technical writing and have a particular interest in user documentation, you may, for example, wish to create a parallel corpus from a collection of computer manuals originally written in Japanese along with the translations of these manuals into English, Spanish and French. If you are learning how to write reports, you may wish to create a parallel corpus from a collection of reports produced by an international organization and translated into all of the official languages of that organization. The International Telecommunications Union, for example, has three official languages, English, French and Spanish, which means that all official documentation must be available in each of the three languages. Similarly, the European Union publishes all of its documentation in all of the official EU languages. In Canada, all federal government documents must be in both English and French. If you are interested in observing what happens in the translation of popular science texts, you may decide to create a parallel corpus from a collection of articles published in *Scientific American,* for example, and the French and German translations of those articles published in *Pour la Science* and *Bild der Wissenschaft.* Whatever type of parallel corpus you choose to create, the same design criteria as those outlined in Chapter 3 should be applied.

Preparing your texts for alignment

Once you have chosen your texts and converted them all to machine-readable or electronic form, you will need to carry out some pre-processing in order to prepare them for alignment. As we will see later in this chapter, alignment programs make a number of assumptions about texts and their translations, and you will need to ensure that your texts meet these assumptions. For example, alignment programs usually assume that source texts and translations have the same number of paragraphs and preferably the same number of sentences. You will therefore need to ensure that this is the case for your source and target texts. The pre-processing will mainly involve deleting superfluous hard returns (i.e. line breaks) because alignment programs tend to interpret hard returns as paragraph breaks. The quickest way to prepare your pairs of texts for alignment and bilingual concordancing is for each student who intends to work with the parallel corpus to edit one or more pairs of texts, using the following procedure.

Take one pair of texts and, using a word processing program, open each of the texts in the pair. To facilitate comparison and to avoid having to switch back and forth between windows, display your texts side by side by resizing the document windows. Select each of the texts in turn and switch on the numbering feature so that all paragraphs are automatically numbered. This makes the task of comparing the two texts much easier (Figure 6.2). If at some stage, you notice that the paragraph numbers no longer correspond, this is probably due to one of the following reasons:

1   There may be an extra line break or hard return in one of the texts. This is what has happened as you can see in the right hand window of Figure 6.3. A paragraph number has been assigned (no. 8), creating a mismatch between the remaining paragraph pairs. To solve the problem, simply remove the offending hard return each time this problem occurs.

2   It may be because one paragraph in the original text is translated as two paragraphs, or because two paragraphs in the original text have been translated as one. This can happen quite frequently. While some alignment programs can handle this, the best solution is to conflate two paragraphs into one to ensure a one-to-one match. To ensure best practice and to maintain the integrity of the texts, you should insert some type of symbol at the point of conflation to indicate that a change has been made. This means that if you ever wish to restore the text to its original layout, you can do so fairly easily. It is best to use a symbol that you would not normally expect to find in this type of text. Can you spot the special symbol that has been used in Figure 6.4 to indicate that two paragraphs have been conflated?

3   You may find that a paragraph that appears in the original text has not been translated at all or that the translation contains a paragraph that has no correspondence in the original. If a paragraph has been omitted from the translation, you should simply create a paragraph in the translation using the words 'paragraph not translated'. If a completely new paragraph has been added to the translation, you should simply insert a paragraph in the original using the words 'additional paragraph in the translation'.

When you have finished scrolling through the document and have ensured that each text in your pair of texts has exactly the same number of paragraphs, simply select each text again, turn off the numbering option,

1.	An Ocean Away	Mers et océans
2.	Some highland areas on Mars contain extensive systems of valleys that drained into sediment-floored depressions.	Des réseaux de vallées qui s'étendent sur certaines hautes terres de Mars débouchent sur des dépressions tapissées de sédiments.
3.	These lowlands were at one time full of water.	Ces plaines auraient été couvertes d'eau.
4.	The largest of these Martian lakes filled two gigantic impact basins called Hellas and Argyre.	Les plus grande de ces lacs martiens remplissaient deux gigantesques basins d'impact, Hellas et Argyre.
5.	We have interpreted many features bordering these ancient basins as marking where glaciers once emptied into these deep bodies of water.	De nombreuses caractéristiques des bords de ces anciens bassins marqueraient les endroits où les glaciers se jetaient.
6.	Tanaka and Moore believe that thick layers of sediment deposited in these seas now stretch across much of the extensive northern plains.	D'épaisses couches sédimentaires déposées dans ces mers recouvriraient aujourd'hui la plus grande partie des plaines septentrionales.
7.	According to several estimates, one of the larger of the northern seas on Mars could have displaced the combined volume of the Gulf of Mexico and the Mediterranean Sea.	Le volume de l'une des plus grandes mers septentrionales de Mars aurait été équivalent à ceux du golfe du Mexique et de la Méditerranée réunis.

Figure 6.2 Parallel texts displayed side by side to facilitate comparison

6.	Giants¶	6.	No heading¶
7.	Those questions have occupied physicists since cosmic rays were first discovered in 1912 (although the entities in question are now known to be particles, the name "ray" persists).¶	7.	Cette question préoccupe les physiciens depuis la découverte des rayons cosmiques, en 1912. À l'époque, on ignorait la nature particulaire des rayons cosmiques, d'où leur nom impropre, qui a subsisté.¶
8.	¶	8.	Le milieu interstellaire contient des noyaux atomiques de tous les éléments, qui se déplacent dans des champs électriques et magnétiques. Sans la protection de l'atmosphère terrestre, beaucoup plus de rayons cosmiques arriveraient jusqu'au sol.
9.	The interstellar medium contains atomic nuclei of every element in the periodic table, all moving under the influence of electrical and magnetic fields. Without the screening effect of the earth's atmosphere, cosmic rays would pose a significant health threat.		

Figure 6.3 Example of superfluous line break

| 34. | It is interesting to speculate what the sources might be. Three recent hypotheses suggest the range of possibilities: galactic black-hole accretion disks, gamma-ray bursts and topological defects in the fabric of the universe. ££ Astrophysicists have predicted that black holes of a billion solar masses or more, accreting matter in the nuclei of active galaxies, are needed to drive relativistic jets of matter far into intergalactic space at speeds approaching that of light; such jets have been mapped with radio telescopes. | 34. | Quelles pourraient être les sources des rayons cosmiques les plus énergétiques ? Trois possibilités sont avancées : les disques d'accrétion autour de trous noirs galactiques, les zones de sursauts gamma, et les défauts topologiques de l'espace-temps. Les astrophysiciens pensent que des trous noirs de un milliard de masses solaires ou plus, qui attirent la matière dans les noyaux actifs de galaxies, émettent des jets dans l'espace intergalactique, à des vitesses approchant celle de la lumière ; de tels jets ont été observés à l'aide de radio télescopes. |

Figure 6.4 Insertion of special symbol to mark paragraph conflation

and save your texts as plain text files. The next step involves using an alignment program to align or mark up your texts so that you can produce bilingual concordances.

How does alignment work?

Once parallel texts have been selected and pre-processed, a program is then used to create links between the texts in order to facilitate linguistic processing. This is an essential part of the corpus compilation process because you cannot create bilingual concordances without such links. The process of creating links is generally referred to as alignment. A number of alignment techniques have been developed and a small number of programs are available. While it is beyond the scope of this book to provide an in-depth description of alignment, mainly because so few of the programs are available, a brief overview is provided in order to give you some idea of what alignment involves, and a reading list is provided at the end of the chapter for those who are interested in reading more about the computational aspects of the various approaches.

Broadly speaking, links between texts are established by identifying and using characteristics which source and target texts have in common. Such characteristics may include the number of paragraphs in the source and target texts, the number of sentences in the source and target texts, and the number of lexical correspondences between source and target text. Some models align sentences based on a statistical model of numbers of characters (see Gale and Church 1993) on the basis that these are better predictors of matches than numbers of words.

As mentioned previously, texts have to be prepared for alignment. One method of preparation or pre-processing is the one that we recommended earlier when we suggested asking each student to pre-process a pair of texts by scrolling down through them using a word processor. As this approach can be tedious for processing large volumes of texts, mechanisms have been devised for carrying out some pre-processing. We call this pre-processing the first stage in the alignment process. What usually happens in this stage is that all texts are automatically marked up using a small set of basic tags (to indicate start and end of documents, paragraph boundaries, page breaks, etc.). Sentence boundaries are marked up next. Sentence boundaries are identified on the basis of the presence of certain punctuation marks (e.g. .?!) followed by a capital letter. Of course, punctuation marks followed by capital letters do not always indicate the end of a sentence. For instance, consider the case of proper nouns such as 'Mr. Gates', 'Dr. Doolittle', 'St. Luke' or the case of acronyms such as 'U.S.A.' and 'M.I.T.' In these examples, a full stop or period followed by a capital letter does not indicate the end of a sentence. Thankfully, the number of commonly used abbreviations and acronyms is limited and alignment programs can be instructed to treat them as exceptions to the sentence boundary rule. Once all of the texts in each language have been marked up, they are then ready for the next stage: alignment proper. Some programs will align (e.g. MultiConcord) during the generation of bilingual concordances but most programs separate the processes of alignment and generation of bilingual concordances. The first stage of alignment usually involves creating links between matching paragraphs and headings in the source and target texts by matching them sequentially. A small number of alignment programs will stop there and will not attempt to align below paragraph level; most, however, will also attempt to align texts at sentence level. To achieve this, a probabilistic score is assigned to each pair of candidate sentence pairs, based on the ratio of lengths of the two sentences (in characters or words) and the variance of this ratio. The probabilistic score is used to calculate the maximum likelihood alignment of sentences. Some models also make use of a bilingual dictionary in order to improve the match ratio (see Peters, Picchi and Biagini 1996). In such instances, whenever a translation equivalent for a source text word is found in the target text during the alignment process, a link is created between the translation equivalent and the original source text word. All links created in this way are then stored in text archives so that they can be used later by a bilingual concordancer. Unfortunately, such programs are not yet available. While most alignment programs that attempt to align sentences will do so within paragraphs, there is at least one alignment program that adopts a slightly different method; this is the aligner developed for the English–Norwegian parallel corpus. This particular program ignores paragraph boundaries and works through the text pairs on the basis of fifteen-sentence chunks. This is an interesting approach because it recognizes that paragraphs may not always be segmented in the same way in source and target texts.

One further aspect of alignment worthy of mention here is its use in the translation memory environment. As mentioned in our earlier discussion of this subject, more and more companies involved in the business of translation have started using software that allows them to store their source texts and translations in a translation memory for re-use at a later stage. Translators using translation memory software translate texts segment by segment (a segment is usually the equivalent of a sentence). Each time a segment has been translated, a translation unit (i.e. source segment and target segment) is created and stored in the translation memory. In other words, translators are creating an aligned parallel corpus as they work. The rationale behind using translation memory systems is that companies can store translations for re-use or adaptation at a later stage.

More recently, some translation memory developers have developed alignment tools to enable companies to align source texts and translations produced before they started to use translation memories. Their alignment programs appear to function along the same lines as other alignment

<p><s>From the fourth through the 14th century, the 7,500-kilometer Silk Road linked China to Rome and to every place in between, including Tibet, India, Turkestan, Afghanistan and the Arabian Peninsula.	<p><s>Du ive au xive siècle, les 7 5C kilomètres de la route de la soie relia Chine à Rome, via le Tibet, l'Inde, le 1 l'Afghanistan et la péninsule arabe.
<s>The road-its name coined by the 19th-century explorer Baron Ferdinand von Richthofen-was more than a trade route.	<s>Son nom, dû au baron Ferdinand Richthofen, explorateur allemand du ; siècle, est trompeur, car il laisse sup qu'elle n'était qu'une voie d'échanges commerciaux ; <s>en réalité, elle fut première autoroute de l'information, s quart de la circonférence terrestre.
<s>It was the first information highway, spanning a quarter of the circumference of the globe and virtually the entire known world at that time	<s>De l'Empire du Milieu arrivaient le étonnantes richesses et innovations techniques de la Chine :

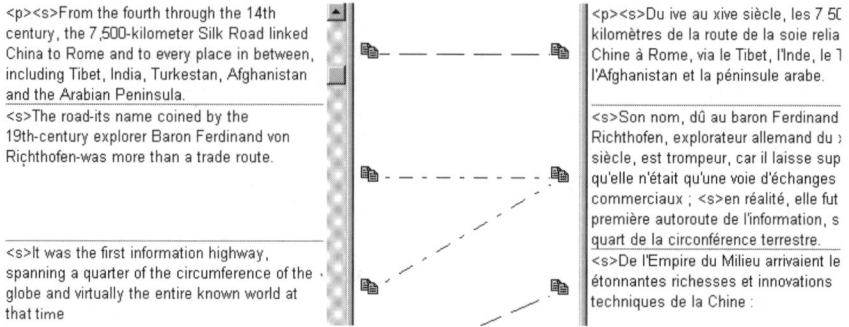

Figure 6.5 View of alignment editor screen from Trados WinAlign

programs, with one important difference: they frequently have an inbuilt editing tool that allows users to confirm and/or rectify the alignments that have been made. As you can see in Figure 6.5, WinAlign has correctly calculated that two of the paragraphs in the English text are conflated into one paragraph in the French translation. When the user confirms that this is correct, the line between the paragraphs is transformed from a dotted line to a continuous line.

Problems with alignment

Some of the assumptions alignment programs make about texts and their translations can be incorrect. For example, there is an assumption that there is generally a sequential one-to-one correspondence between source and target text, at the very least at paragraph level and ideally at sentence level. This means that sentence 1 in the source text is assumed to correspond to sentence 1 in the target text, sentence 2 to sentence 2 and so on throughout each paragraph or text. This notion of a sequential correspondence is a prerequisite for successful alignment. Unfortunately, however, as translations do not always follow the sequential progression of the source texts, you will sometimes encounter strange sentence pairs when you are reviewing a set of concordance lines. Another assumption that alignment programs will make is that each sentence in the source text is translated in the target text, i.e. that all of the information contained in the source text will be carried over to the target text. Yet, this is not always the case. In our experience, it is not uncommon for sentences and even entire paragraphs in the source texts not to be translated at all. For example, cultural references in the source text that would have little meaning for the target audience may be eliminated. The output will therefore contain mismatches. This is certainly a very real problem. However, the benefits of having access to parallel texts, even when there are mismatches, are such that the inconveniences are only a minor irritation in comparison.

Furthermore, it is likely that, in the future, most alignment tools will build in an alignment editor to help us overcome this type of problem.

Using your parallel corpus

As already mentioned, the types of people who use parallel corpora are software developers (to develop alignment tools), language learners and translators. In this section, we propose to focus on the language teacher/ student and the translation teacher/student. If you are a translation teacher/student, you may be interested in examining how translators have handled certain linguistic features. You may be interested in examining how cohesive devices have been translated. You may wish to look more closely at what happens to culture specific references in translation. You may wish to examine what has not been translated and ponder the reasons for it. You may wish to look what has been added to translations. Laviosa (1998) is an excellent starting point for a wide ranging discussion of the applications of parallel corpora in translation studies.

If you are a language learner, you can use your corpus in much the same way as you would use a bilingual dictionary. Thus, you can use it to establish whether a particular translation you have found in the dictionary is actually used, and also to establish how words are used, i.e. whether a particular word favours a certain syntactic pattern, whether it prefers certain groups of adjectives, etc. You can use your corpus to find out how to present something in another language. For example, science texts in English favour the use of the passive voice; you may wish to see whether the same applies in your other language. The possibilities are really quite exciting and we would suggest that as you work with your parallel corpus, you will find that there are more and more things which you would like to investigate. You may have your own ideas about how to start your investigation but we thought it would be useful to provide some examples here for those of you who might not know how to get started. We have taken a small set of examples and checked them against a parallel corpus which we have created. In the first example, we take a noun ('finding/findings') from what is often described as subtechnical vocabulary, i.e. vocabulary that is used in specialized domains but not exclusively in any one domain, and we try to see how this word is translated into French. In the second example, we take the verb 'suggest', a verb commonly used in reporting research and examine how it can be translated. In the third and final example, we take an adjective ('genetic') and try to identify all of the terms in which this adjective appears.

Translating 'finding/findings'

Let us imagine that you are a science student and that you have been asked to write up a report on a laboratory experiment in French. You

1 Pasteur's **findings** had a widespread	Les découvertes de Pasteur ont eu
2 Have confirmed these **findings** in animals and expanded them into the development	ont confirmé ces observations et les ont utilisées pour mettre au point
3 But our encouraging preliminary **findings** indicate that lipoplexes might help treat	mais nos résultats préliminaires indiquent que les lipoplexes font
4 This latter **finding** is puzzling if one regards schizophrenia as only	Cette dernière observation devrait troubler ceux qui considèrent la
5 Despite the **findings** of many anthropological and epidemiological	bien que les études anthropologiques et épidémiologiques aient établi que
6 Recent **findings** suggest that acid rain is a much more complex phenomenon than	Les spécialistes de l'atmosphère ont récemment découvert que le

Figure 6.6 Extract from bilingual concordance for 'finding*'

already have some experience of writing these reports in English and are therefore familiar with the type of language usually used. You want to describe your findings but do not know which word to use in French. Your bilingual dictionary has only offered you one possibility (i.e. 'conclusion') but you would like to establish if there are other words you could use as well. This is where your specialized parallel corpus will come into its own. You simply enter your searchword, and the bilingual output will be displayed, as illustrated in Figure 6.6. You may observe that the concordance lines are not complete sentences; this is quite normal and you should use the numbers in the left hand column to help you to distinguish one example from the next one.

The extract in Figure 6.6 shows that 'finding/findings' can be translated in a number of different ways and, interestingly, the dictionary equivalent (i.e. *conclusion*) is not one of these. Thus, it can be translated by *découvertes, résultats, observation, études* or by converting it to a verb, as has happened in concordance line 6 (Figure 6.6). We would suggest that one of the solutions, namely *découvertes,* may not be an appropriate solution for your purposes. Can you guess why?

Translating 'suggest/suggests'

The verb 'suggest' is commonly encountered in research papers. If you look the verb up in a bilingual dictionary, you will probably find equivalents

1	Their blue colors again **suggest** that they are forming stars rapidly.	Leur couleur bleue suggère à nouveau que des étoiles s'y forment rapidement.
3	The fossil evidence, thin as it is, **suggests** that this place of origin was	Les fossiles, bien que ne constituant que de minces preuves, suggèrent que
4	Evidence from a wide variety of insect species **suggests** that, as	L'étude de nombreuses espèces d'insectes montre que la
5	But our experience **suggests** that many compensated dyslexics have a distinct	Nos expériences indiquent toutefois que nombre de dyslexiques compensés
6	This unusual prevalence, here and elsewhere, **suggests** that some	Cette prédominance inhabituelle indiquerait que le site aurait abrité des
7	Taken together, all these facts **suggest** that mountains evolve their own	Au total, les montagnes modifieraient leur propre climat à mesure qu'elles
8	at levels in excess of those expected would **suggest** the existence of a	des concentrations élevées en plutonium signaleraient qu'un
9	Some evidence **suggests** that the patients who became infected even	Les patients homozygotes qui ont été infectés auraient été particulièrement

Figure 6.7 Extract from bilingual concordance for 'suggest/suggests'

such as *suggérer* and *indiquer*. It is interesting to note in the concordance lines in Figure 6.7 that while these verbs are indeed used to translate 'suggest', other verbs or means are also used. Thus, we find *montrer,* and we also find that in the translations the conditional tense is sometimes being used, to convey the notion of tentativeness or suggestion. This is particularly interesting, as you could not expect a dictionary to provide you with this type of information. If you have not encountered this use of the conditional before and wish to find out more about it, you can simply continue your search by looking for other verbs in the conditional. You can do this in a very general way by using a wildcard search, e.g. *rait and/or *raient which will retrieve all words ending with -rait or -raient.

Terminological equivalents

When you are studying a particular domain in a foreign language, you will need to find out what the equivalents are for terms you already know

1 has a **genetic** basis.	est d'origine génétique.
2 focused on **genetic** characteristics of the	intéressés aux caractéristiques génétiques
3 demonstrated a **genetic** component to	qu'il existe une composante génétique
4 localized alteration in **genetic** content	locales du matériel génétique
5 we thought we noted **genetic** differences,	avoir détecté des différences génétiques,
6 it thereby increases **genetic** diversity,	augmentant la diversité génétique de
7 to look for other **genetic** factors	chercher d'autres facteurs génétiques de
8 store and transfer **genetic** information.	transfèrent l'information génétique de
9 This **genetic** material is then "read out" to	Ce matériel génétique est alors décodé, et
10 same kind of **genetic** mechanisms that	mêmes mécanismes génétiques que ceux
11 our knowledge of **genetic** mechanisms	connaît bien les mécanismes génétiques,
12 their **genetic** message is read out and	avant que le message génétique ne soit
13 cell a **genetic** process that has both	un mécanisme génétique, qui associe des
14 Screening for **genetic** susceptibility to	le dépistage de prédispositions génétiques
15 supply of DNA for **genetic** testing.	illimitées d'adn pour les tests génétiques.
16 A **genetic** trait that protects against	La découverte d'un gène qui protège
17 Finally, to pinpoint **genetic** traits that	pour identifier des gènes de résistance au
18 Searching for **genetic** traits that provide	Nous cherchons des gènes de protection

Figure 6.8 Extract from bilingual concordance for 'genetic'

in English. As you may not have access to an appropriate specialized dictionary, you can treat your parallel corpus as a dictionary and simply look up terms as and when the need arises. Alternatively, if you know that you will not have access to the parallel corpus while you are drafting the document, you may decide to use the corpus to help you compile a small bilingual wordlist. If, for example, you are writing a document that deals with genetic engineering, you may wish to compile a wordlist of all of the terms you are likely to need. You could start by looking for all of the terms containing the words 'genetic' (see Figure 6.8) and 'gene'.

Figure 6.8 shows an extract from the bilingual concordance for 'genetic'. For reasons of space, the concordance lines have been reduced from their original length of full sentences to single lines. In this small extract alone, you can find some very interesting information. For example, if you had wanted to use the term 'genetic trait' in French, you might have been tempted to create a term in French by translating each of the components of the English term. If, however, you look at the last three concordance lines in Figure 6.8, you will see that 'genetic trait(s)' is usually translated as *gène(s)* in French. As you start to read through the concordance lines, you may spot other words or phrases which you think might be useful (e.g. 'pinpoint' = *identifier*). You should add these to your list so that by the time you have worked your way through all of the concordance lines for 'gene(s)' and 'genetic', you will have quite an extensive list of the vocabulary which you may require.

Key points

- Parallel corpora contain texts and their translations into one or more languages.
- Comparable corpora consist of sets of texts in different languages that are not translations of each other.
- Alignment involves matching source and target text segments in a parallel corpus.
- A parallel corpus needs to be aligned if you wish to use bilingual concordancing software.
- You can use a parallel corpus to learn how to translate words or phrases.
- You can use parallel corpora to learn how to say something in another language.
- You can use a parallel corpus to identify terminological equivalents in another language.

Further reading

Barlow, Michael (1996) 'Parallel texts in language teaching', in S. Botley, J. Glass, T. McEnery and A. Wilson (eds) *Proceedings of Teaching and Language Corpora 1996*. Vol. 9, special issue, Lancaster: UCREL, 45–56.

Botley, Simon P., McEnery, Anthony and Wilson, Andrew (eds) (2000) *Multilingual Corpora in Teaching and Research*, Amsterdam: Rodopi.

Gale, William A. and Church, Kenneth W. (1993) 'A program for aligning sentences in bilingual corpora', *Computational Linguistics*, 19(1): 75–90.

Johansson, Stig, Ebeling, Jarle and Hofland, Knut (1996) 'Coding and aligning the English–Norwegian parallel corpus' in Karin Aijmer and Bengt Altenberg (eds) *Languages in Contrast: Papers from a Symposium on Text-Based Cross-linguistic Studies, Lund 4–5 March 1994*, Lund: Lund University Press, 87–112.

Malmkjær, Kirsten (1998) 'Love thy neighbour: will parallel corpora endear linguists to translators?', *Meta* 43(4): 534–41.

Monachini, Monica, Peters, Carol and Picchi, Eugenio (1993) 'The PISA tools: a survey of computational tools for corpus-based lexicon building', *DELIS Working Paper for TR01/1–2*.

Peters, Carol, Picchi, Eugenio and Biagini, Lisa (1996) 'Parallel and comparable bilingual corpora in language teaching and learning', in S. Botley, J. Glass, T. McEnery and A. Wilson (eds) *Proceedings of Teaching and Language Corpora 1996*, Vol. 9, special issue. Lancaster: UCREL, 68–82.

Ulrych, Margherita (1997) 'The impact of multilingual parallel concordancing on translation', in Barbara Lewandowska-Tomaszczyk and Patrick James Melia (eds) *PALC'97: Practical Applications in Language Corpora*, Lodz: University of Lodz. 421–35.

Where to get information about corpus resources

See Appendix for list of organizations offering corpus resources.

Where to find out more about bilingual concordancers

TransSearch: RALI (Laboratoire de Recherche Appliquée en Linguistique Informatique) at the University of Montreal has developed a number of tools, including TransSearch, the concordancer used for accessing the Canadian Hansard online. More information about RALI at http://www. rali.iro.umontreal.ca/Accueil.en.html. You can try using TransSearch at http://www.tsrali.com where you can download a five-day trial for free, but after that it is a subscription service.

MultiConcord: a multilingual concordancing program for parallel texts developed by David Woolls and others in the Lingua project. Platform: MS Windows. More information at http://www.copycatch.freeserve.co.uk

ParaConc: a bilingual/multilingual concordance program designed to be used for contrastive corpus-based language research and for training and analysis related to translation studies. More information at http://www.ruf. rice.edu/~barlow/parac.html

Exercises

Exercise 1

Locate two parallel texts, i.e. one source text and its translation into another language. Ideally, you should be able to locate these texts on the Internet. The texts can be in the domain of your choice. Pre-process and align the texts as outlined in this chapter.

Exercise 2

Create a frequency ranked word list for the source text (see Chapter 7 for information on how to do this). Select one of the most frequently occurring lexical words in your list (i.e. words which have definable meaning).

Exercise 3

Produce a bilingual concordance using this word as your search pattern. Try to ascertain from the concordance lines whether and how this word is usually translated. Compare your findings with the findings from a general bilingual dictionary.

7   Introduction to basic corpus processing tools

This chapter will introduce the basic processing tools used in corpus linguistics. Using practical examples, we will explain how to produce and interpret word lists and concordances. From our own experience, we know how daunting a prospect it can be to take your first steps towards using a corpus-based approach to learning or studying a language. It is for this reason that we start this chapter with some very simple techniques, which should tempt even the most technophobic learner. These will enable you to become familiar with the software and they may even give you some ideas about how to proceed with your investigation. We then move gradually towards outlining more complex processes and searches, which should challenge and stimulate all students, from the technology shy to the technologically literate.

Producing word lists

When you embark upon your first corpus-based activity, perhaps the best way to start is by producing a list of all of the words in your corpus. This will enable you to familiarize yourself with one particular type of corpus processing software and should also give you some ideas about what to do next. The software that we will use in this section is called WordLister and it belongs to a suite of tools called WordSmith Tools.[1] To create a word list, you simply select the texts you wish to examine and apply the WordList function. WordLister will allow you to produce a batch word list, i.e. one list of all of the words in all of the selected files, or multiple word lists, i.e. a separate word list for each of the selected files. The output comes in three different formats: a statistical analysis, a frequency-ranked word list and an alphabetically ordered word list. We will look at each of these in turn.

---

1   WordSmith Tools: developed by Mike Scott of the University of Liverpool and available from http://www.oup.com/elt/global/isbn/6890/

N	1	2	3	4	5
Text File	Overall	youdim.en	webb.en	wallace.en	villas.en
Tokens	187,157	4175	3353	4130	2481
Types	15,615	1268	906	1187	815
Type/Token Ratio	8.34	30.37	27.02	28.74	32.85
Standardized Type/Token Ratio	45.27	46.33	39.90	43.92	43.15
Ave. Word Length	5.11	5.25	4.84	5.51	5.33
Sentences	6.998	154	119	120	75
Sent. Length	26.58	27.03	28.03	34.15	32.83

Figure 7.1 Statistical summary for *Scientific American* corpus

Statistics

Figure 7.1 contains the statistical information about the words in a batch of sixty-three articles from *Scientific American*. What does the figure reveal?

In column 1, you can see that there is a total of 187,157 words or tokens in the batch of files and that there are 15,615 different words or types. Each of the columns to the right of column 1 contains details about individual files in the corpus. Thus, we can see in column 2 that a file called youdim.en has 4175 tokens and 1268 types, that a file called webb.en has 3353 tokens and 906 types, etc. The table of statistics tells us that the standardized type/token ratio, i.e. the number of different types or word forms per 1000 words is 45.27. The **standardized type/token ratio** is obtained by calculating the type/token ratio for the first 1000 words in a text, and for the next 1000 words and so on. A running average is then computed giving you a standardized type/token ratio based on consecutive 1000-word chunks of text. The standardized type/token ratio may be of interest to you if you are comparing different text types. You may find that some text types systematically have a much higher standardized

1-letter words	5,589
2-letter words	29,438
3-letter words	31,327
4-letter words	28,059
5-letter words	20,288
6-letter words	15,724
7-letter words	17,690
8-letter words	13,379
9-letter words	9734
10-letter words	7050
11-letter words	4238
12-letter words	2417
13-letter words	1389
14(+)-letter words	459

Figure 7.2 Statistics concerning numbers of short and long words

type/token ratio than others; this is the sort of difference you might expect to find when comparing specialized language texts and general language texts. The statistics table also tells you what the average word length is, how many sentences there are in the corpus and what the average sentence length is; in all cases, it does this for the corpus as a whole and for each individual file.

The statistical information that seems to interest students most initially is the information about the number of long words in a corpus.

If you look at Figure 7.2, you will see that the corpus contains 459 words with fourteen or more letters. While these are not necessarily all different words (i.e. types) in that some words will appear more than once, most of us would find it difficult to think of even a handful. If you searched the corpus, you would find that they include 'ordinary' words such as 'characteristic', 'straightforward', 'administration', 'representation' and so-called technical words such as 'thermoregulate', 'spectrographic', 'semiconductors', 'histocompatibility', 'extraterrestrial', 'xenotransplanta-tion'. You would also probably notice that many of the words are in fact derived from much shorter ones. This is particularly true of adverbs, as the following examples should indicate: 'unrecognizably', 'unhesitatingly', 'excruciatingly', 'correspondingly'.

In summary, the statistics function in WordLister provides you with facts and figures about your corpus and about individual files in your corpus.

Frequency lists

To produce a frequency list, WordLister processes all of the files in your corpus and produces a list of all of the different types (different word-forms) ranked according to frequency of occurrence. If you are unsure about the distinction between types and tokens, please refer to Chapter 1 (page 13). Figure 7.3 shows the frequency-ranked count, i.e. total number of occurrences for the first twenty-five types in the *Scientific American* corpus and the Cobuild corpus (Sinclair 1991: 143).

As you can see from this figure, the rankings are identical for the first two types but start to diverge from the third type onwards. However, the same types occur in the top seven most frequently occurring types in both

Scientific American				Cobuild Corpus			
type	freq	type	freq	type	freq	type	freq
the	11,954	with	1225	the	309,497	you	37,477
of	7177	have	1084	of	155,044	on	35,951
to	4753	be	1066	and	153,801	with	35,844
in	4316	it	1003	to	137,056	as	34,755
and	4285	at	969	a	129,928	,	30,952
a	4028	on	950	in	100,138	be	29,799
that	2750	or	893	that	67,042	had	29,592
for	1696	this	867	I	64,849	but	29,572
is	1589	can	773	it	61,379	they	29,512
as	1560	an	765	was	54,722	at	28,958
by	1218	not	704	is	49,186	his	26,491
are	1188	these	696	he	42,057	have	26,113
from	150			for	40,857		

Figure 7.3 Comparison of 25 most common types in *Scientific American* corpus with most common types in the Cobuild corpus

lists. All of the types in the top twenty-five are what are generally called grammatical words or function words. The personal pronouns 'I' and 'you' are in eighth and fourteenth position in the Cobuild corpus but do not appear at all in the top twenty-five types in the *Scientific American* corpus. If you are familiar with scientific writing, you will realize that this is not very surprising as science writers tend to avoid using the first person. Interestingly, 'was' and 'had' are in tenth and twentieth positions in the Cobuild corpus but do not appear in the top twenty-five in the *Scientific American* corpus. On the other hand, 'are' is in twelfth position in the top twenty-five in the *Scientific American* corpus but does not appear at all in the Cobuild top twenty-five. What may surprise you most of all is the fact that there are no lexical words, i.e. words with referential meaning, in the top twenty-five of either corpus. As a student, you spend a lot of time acquiring and learning to use lexical vocabulary and you probably pay little attention to the non-lexical or function words such as those listed in the top twenty-five. Yet, these are often the very words that set native speakers apart from advanced language learners and advanced language learners from beginners. You might find it useful to pay a little more attention to them in the future.

Using a stop list

If you are interested in focusing on the lexical words in your frequency list, you can create something called a **stop list**. A stop list contains the words you wish to exclude from your analysis. Thus, you might create a stop list containing all of the function words in your corpus (e.g. you could start with the top twenty-five listed in Figure 7.3). When you apply the stop list, WordLister will produce a frequency ranking of all of the words in your corpus except those you have chosen to put in your stop list. By applying our own stop list to the *Scientific American* corpus, we get the results contained in Figure 7.4. To give you some idea of the difference a stop list can make, we have included, in the columns to the left of each type, the new (columns 1 and 5) and original (columns 2 and 6) rankings for each type prior to application of the stop list. You can see, therefore, that 'cells' which is now ranked 1 was originally ranked 43 and that 'years', which is now ranked 2, was previously ranked 60.

Word lists do not tell the whole story

One word of caution about word lists and frequency lists in particular: they do not tell the whole story. Take a look again at Figure 7.4 and ask yourself how you interpreted the types 'time', 'use' and 'work'. Did you perceive them to be verbs or nouns? It is very probable that you perceived them to be either a noun or a verb but that both possibilities did not occur to you. Frequency lists do not discriminate between words that have

new	old	type	frequency	new	old	type	frequency
rank	rank			rank	rank		
1	43	cells	417	14	93	university	185
2	60	years	273	15	96	animals	182
3	62	first	270	16	98	research	181
4	64	new	262	17	99	use	181
5	69	gene	234	18	105	molecules	174
6	70	genes	226	19	106	way	174
7	71	found	223	20	107	work	170
8	76	human	212	21	112	called	165
9	77	known	211	22	114	percent	164
10	78	time	209	23	116	researchers	163
11	79	animal	208	24	117	DNA	162
12	80	system	205	25	120	scientists	157
13	82	people	200				

Figure 7.4 Frequency list after application of stop list

the same form but belong to different grammatical categories, and it can be difficult to spot all instances of categorial ambiguity, as this phenomenon is called. And how did you interpret the type 'can' in Figure 7.3? Did you interpret it as a noun or as a modal verb? Both interpretations are possible but, as it happens, 'can' occurs exclusively as a modal verb in this corpus. It is worth bearing in mind that frequency lists do not discriminate between words which are spelt the same but have completely different meanings, as is the case with 'can'. As frequency lists show us words out of context, all of the possible interpretations of a particular word will not be immediately apparent. You should therefore avoid making claims about the frequency of any word without checking how it is actually used in context. This is why concordancing tools are so useful. We will discuss these later in this chapter.

Identifying keywords

While frequency lists are very useful for giving you an indication of what a text or corpus is about, some suites of corpus processing tools (e.g. WordSmith Tools) have another facility called KeyWord which will identify words which occur with an unusually high frequency in a text or corpus when that text or corpus is compared with another corpus. These are called 'key types'. The KeyWord feature will therefore give you an even better indication of what a text is about.

It can also be useful for the purposes of discourse analysis or stylistics studies. For example, you may be interested in comparing two versions of the same event reported in two different publications. The KeyWord tool will highlight what is unique about each of the versions. To illustrate the differences between a conventional frequency list and a **key word list**, we took one of the articles from our corpus and produced a conventional word list. We then used KeyWord to compare the word list for this one article with the word list for the entire corpus. The results are provided in Figure 7.5. In the left-hand column, you have output from the conventional frequency list, consisting of the ten most frequently occurring types; as you can see, these only give you a glimpse of what the text is about. The right-hand column contains the ten most frequent key words in the article – i.e. the ten words with the most unusually high frequency when compared with the corpus as a whole. It should be fairly obvious to you that the right-hand column is much more informative.

At this stage, you may be wondering whether there is any difference between a frequency list produced using a stop list and a key word list. The answer is that the conventional frequency list simply gives you the most frequently occurring words in your text or corpus ranked by frequency. The key word feature compares the word list for your text or corpus with a word list from another corpus and considers any word that is outstanding in its frequency to be 'key'. The words are then ranked according to 'keyness' rather than according to frequency. In other words, the 'key' words float to the top.

10 most frequent types in conventional list	10 most key words using KeyWord
the	mitochondrial
of	mutations
in	DNA
and	mitochondria
to	mutation
mitochondrial	somatic
a	muscle
DNA	inherited
that	energy
mutations	aging

Figure 7.5 Ten most frequent and most key types in a single text

REPRESENT	18
REPRESENTATION	8
REPRESENTATIONS	4
REPRESENTATIVE	1
REPRESENTATIVES	6
REPRESENTED	3
REPRESENTING	5
REPRESENTS	11
REPRESSED	1
REPRIEVE	1
REPROCESSING	3
REPRODUCE	9
REPRODUCED	2
REPRODUCES	2
REPRODUCING	2
REPRODUCTION	6
REPRODUCTIVE	9
REPROGRAM	1
REPROGRAMMED	1
REPROGRAMMING	2

Figure 7.6 Alphabetical listing of types beginning with repr*

Alphabetical lists

In addition to frequency lists, WordLister can produce alphabetically ordered lists, i.e. lists of all of the types in your corpus arranged in alphabetical order. Figure 7.6 shows, in alphabetical order, all of the types in the corpus that begin with 'repr-'. Here, we used the wildcard* in order to retrieve all wordforms beginning with 'repr-'.

Alphabetically ordered lists, which also include information about how often each word-form occurs, can be very useful from a number of points of view. First and foremost, all types commencing with the same letters are grouped together. This gives you easy access to individual word forms that begin with similar sets of letters. It also usually allows you to see whether all forms of a particular **lemma** are actually used in your corpus.[2]

2   This will not work for irregular forms; i.e. do* will find 'do', 'does', 'doing', 'done'; but not 'did'.

For example, in Figure 7.6, you can see that the verb form 'repress*' only occurs as 'repressed' and never as 'repressing' or 'represses'. The type 'reprieve*' occurs as 'reprieve' but never as 'reprieves', 'reprieving', 'reprieved'. (Note: 'reprieve' can be either a verb or a noun and we are unable to tell from the list in which form it appears in the corpus.) The verb form 'represent*' occurs in all its forms but 'represent' (infinitive and third person singular indicative) and 'represents' are much more common than 'represented' and 'representing'. 'Represent*' also occurs in derived forms as 'representative', 'representatives', 'representation' and 'representations'. 'Reproduc*' also occurs in all its verbal forms and as 'reproduction' and 'reproductive'.

Another advantage of **alphabetical lists** is that related word-forms will often appear in the vicinity of each other. Thus, types such as 'reproduce', 'reproduced', 'reproduces', 'reproducing', 'reproduction', 'reproductive', are listed in close proximity. Your alphabetically ordered lists can therefore help you to make a more judicious choice when deciding how to search your corpus using the concordancing tool. You can also judge the commonality of one form versus another by looking at how frequently each of the forms is used.

Reverse alphabetical ordering

You can also order your alphabetical lists by word endings. This is particularly useful if you wish to identify families of words (verbs, adverbs, adjectives, nouns) ending with the same letters. With the reverse order facility, all words with the same suffix are ranked together and you can therefore select and work with the suffixes of your choice. Figure 7.7 contains a selection from the list ranked in reverse alphabetical order. As you can see, words with similar endings are grouped together, thereby allowing you to identify all adjectives ending with '-able'. It can be difficult at first to read a list that has been ordered in reverse but you should treat it as if you were consulting a dictionary (albeit organized in reverse). Thus words, ending in '-bable' ('probable', 'improbable', 'imperturbable') will be listed before words ending in -cable ('implacable', 'applicable', 'inapplicable') etc.

Producing word clusters

In addition to producing lists of single words, WordLister can produce lists of clusters, again ranked alphabetically and by frequency. This is particularly important when you are working with LSP texts as the lexical unit is very often longer than a single word. The clustering facility enables you to identify multiword units. It will therefore help you with identifying units such as noun phrases and phrasal verbs. Lists of clusters can also be ordered in reverse alphabetical order which means that you can

probable	permeable	tenable	desirable	creditable
im**probable**	unquenchable	impregnable	undesirable	profitable
imper**turbable**	searchable	obtainable	memorable	suitable
implacable	switchable	sustainable	inexorable	inevitable
applicable	distinguishable	unsustainable	durable	lamentable
inapplicable	indistinguishable	attainable	curable	notable

Figure 7.7 Reverse order word list for types ending in -able

identify not only noun phrases with the same first element but also noun phrases with the same final element. Figure 7.8 shows you an extract from an alphabetically ordered list of three-word clusters in one of the texts in our corpus. The multiword units in column 1 are sorted in normal alphabetical order, and the units in column 2 are sorted in reverse order.

When you look at the figure, you can see that there are a number of clusters that are not of interest to us as three-word clusters because they do not form what we would consider to be a fixed unit. These include 'mitochondrial DNA in', and 'of somatic mutations'; this kind of irrelevant example is perfectly normal because the facility simply lists all three-word clusters and it is up to you to decide which of them are valid units. You can then simply delete any clusters you consider to be non-relevant so that you can concentrate on those which appear to be important to you. A word of caution here: always think twice before deleting any lines because you may find in your subsequent investigations that what appeared to be uninteresting initially is in fact directly relevant to your investigation (e.g it might be part of a larger unit).

Now, if you look more closely at the contents of Figure 7.8, you will note the following: in column 1, all noun phrases <u>starting</u> with 'mitochondrial' cluster together, while in column 2, all noun phrases <u>ending</u> in 'mutations' or in 'defects' cluster together. Thus, conventional alphabetical ordering allows you to see that there are several multiword terms containing the word 'mitochondrial', that many of these are associated with the term 'DNA' and that 'mitochondrial DNA' is in fact functioning as a unit which combines with words such as 'damage', 'defects', 'diseases', for example. Reverse alphabetical ordering, on the other hand, allows you to see that the word 'mutations' associates with 'mitochondrial DNA', 'base-substitution', 'protein synthesis', and that 'defects' is associated with 'genetic' and 'mitochondrial DNA'.

Conventional alphabetical order	Reverse alphabetical order
mitochondrial DNA damage	oxygen free radicals
mitochondrial DNA defects	mitochondrial DNA mutations
mitochondrial DNA diseases	of somatic mutations
mitochondrial DNA in	base-substitution mutations
mitochondrial DNA molecules	protein synthesis mutations
mitochondrial DNA mutation	the aging process
mitochondrial DNA of	mitochondrial DNA defects
mitochondrial energy production	the genetic defects

Figure 7.8 Three-word clusters ordered in alphabetical and reverse alphabetical order

Summary of what you can learn from word lists

By using WordLister and examining alphabetically ordered and frequency-ranked lists, you can gradually begin to familiarize yourself with the language used in your corpus. Frequency lists, with or without stop lists, and keyword lists can be used as the basis for a preliminary survey of a text or corpus. They allow you to see which lexical words occur most frequently and give you some idea of what the text is about. On observing a particular word in a list, you may be prompted to produce a concordance of this word in order to find out more about it.

Lists of word clusters have further advantages; they allow you to identify larger units. By looking at lists of larger units, you may start to see similarities between some units and decide to investigate them further. If you look again at Figure 7.8, you will see that there are three units associated with 'mitochondrial DNA', which may be related in some way. These are 'mitochondrial DNA damage', 'mitochondrial DNA defects' and 'mitochondrial DNA diseases'. It is only by examining the concordances for each of these clusters that you will be able to ascertain whether they are indeed related in meaning or only apparently so. You may notice that certain verbs appear to co-occur more frequently with one preposition rather than another. Again, you will need to use the concordancing tool in order to investigate further.

You can therefore use word lists for a number of purposes: to familiarize yourself with the terminology of your corpus, to identify words which are related to each other or similar to each other in form and/or meaning, and to observe typical co-occurrence patterns in word clusters. The most important consideration of all is that word lists enable you to consider investigating patterns that you might not otherwise have even observed.

Concordances

In this section, we discuss two different types of concordancing tools: monolingual concordancers and bilingual concordancers. Monolingual concordancers are used on monolingual texts, i.e. texts in one language; they allow you to retrieve all of the occurrences of a search pattern in your corpus together with its immediate contexts. The output is displayed in KWIC (keyword in context) format (see Figure 7.9). Bilingual concordancers are used on aligned parallel corpora; they allow you to search for a pattern in one language and will retrieve all of the occurrences of that word and its immediate contexts and will also retrieve the matching segments in the translation. The output is generally displayed in a split screen (see Figures 7.15 and 7.17), and the display format will vary according to the software being used.

Monolingual concordances

To create a **monolingual concordance**, you need to have a corpus or a text with which you want to work and you need to enter a search pattern. Here, to begin with, we have chosen to work with one text from our corpus and we have chosen 'diseases' as our search pattern. We are interested in establishing what words are associated with 'diseases' in our corpus.

Displaying monolingual concordances

Figure 7.9 contains an unsorted extract from the concordance for 'diseases'. If you have not seen a concordance before, you are probably surprised

```
osis and certain other neurological  diseases result from the destructively
mid-19th century, most debilitating  diseases resulted from bacterial or vi
  and other progressive degenerative  diseases of the brain.    Gene therap
ght be achieved by attacking inborn  diseases at their source.    Among th
ely to be useful for intervening in  diseases affecting those tissues.    O
  of the body.   The proof that such  diseases did in fact derive from exter
    ppeal because they cause no known  diseases in people.    What is more,
   n the cells of people with genetic  diseases or cancer.    A technique k
  t their source.   Among the genetic  diseases that have been studied are
    rearrangement" mutations can cause  diseases of varying seriousness.
jury, as well as during progressive  diseases such as Parkinson's or Alz
The characteristic worsening of the  diseases over time is thought to occ
```

Figure 7.9 Unsorted KWIC display of the search pattern 'diseases'

to see that the concordance or KWIC display does not show full sentences. You will probably be even more surprised to note that the cut-off point does not even appear to be at the beginning or end of a word. This is because concordancers are designed to display the search word in the centre of the concordance line.

The cut-off point for the beginning or end of concordance lines is within a specified number of characters to the right and left of the search pattern, regardless of punctuation marks, and regardless of the beginnings and endings of words. You can, however, vary the line length, and concordancers will usually allow you to specify how many characters you would like to display. For example, the number of characters that we have chosen to display for each of the concordances in this chapter varies from one concordance to another; some of the concordances are eighty characters long (the standard concordance length), and others are longer. Concordancers will also allow you to display entire sentences and even paragraphs if you wish.

Re-sorting monolingual concordances

Most concordancers will allow you to re-sort or rearrange your concordances. While the concordance lines in Figure 7.9 are displayed in the order in which they appear in the original text, the concordance lines in Figure 7.10 have been re-sorted by the first word to the left, and the lines in Figure 7.11 one word to the right. The concordancer rearranges the data to present the lines in the alphabetical order of the word preceding or following the search pattern, depending on whether you have sorted to the left or to the right of the search pattern. You can usually sort up

```
e an array of inherited and acquired diseases.    Preparing for a radical
  rearrangement" mutations can cause diseases of varying seriousness.
 mid-19th century, most debilitating diseases resulted from bacterial or v
 and the appearance of AIDS-defining diseases, we found that the onset of
t a number of late-life degenerative diseases have been associated with
  to various age-related degenerative diseases.    Aging and Age-Relate
s and other progressive degenerative diseases of the brain.    Gene thera
nd a variety of chronic degenerative diseases.    Today study of this DN
cated in inherited mitochondrial DNA diseases may accumulate as well.
tion (just as many mitochondrial DNA diseases are)-suggest that progressiv
erved in inherited mitochondrial DNA diseases.    People born with mitoch
```

Figure 7.10 KWIC display of the search pattern 'diseases' sorted one word to the left

```
urvive into childhood or later. Milder diseases can stem from either a hea

eletions that probably explain why the diseases can be serious from the st

nt antibacterial drugs; new infectious diseases continue to emerge.   It i

ents of the body.  The proof that such diseases did in fact derive from ex

   and even Alzheimer's and Parkinson's diseases might well be treated usin

lerosis and certain other neurological diseases result from the destructiv

he mid-19th century, most debilitating diseases resulted from bacterial or
```

Figure 7.11 KWIC display of the search pattern 'diseases' sorted one word to the
        right

to five words to the left or the right. As you re-sort your concordance using different sort options, different lexical and syntactic patterns will become apparent to you. Thus, in Figure 7.10 where the concordance is sorted one word to the left, you get an insight into different types or different descriptions of diseases ('acquired', 'debilitating', 'degenerative').

In Figure 7.11 where the concordance is sorted one word to the right, you can spot verbs that co-occur with 'diseases' ('stem from', 'derive from', 'emerge', 'result from').

Some concordancers will also allow you to apply a secondary sort. This means that the software will carry out two consecutive sorts and display the results simultaneously. Thus, in Figure 7.12, the concordance has first been sorted one word to the left and then two words to the left.

As you can see from Figure 7.12, re-sorting is not always useful, as it will not always provide you with additional information. It is nonetheless advisable to make use of the re-sorting facility.

Choosing your search pattern

Your search pattern can consist of a single word, a phrase, alternate words, alternate phrases. You can widen your search in a number of ways: by using the wildcard*, by using '/' to look for alternates (e.g. 'cell/cells' will retrieve all occurrences of 'cell' and 'cells'), by using '?' to specify any single character (e.g. 'wa?e' will retrieve 'wade', 'wake', 'ware', etc.). Your concordancer will usually contain detailed help on the different options available. In this section, we plan to look at one sample search to show you why and how to expand your search to retrieve all possible occurrences of a particular pattern.

We saw previously that frequency lists can be useful starting points for deciding which searches you want to make because you will probably want to start by investigating the most frequently occurring words. As 'cells' is the most common lexical word in our science corpus, we have

```
in ways that will enable them to cause disease. This consideration and o

ot be sufficient in themselves to cause disease. Acquired mitochondrial m

f the revolution-the ability to correct disease-is another story. Investi

earlier and would progress to fullblown disease more rapidly than would p

n increase susceptibility to infectious disease and certain tumors as wel

 ated a genetic component to infectious disease. Inbred mice, rats and li

neuromelanin contributes to Parkinson's disease, we and our colleagues ha

olish to take up smoking to try to slow disease progression. Data on the

onmental factors that contribute to the disease or provide resistance to

uccessfully use this knowledge to treat disease. Our analyses predict, ho
```

Figure 7.12 KWIC display of 'disease' first sorted one word to the left and then two words to the left

chosen to use it as the basis for this search. When we enter 'cells' as our search pattern, we retrieve all 417 occurrences of 'cells'. Remember that by specifying 'cells' as our search pattern, we will only retrieve occurrences of 'cells'. We may, however, also be interested in looking at occurrences of 'cell'. The obvious way to do this would appear to be to simply change our search pattern to 'cell/cells'. The concordancer will then search the corpus for all occurrences of 'cell' and 'cells' (there were 590 occurrences). We might, however, want to be absolutely sure that we had indeed retrieved all occurrences of patterns containing 'cell' and 'cells'. We can do this by entering a new search pattern using a wildcard, namely 'cell*', this time. By entering 'cell*' we will retrieve all types beginning with 'cell-'. This search yielded 634 occurrences. The wildcard search produced quite a lot of unnecessary noise, i.e. words which are neither 'cell' nor 'cells'. The noise included the following: 'cell-binding', 'cell-equipped', 'cell-like', 'cell-surface', 'cellsurface', 'cellular' and 'cellulose'. We also found, however, that the wildcard search retrieved occurrences of 'cell's' and 'cells'', thereby confirming that we were right not to settle for a search with just 'cell/cells'. You now have two options if you wish to ensure that you retrieve all relevant concordance lines. You can either edit the output from the wildcard search by deleting the non-relevant lines, or you can enter a new search. Your decision will depend on the amount of noise in the concordance produced using the wildcard. If you enter a new search, it will look as follows: 'cell/cells/cell's/cells''. This will finally give you all occurrences (there are 611 in our corpus). As mentioned previously, the alphabetical word list is also a good place to start when you want to identify all of the different forms that you wish to include in your search pattern.

```
ces microglia - the brain's immune cells - high up in the destructive pat

he robust attacks that white blood cells of the immune system often mount

hagocytes and by activating immune cells or complement.       And although

s activated immune (and nonimmune) cells that can either stimulate or inh

nt or, worse, can cause the immune cells in the donor marrow to attack th

other class of CD4-carrying immune cells called macrophages.     HIV does

cids responsible for luring immune cells to injured or diseased tissues.

mmune system is distinguishing the cells, tissues and organs that are a l

t during an immune response.     T cells, for example, help to regulate t

cules that stimulate immune system cells.       Developing pharmaceuticals
```

Figure 7.13 KWIC display for 'immune' co-occurring with 'cell/cell's/cells/cells"
    within five words to the left or right of the search pattern

Looking for words in context

Once you have produced a concordance, you may decide to look only at
concordance lines that contain a particular word, called a context word,
in the vicinity of your search pattern. Most concordancers will allow
you to specify a context word that must appear within a certain number
of words of your search pattern. Let us take our previous example of
'cell/cell's/cells/cells" and let us assume that we wish to look for the context
word 'immune' within five words to the left or right of the search pattern.
We will find that instead of the original 611 entries with all occurrences,
we now have just twenty-one. An extract from the KWIC display is
provided in Figure 7.13.

Displaying collocates

Some concordancers offer an additional facility which frequency ranks the
words that appear in the vicinity of your search pattern. This facility
computes and displays the most frequently occurring **collocates**. Collocates
are words which typically occur in the vicinity of your search pattern.
Figure 7.14 shows an extract from the collocates for 'cells'.

When you first use this facility, you may find the results difficult to interpret but it is worth persevering, particularly if you have a special interest
in identifying typical collocates. The collocate display shows the search
pattern ('cells') in the middle column and then shows, for each position to
the left and right of the search pattern, which word occurs most frequently.
Thus, 'cells' appears in line 1 of Figure 7.14, occurring a total of 454 times.
Of these, it occurs 417 times in the centre, twenty-two times to the left of

N	Word	Total	Left	Right	L5	L4	L3	L2	L1	*	R1	R2	R3	R4	R5
1	cells	454	22	15	8	3	5	5	1	417	0	2	6	3	4
2	the	275	160	115	26	41	28	30	35	0	0	42	24	24	25
3	and	105	29	76	5	7	8	7	2	0	29	11	7	14	15
4	that	82	32	50	9	5	8	5	5	0	27	3	8	5	7
5	from	42	16	26	4	6	2	3	1	0	15	2	4	2	3
6	are	40	8	32	4	1	2	5	0	0	8	5	1	9	9
7	into	40	29	11	6	1	5	1	12	0	3	1	2	2	3
8	for	38	19	19	3	5	4	7	0	0	1	7	6	2	3
9	blood	33	27	6	2	1	2	1	21	0	1	2	0	1	2
10	their	28	10	18	1	2	5	0	2	0	1	2	5	7	3
11	genes	27	17	10	2	2	4	9	0	0	1	1	1	5	2
12	these	23	16	7	2	1	1	2	10	0	0	3	0	3	1
13	immune	21	14	7	1	1	2	1	9	0	0	0	6	1	0

Figure 7.14 Collocates of 'cells'

the search pattern, and fifteen times to the right of the search pattern. 'The' is the next most frequently occurring collocate, 'and' the next, 'that' the next, and so on until you reach the first lexical collocate. You will notice that 'blood' is the most frequently occurring lexical collocate. It appears a total of thirty-three times, twenty-seven times to the left of the search pattern and just six times to the right. Moreover, when it appears to the left of the search pattern, it occurs most frequently just one word to the left of the search pattern ('blood cells'), as you can see by looking at the column L1.

The advantage of using a collocate viewer is that it does a lot of the hard work for you and saves you having to sort and re-sort your concordances in order to bring typical patterns into relief. If we take an ordinary word like 'experiment', for example, we may want to find out which words to use with it. By computing the collocates for 'experiment' in our corpus, we were able to ascertain that it is more usual to 'conduct' an experiment than to 'do' an experiment, and that an experiment 'provides evidence' of something rather than 'shows' something.

Uses of monolingual concordances

As you may have gathered from the discussion so far, monolingual concordances can be used for a variety of purposes. By enabling you to see a search pattern in not one but several contexts, they give you critical information about the meaning and usage of words and phrases, insights that you are unlikely to find in such detail in dictionaries. Dictionaries will provide you with grammatical information, definitions, a small number of examples of usage but they will never be able to give you the wealth of information that you can find in a concordance. The difference between concordances and dictionary entries is that the information in dictionaries has been prepared for you whereas you have to do your own analysis and preparation when working with concordances. In addition to allowing you to gain greater insight into the meaning and usage of words, concordances will give you an idea of which words typically belong together. For example, if you were working with a corpus of academic writing, you would discover that a 'paper' can 'describe', 'claim' or 'show' but it does not 'believe' or 'want' (e.g. 'this paper wants to demonstrate' is not usual). You will start to see patterns that will inform your own use of language. You will be able to use concordancers to identify which verbs go with which nouns, which prepositions with which verbs, which adjectives with which nouns, whether active or passive voice is more appropriate in a particular context. As you will see, the exercises at the end of this chapter and the case studies in our later chapters are designed to give you further ideas for uses of monolingual concordancers.

Bilingual concordances

Bilingual concordancers allow you to work with parallel corpora. Parallel corpora, as explained in Chapter 6, contain texts and their translations into one or more languages. They are usually aligned at paragraph and/or sentence level. In many respects, bilingual concordancers are very similar to monolingual concordancers in that they allow you to retrieve all occurrences of a search pattern together with their immediate contexts. They also offer the same sorting features as monolingual concordancers and they allow you to search for words in context. The difference is that bilingual concordancers also retrieve the corresponding translation segments. They retrieve all of the segments in which the search pattern appears in one language together with all of the corresponding segments in the other language, and the two sets of results are displayed simultaneously. (We use the word 'segment' rather loosely here, sometimes to refer to a single concordance line of a specified length, sometimes to refer to complete sentences.) The results can be displayed side by side, as in Figure 7.15, or in a split screen, as in Figure 7.17. The presentation format is determined by the program used.

As you can see from Figure 7.15, the top half of the window displays the search pattern and, in this instance, the words immediately to the

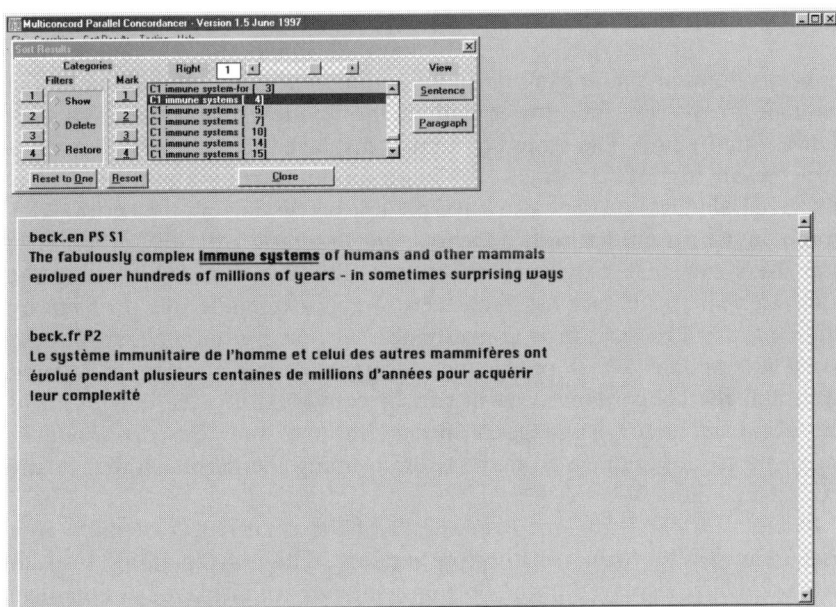

Figure 7.15 One concordance line from bilingual concordance of 'immune' produced using MultiConcord

In the nearer term, naked DNA has promise for use in vaccines, because even minute amounts of protein can stimulate a protective <u>immune</u> response.	À plus court terme, l'adn nu semble être un composé de vaccin prometteur, car même des quantités infimes de protéines stimulent une réaction immunitaire protectrice.
Two other features of the vertebrate <u>immune</u> system – complement and lymphocytes – are also missing from invertebrates, but for both there seem to be invertebrate analogues.	Les invertébrés sont privés de deux autres particularités immunitaires des vertébrés – le complément et les lymphocytes –, mais ils possèdent des systèmes analogues.
Invertebrates lack lymphyocytes and an antibody-based humoral <u>immune</u> system.	Les invertébrés n'ont pas de lymphocytes ni de système immunitaire humoral fondé sur les anticorps.

Figure 7.16 Extract from concordance for 'immune' converted to table format

right of 'immune'. You can adjust the settings to see words further to the right or to the left. The lower half of the window displays the concordance, line by line. The search pattern is displayed in a complete sentence rather than in KWIC format. The corresponding translation segment is displayed alongside. Users also have the option of viewing the entire paragraph in which the pattern appears. One limitation of this program is that users can only view one concordance line at a time while using the software. The developer has, however, largely overcome this problem by allowing users to save their concordances in text for subsequent viewing using a standard word processing program. Using a word processing program, the concordance output can be converted to a table with all of the occurrences for language A in one column and the corresponding segments from language B in the column alongside, as illustrated in the extract in Figure 7.16.

In Figure 7.17, ParaConc displays all of the occurrences of the search pattern in KWIC format in the top window. The corresponding translation segments, displayed in the bottom window, are displayed as complete sentences. While this does mean that users have to read through the sentences in the lower window in order to identify the equivalents in the other language, the findings are usually more than worth the effort.

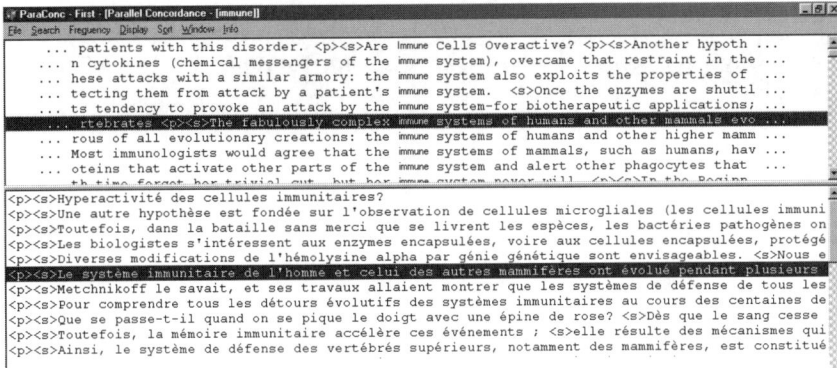

```
ParaConc - First - [Parallel Concordance - [immune]]
File  Search  Frequency  Display  Sort  Window  Info
    ... patients with this disorder. <p><s>Are immune Cells Overactive? <p><s>Another hypoth ...
    ... n cytokines (chemical messengers of the immune system), overcame that restraint in the ...
    ... hese attacks with a similar armory: the immune system also exploits the properties of  ...
    ... tecting them from attack by a patient's immune system.  <s>Once the enzymes are shuttl ...
    ... ts tendency to provoke an attack by the immune system-for biotherapeutic applications; ...
    ... rtebrates <p><s>The fabulously complex immune systems of humans and other mammals evo ...
    ... rous of all evolutionary creations: the immune systems of humans and other higher mamm ...
    ... Most immunologists would agree that the immune systems of mammals, such as humans, hav ...
    ... oteins that activate other parts of the immune system and alert other phagocytes that  ...
    ... th time forgot her trivial cut, but her immune system never will. <p><s>In the Beginn
<p><s>Hyperactivité des cellules immunitaires?
<p><s>Une autre hypothèse est fondée sur l'observation de cellules microgliales (les cellules immuni
<p><s>Toutefois, dans la bataille sans merci que se livrent les espèces, les bactéries pathogènes on
<p><s>Les biologistes s'intéressent aux enzymes encapsulées, voire aux cellules encapsulées, protégé
<p><s>Diverses modifications de l'hémolysine alpha par génie génétique sont envisageables. <s>Nous e
<p><s>Le système immunitaire de l'homme et celui des autres mammifères ont évolué pendant plusieurs
<p><s>Metchnikoff le savait, et ses travaux allaient montrer que les systèmes de défense de tous les
<p><s>Pour comprendre tous les détours évolutifs des systèmes immunitaires au cours des centaines de
<p><s>Que se passe-t-il quand on se pique le doigt avec une épine de rose? <s>Dès que le sang cesse
<p><s>Toutefois, la mémoire immunitaire accélère ces événements ; <s>elle résulte des mécanismes qui
<p><s>Ainsi, le système de défense des vertébrés supérieurs, notamment des mammifères, est constitué
```

Figure 7.17 One concordance line from bilingual concordance of 'immune' produced using ParaConc

Uses of bilingual concordancers

As we explained in some detail in Chapter 6, you can use bilingual concordancers for a variety of investigations. If you are a translation teacher/student, you might want to know how translators have handled certain linguistic features. You might want to look more closely at what happens to culture specific references in translation. You might want to see how certain terms are translated. If you are a language learner, you can use a bilingual concordancer to access your corpus in much the same way as you would use a bilingual dictionary. Thus, you can use it to identify translations for words, terms and phrases. You can use it to establish how words are used, i.e. whether a particular word favours a certain syntactic pattern, whether it prefers certain groups of adjectives, etc. As we suggest in Chapter 6, the possibilities are endless, and we would suggest that as you work with your parallel corpus, you will find that there are more and more things that you would like to investigate.

Key points

- You can use concordancing tools to produce word lists and concordances.
- Word lists will tell you something about what your text is about.
- Keyword lists will tell you more about what your text is about.
- You can use word clusters to identify term candidates.
- You can use word clusters to find out which words belong together.
- You can use concordances to learn how to use a particular word or phrase.
- You can use concordances to understand the meaning of a word or phrase.

Further reading

Aston, Guy (ed.) (2001) *Learning with Corpora*, Houston: Athelstan; Bologna: CLUEB.
Tribble, C. and Jones, G. (1997) *Concordances in the Classroom*, Houston: Athelstan.

Concordancing software

KWiCFinder (Keyword in Context Finder): a stand-alone search agent which retrieves and excerpts relevant documents identified by AltaVista's search engine. More information at http://miniappolis.com/KwiCFinder/KwiCFinderHome.html

Logi Term: a bilingual concordancer and terminology manager. More information at http://www.terminotix.com

MultiConcord: a multilingual concordancing program for parallel texts developed by David Woolls and others in the Lingua project. More information at http://www.copycatch.freeserve.co.uk

ParaConc: a bilingual/multilingual concordance program designed to be used for contrastive corpus-based language research and for training and analysis related to translation studies. More information at http://www.ruf.rice.edu/~barlow/parac.html

WordSmith Tools: suite of corpus processing tools available for sale, and in demo mode, from Oxford University Press at http://www.oup.com/elt/global/isbn/6890/

Exercises

Here, we provide a small number of sample exercises to give you an idea of the kinds of investigations you can undertake using corpus processing tools.

Working with word lists

Select a text for investigation. Create a word list. Using either the frequency-ranked or alphabetically ordered list, identify and make a note of all of the nouns in your word list. This involves literally reading down through the list and making a note of all nouns. Now create a new word list, this time applying the clustering facility so that you obtain two-word lists. Identify and make a note of all of the two-word noun phrases in your new list by reading down through the list. Compare these with the first list which you drew up. What do you notice? Perhaps some of the nouns which you assumed to be single-word nouns in the first list are in fact always part of a larger group, i.e. a two-word cluster? At this stage, it might be worth re-setting the cluster to three words to see what you retrieve.

Working with key words

Following the guidelines in Chapters 3 and 4, create a small corpus (*c.* 50,000 words) of your choice. Now create and save a word list for the entire corpus. Next, create and save a word list for one of the texts in your corpus. Using the key word facility, compare the word list for your single text with the word list for the corpus as a whole. Finally, compare the key word list with the original word list for the single text. What do you notice? What you should find is that lexical words will float to the top much more easily in the key word list than in the conventional word list. You may also find that some non-lexical words are listed as being key. If so, these are very likely to be worthy of further investigation because they may tell you something about the author's style.

Reading and interpreting concordances

Exercise 1

Examine the concordance for 'prices' in Figure 7.18, by focusing in particular on the part of the line which precedes the search pattern. The lines

```
thorities there capped consumer prices, thereby discouraging  inv
to Christmas in the US, Dell cut prices on its Latitude  notebooks
er.  A 3 per cent fall in energy prices, which knocked almost 0
lation (ODTR) hopes to  finalise prices by the end of February. T
 February 1st to boost  flagging prices, ministers said yesterday.
ll merely mask continuing higher prices in domestic economy The
 and other economies. Rising oil prices not only push up inflation
tically in trying to improve oil prices when it meets in Vienna t
 of the euro and the rise in oil prices, have proven to be more t
onth, reflecting the fall in oil prices and the impact of the Jan
ell by 3.4 per cent. Falling oil prices were reflected in a drop o
 company's strategy of  reducing prices to gain market share.  Th
alting the recovery in the share prices of the Irish financial secto
oduction is aimed at stabilising prices within the $22-$28 price
 round effects that will push up prices. In view of these concern
 will cut production to shore up prices in the face of falling winte
```

Figure 7.18 KWIC display for 'prices', sorted one word to the left

contain different descriptions of 'prices' and of what can happen to 'prices'. How many can you find? For example, in line 1, there is a reference to 'capped consumer prices'.

Exercise 2

Examine the concordance for 'prices' in Figure 7.19, by focusing in particular on the part of the line which follows the search pattern. In the concordance, you will find different ways of saying that prices have increased or fallen. How many can you find? Remember to make a note of any accompanying words which you think might be useful.

```
operator enters the market is that prices are reduced by anywhere b
 weeks of last year," he said. Oil prices barely reacted to the widely
he costs of imports steady and oil prices continue to hold steady or f
ices fallen. Household electricity prices decreased by  20 per cent
      ministers on Monday. Consumer prices fell by 0.8 per cent last mo
ices and a deteriorating euro. Oil prices have begun to fall although
n it meets in Vienna tomorrow. Oil prices have been rising for more th
e past year. Clothing and footwear prices in contrast are down 4.8 pe
    the 12 months to January, house prices nationally were up by 20.6
  S and other economies. Rising oil prices not only push up inflation b
   in December to below 6 per cent. Prices rose by 0.1 per cent during
   cut output for fear it would send prices spiralling, stoking inflation
iends  First, pointed out that oil prices were also moving up again
   r. Outside Dublin city and county, prices were up by 1.1 per cent aft
 e  economy, there is a danger that prices will rise to what the market
```

Figure 7.19 KWIC display for 'prices', sorted one word to the right

Exercise 3

Examine the concordance for 'findings' in Figure 7.20, by focusing in particular on the part of the line which follows the search pattern. Can you identify which verbs or verb phrases are associated with 'findings'?

Exercise 4

Examine the concordance for 'paper' in Figure 7.21. Is 'paper' being used in the same way in each of the concordance lines? If not, what are the different meanings? What information are you using in the concordance lines to support your answers?

```
o processes are related.     These findings also converge with data from
isibility.  Whatever the case, the findings also tell scientists that the
y were merely fantasies.     These findings confirm earlier studies that
trated unequivocally. Indeed, our findings constitute the first concrete
tudies, the new chemokine receptor findings critically refined understand
ubunits in mitochondria.     These findings implied that mitochondrial
   But our encouraging preliminary findings indicate that lipoplexes migh
I g for untoward reactions.  Their findings led to the test being dropped
potheses that better explain their findings.   Many of the apparent a
ed, and others are emerging.   The findings open entirely new avenues
f 15 years or more.    The recent findings reveal that some people w
   improvements in reading.  Such findings set the stage for our own s
  cannot he made to boom.   These findings show that although smooth
s originally predicted?    Recent findings suggest that acid rain is a
ey move through the pore.    The findings with H5 offer an illustration
```

Figure 7.20 KWIC display for 'findings' sorted one word to the right

```
   Academy of Sciences had written a paper in English in which they subscr
thin a few weeks after submitting a paper on these remarkable findings to
rty," printed with gold on asbestos paper.   Credit for another use belon
st of us thought it was a very good paper, the result of an excellent, de
sidents of these sites manufactured paper out of the bark of the wild fig
 carried out in the distribution of paper copies.   Suppose that Morgan
ichord, read Shakespeare's plays on paper as well as recite them aloud, a
aca, that served as a sort of scrap paper for the community.      These
s, developed a  flame-resistant tar paper tailor-made for an era all too
994, when we finally  submitted the paper for publication, most of us tho
s and dissected the organs;   their paper, published in 1996, arrived at
 made of basalt.    The Aztecs used paper to make books of picture-writin
```

Figure 7.21 KWIC display of 'paper'

Part III

Corpus-based applications in LSP

8   Building useful glossaries

This chapter will show you how to use corpora and corpus processing tools to produce glossaries. We start by considering what glossaries are and why you might need to produce them. We take a look at how professional terminologists work and model our own approach on the professional model. We work our way step by step through two different but related scenarios in order to show you how to adopt a corpus-based approach to your own terminology work.

As a language student, you have probably been compiling vocabulary lists ever since you first started learning a new language. While your vocabulary lists may vary in the amount of detail they contain, and some of them may just be simple lists of words and their equivalents, they are very probably already embryonic or potential glossaries. In other words, it is very likely that you already have some experience of glossary preparation, even though you might not have been aware that that is what you were doing. The difference between the approach that you have been using and the approach that we propose in this chapter lies in the fact that (a) we use corpus processing tools to help us in our task, and (b) we favour a systematic approach. What we are trying to achieve here is to show you how to create glossaries that will enable you to collate all of the information you have gleaned from different sources. We aim to show you where to start, how to proceed and how to use a range of tools to collect the information you need.

What is a glossary?

A glossary is essentially a list of terms in one or more languages. The amount of information contained in glossaries can vary greatly, and the level of detail in any glossary will usually depend on the purpose for which it is intended. Thus, at one end of the spectrum, the most basic glossary will simply contain lists of terms and their equivalents in one or more foreign languages. In this situation, the glossary producer is assuming that the person consulting the glossary is already familiar with the domain and just needs to know how to translate a particular term. Some basic glossaries may also have a rudimentary classification system which groups related terms together (i.e. terms from the same subfield). At the other end of the glossary spectrum, you will find richly detailed glossaries containing definitions, examples of usage, synonyms, related terms, usage notes, etc. These are the glossaries which every translation student and language student dreams of having because they can use them to understand terms, to identify equivalents, to learn how to use terms, to identify synonyms if they exist, to identify related terms and their equivalents. Unfortunately, such richly detailed glossaries are a rarity, mainly because glossary compilation can be very time consuming. Commercial glossary publishers will rarely have the resources to produce such detailed glossaries and will prefer instead to produce glossaries that fall somewhere in the middle of the spectrum. These will usually contain definitions, equivalents and, much more rarely, some information on usage. If you have never seen a glossary before, you might try looking for some in your library or on the Internet. Try entering 'bilingual glossary', or 'multilingual glossary' as your search pattern and you should get a large number of hits. Take a look at some of the glossaries and you will see that there is a huge variety both in relation to content and in relation to the presentation of the information. These might give you some ideas for how you will eventually structure your own glossary.

Why do you need to produce a glossary?

You may be asked to build a glossary for any number of reasons. As a student of a particular discipline (e.g. engineering, business, law, science) already familiar with the terminology of the discipline in your own language, you may need to acquire the terminology in another language. You will therefore be particularly interested in identifying equivalents in the other language for the terms you already know in your own language and you will want to know how to use these terms in the other language. As a student of technical writing or journalism, for example, you may be asked to produce a document or article in your own language on a domain in which you have little or no expertise. You will want to read up on the area and make a note of the terminology and language used so that you can use these appropriately in your document or article. As a student of translation you may be asked to translate a text dealing with a topic that is unfamiliar to you. Here, you will need not only to understand the terminology and language used in the source text but also to have a grasp of the appropriate terminology and language in the **target language** in order to produce an adequate translation.

What about dictionaries and comparable documents?

Some of you might wonder if there is any need for glossaries in domains for which monolingual, bilingual and multilingual dictionaries exist. You may be quite happy to prepare your language and translation assignments by relying on appropriate dictionaries and doing some background reading into the topic by consulting comparable documents. If you can honestly say that you have always found exactly what you wanted by consulting dictionaries and comparable documents, you are a rare person indeed and also very fortunate. The reality, we believe, is that students frequently have problems consulting dictionaries and using background material. The reasons for this can vary.

Shortcomings of dictionaries

Let us look at dictionaries first. How often do you have to consult more than one dictionary in order to find the information you are seeking? How often do you find that the information you are seeking is simply not there? How often do you choose a word in the dictionary without really knowing whether it is the right one? While dictionaries are an essential part of any language student's toolkit, they rarely provide the answer to all your questions.

Dictionaries generally fall into the following categories: monolingual general language dictionaries, monolingual specialized dictionaries, bi-/ multilingual general language dictionaries, bi-/multilingual specialized language dictionaries. Monolingual general language dictionaries will provide you with grammatical information, definitions, synonyms, antonyms, examples of usage. While they tend to focus mainly on LGP (language for general purpose) words, they will often contain some entries for general technical terms. If, however, you are looking for information about the meaning and usage of more specialized terms, monolingual general language dictionaries will be of little use. Monolingual specialized dictionaries, i.e. dictionaries dealing with a particular domain, tend to concentrate on providing information about the meaning rather than the usage of terms. Consequently, they will not usually provide grammatical information or examples of usage. Bi-/multilingual general language dictionaries tend to concentrate on the usage of terms and do not provide definitions. This can be problematic, particularly in cases where a word has more than one meaning (e.g. a word like 'bridge', 'foot' or 'nursery' in English). If a definition is not provided, how can you tell which of the equivalents is appropriate? Take the word 'nursery', for example: it has two French equivalents i.e. *crèche* or *pépinière* which are used in quite different circumstances (*crèche* is used in the context of childcare and *pépinière* is used in the context of plants). The content of bi-/multilingual specialized language dictionaries can range from one-word entries with equivalents in a large number of languages (e.g. some dictionaries published by Elsevier) to publications covering fewer languages and providing more detailed information. As with bi-/multilingual dictionaries, definitions are rarely provided and the emphasis is mainly on providing equivalents and examples of usage. As you can gather from this discussion, no single dictionary will ever provide you with all of the information you require as a language student.

Problems with reading comparable texts

Traditionally, comparable texts, texts dealing with the domain you are studying, have been another useful tool in the language learning environment. Generally, students read them on paper or online, in their own language or in the language they are studying. By doing so, they familiarize themselves with a particular domain and with the terminology and phraseology used in that domain. In other words, they acquire the special vocabulary of a domain and they also learn the most typical ways of saying or writing something in a particular domain.

There are, however, drawbacks to reading comparable texts, the first being that it can take quite a lot of time to locate the texts you need, particularly if you are focusing on paper resources. The task is made slightly easier if you are fortunate enough to have good CD-ROM sources or ready access to the Internet. When you do locate texts on the subject, you may then find that you have to read five or six articles before finding one that is strictly relevant to the work you are doing. Second, reading comparable documents takes time; this is a problem, as you do not often have that much time to prepare assignments. Consequently, you will often only read quickly through one or two articles. The main problem with reading is that it is very easy to overlook important information. For example, if you are looking for a particular term, it is quite possible that it may only appear once or twice in each of the articles you are reading. The chances of your finding it by reading the document in the normal way (i.e. starting at the beginning and working your way through) are therefore not great. If you are going to use comparable texts to help you with language assignments, and we strongly recommend that you do so, you should consider 'reading' them using corpus processing tools. As we saw earlier in Chapter 7, corpus processing tools will help you to see patterns in texts far more quickly than if you were reading through documents in the more conventional way.

Traditional methods of producing a glossary

In this section, we propose to give a brief overview of how professional terminologists usually proceed with their work. Professional terminologists are people whose job it is to produce glossaries and specialized dictionaries. While we are not aiming in this chapter to train you to be professional terminologists, we believe that there is much to be learnt from the way they approach their work. The method which we propose on pages 143–4 will be modelled on the traditional professional approach described here.

When professional terminologists start work on a completely new glossary, they start by deciding on the domain and working language for the glossary. They then identify a subject expert whom they can consult for advice. The type of advice they might need would relate to the selection of terms (the specialized words of a domain), the definition of terms, the scope of one particular term compared with another, etc. If the domain that has been chosen is very large, for example, if the domain of computing has been chosen, the terminologists will identify a subfield within the domain and use this as their starting point. The scope of the subfield can be revised (i.e. expanded or restricted) if necessary. Once the subfield has been agreed, the terminologists then start to collect documentation for use during the terminology project. The documentation will consist of different types of texts dealing with the domain. The documentation will be used to select terms and to note evidence of unusual or typical usage. Traditionally, terminologists will read through the documentation, underlining or highlighting term candidates and unusual and typical collocates as they go. The term candidates may be single-word terms or terms consisting of two or more words (commonly referred to as multiword terms). As the terminologists work their way through the documentation, they will start to think about how the individual term candidates relate to each other and may already start to sketch a rough outline of the structure of the subfield. A number of different terms are used to describe this, namely system of concepts (the name preferred by terminologists), hierarchical representation and tree diagram. A very simple system of concepts is provided in Figure 8.1 to give you an idea of what we are talking about.

Once all term candidates have been retrieved, the terminologists will then continue to work on the system of concepts. They may now decide that some of the term candidates are in fact not terms or that they do not belong in the subfield under investigation; they may also realize that there are still some gaps in the system of concepts. At this stage, this does not really matter. What is important, however, is that the terminologists now have a reasonable idea of the number of terms in the subfield. This helps them to gauge the amount of time that is going to be required to complete the project.

During the next stage, terminologists will try to finalize their list of terms by consulting with their subject experts. The subject experts will be able to help with problem cases, i.e. cases where the terminologists are not sure, for example, whether or not a particular word or phrase should be treated as a term. The terminologists will also show their draft

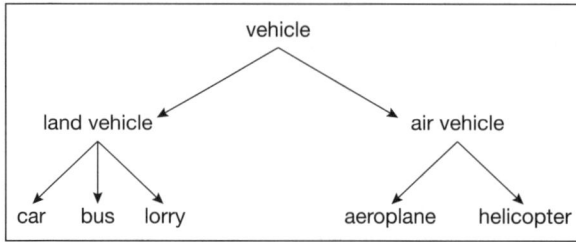

Figure 8.1 Simple system of concepts

system of concepts to the experts, and the experts will advise on the validity of the system proposed and may be able to fill in some of the gaps. Following consultation with the subject experts, the terminologists will then refine their list of terms and their system of concepts and will move onto the next stage.

In this next stage, the terminologists will start to collect information about the terms that have been selected. This information will be stored in what is known as a terminological record sheet. The terminological record sheet will have a number of slots (e.g. definition, subject field, grammatical information, phraseological information, related terms, notes about usage, synonyms (words with the same meaning, e.g. 'equilateral triangle' and 'equiangular triangle'), antonyms (words with opposite meaning, e.g. 'hot' and 'cold'), pseudo-synonyms) that the terminologists will try to fill. Not all slots will be filled immediately and some slots may never be filled for some terms (e.g. not all terms will have synonyms or will require additional information about usage). A sample record sheet is provided in Figure 8.2. As you can see, this sample record sheet is designed for a monolingual glossary. This is because terminologists tend to complete their projects for one language first and then move on to identify equivalents in another language.

The definition slot is one of the most difficult slots to fill because terminologists are usually constrained by guidelines that specify how definitions should be formulated. This means that they can rarely borrow a ready-made definition directly from an existing source. Instead, they usually have to try and conflate a number of existing definitions or try to create an entirely new definition that complies with the guidelines. Essentially, the guidelines usually stipulate that all definitions must relate the term being defined upwards to the next nearest concept/term in the system of concepts. In other words, the hierarchical structure of the domain should be reflected in the definition, making it easier to understand the term. By structuring definitions in this way, a term at the bottom of the system of concepts automatically inherits all of the characteristics of the terms to which it is related further up the hierarchical structure. If you look at the sample completed record sheet for the term 'gene' in Figure 8.3, you will see that

---

Domain (subject field)

Subfield (sub-domain of subject field)

Language (working language)

Term (in its base form, entered in lower case) + gender (if applicable)
(m, f, n)

Grammatical category (noun, verb, etc.)

Definition (ideally in accordance with fairly strict guidelines)

Synonym (if applicable; in fact, few real synonyms exist)

Abbreviated form (e.g. if term is World Wide Web, insert WWW here)

Short for (e.g. if term is WWW, insert World Wide Web here)

Contextual fragments (one or more samples of usage, frequently full sentences)

Usage notes (if applicable)

Figure 8.2 Sample record sheet for professional terminology work

'gene' is defined as a 'unit of DNA'. 'Gene' is at the top of the hierarchy of 'genes' and must therefore be defined using a more generic term, in this case a 'unit'. If we were to produce a record sheet for 'recessive gene', 'recessive gene' should ideally be defined by 'a gene which . . .'. In this way, 'recessive gene' would automatically inherit the characteristics of 'gene'.

By the end of the glossary compilation process, the terminologists will have filled as many slots as are required by the particular terminology project.

Practical terminology work

In this section, we propose to look at two scenarios that are designed to help you produce your own glossary. In the first scenario, you have been asked to translate/write a text on the likelihood of transgenes escaping from transgenic plants into related wild plants in the style of a popular science article in English. You are a translation or communications student with little scientific training (we assume that you did some science in school) and you do not have any in-depth knowledge of the area in question. You are a native speaker of English and you always translate into or write in your mother tongue. Your first objective will therefore be to read up on the topic in your own language in order to familiarize

---

Domain *biotechnology*

Subfield *n/a*

Language *English*

Term *gene*

Grammatical category *noun*

Definition *A unit of DNA that carries information for the bio-synthesis of a specific product.*

Synonym *n/a*

Abbreviated form *n/a*

Short for *n/a*

Contextual fragments *When a gene is active, or as a geneticist would say, "expressed," the sequence of the chemical units, or bases, in its DNA is used as a blueprint to produce a specific protein.*

Figure 8.3 Sample record sheet for 'gene'

yourself with the domain and its terminology; you will record the information you have found in a glossary. In the second scenario, you are a language or translation student and you have been asked to produce a bilingual glossary, on the same topic as the first scenario, for yourself and your fellow students. This means that you will need not only to familiarize yourself with the domain and terminology in your own language but you will also need to identify the terminological equivalents in another language. For both scenarios, you will need to begin by producing a monolingual glossary. Our aim, while working our way through the two scenarios, is to show you how a small corpus and corpus processing tools can be of use in compiling a glossary.

Getting started: selecting your documents

You will need to collect a reasonable number of relevant texts on the domain in order to start your terminology work. Obviously, the more relevant texts you can find the better, but you would be surprised at how much you can achieve with a corpus of *c.* 30,000 words (i.e. the equivalent of ten articles of *c.* 3,000 words each). You may remember that Chapters 3 and 4 provided comprehensive coverage of what is involved in designing and compiling a corpus. At this stage, we suggest that you re-read Chapters 3 and 4 in order to refresh your memory on issues such as corpus design, text selection, text sourcing, text formats, etc. Once you have re-read the chapters, you will be in a better position to decide on where to source your texts, how to evaluate them and how to save them.

Given that you have been asked to produce a text in the style of a popular science article, the ideal solution for you is to locate relevant comparable texts that have been published in popular science journals. Two well-known candidates spring to mind. These are *Scientific American*, published in the US, and *New Scientist*, published in the UK They each have extensive text archives on their web sites; *New Scientist* is also available on CD-ROM. There may be other popular science journals with which you are familiar that are also available in electronic form. To select the texts, it will be necessary to use a number of relevant keywords; we chose to use 'transgenic plants', 'gene' and 'wild species', as our keywords. We then selected the fifteen most relevant articles, saved them as text files and considered that these would make a good starting point for our purposes.

Identifying term candidates

Once you have selected the texts with which you want to work, the next step involves identifying term candidates in your text collection. Terms are words (single words or compounds) that are used in a specialized domain and have a clearly defined meaning. When we speak about 'term candidates', we mean words or phrases that appear to be terms. As we mentioned earlier, you can of course identify term candidates manually, simply by reading through the texts and highlighting all term candidates. Manual term identification is, however, very time consuming and we are assuming that you do not have the time to do this. Moreover, it is difficult to tell which are the most typical or most common terms in a domain. We are going to look at two different ways of semi-automatically identifying term candidates using corpus processing tools.

Using frequency lists

You may remember that we discussed wordlists in Chapter 7 and showed how frequency lists can give us some idea of what a text is about because they rank the words in a corpus in descending order of frequency. (If you are unclear about how to create and manipulate wordlists, you should read over the relevant sections in Chapter 7 again (pages 112–19).) We start by creating simple frequency lists of single words, two-word clusters and three-word clusters. The results are displayed in Figures 8.4, 8.5, 8.6. Figure 8.4 shows the twenty-five most frequently occurring types or single words in our mini-corpus. Take a look at this figure and make a note of how many of these types you think might belong to the subject of transgenic plants and the likelihood of transgenes escaping into related wild species. We believe that the relevant lexical types here may be: 'wild',

the	a	from	genes	with
of	that	wild	by	pollen
and	is	gene	as	on
to	for	be	genetic	this
in	are	plants	plant	it

Figure 8.4 Twenty-five most frequently occurring types

'gene', 'plants', 'genes', 'genetic', 'plant', 'pollen'. We make a note of these.

We could simply stop here and decide to work further with the most frequent single words by producing concordances that would allow us to see which other words co-occur with them. This would enable us gradually to build up a picture of candidate terms in the domain. We believed, however, that we might be able to get results more quickly by producing frequency lists of two- and three-word clusters.

The most frequent two-word clusters are displayed in Figure 8.5. As you can see, there are a lot of two-word clusters that would not be considered to be terms (e.g. 'to the', 'in a', 'on the') but there are also some that may be (e.g. 'gene flow', 'genetic engineering', 'F. Virginiana' and 'wild weedy'). The last two, i.e. 'F. Virginiana' and 'wild weedy' are in fact parts of larger multiword units, as you can see from Figure 8.6.

If we now look at Figure 8.6, we see that quite a few of the most frequently occurring three-word clusters appear to be multiword term candidates or parts of multiword terms (e.g. 'F. Virginiana plants', 'wild weedy plants', 'rapa subsp campestris', 'brassica rapa subsp', 'wild weedy relatives'). By combining the results of all three lists, we begin to get some idea of the most frequently occurring lexical words (and possibly term candidates) in our collection of texts. If we exclude all non-lexical words or words/phrases which we think are not directly relevant to the topic (e.g. 'the United States') in each of the Figures 8.4, 8.5 and 8.6, we find that we have the following list: 'wild', 'gene', 'plants', 'genes', 'genetic', 'plant', 'pollen' (from Figure 8.4), 'gene flow', 'F. Virginiana', 'wild weedy', 'genetic engineering', (from Figure 8.5), 'wild weedy plants', 'rapa subsp campestris', 'brassica rapa subsp', 'wild weedy relatives', 'wild species', 'centers of diversity', 'F. Virginiana plants', 'the cultivar', 'wild relative', 'related wild species', 'transgenic wild weedy' (from Figure 8.6). To make the list more accessible for you, we have sorted it alphabetically in Figure 8.7.

We could now start to work with the words and phrases in Figure 8.7 by producing concordances to establish (a) whether any or all of these

of the	F. Virginiana	and the	will be
in the	wild weedy	for example	of a
gene flow	the wild	in a	that the
from the	et al	of genes	of gene
to the	at the	genetic engineering	such as
to be	into the	it is	can be
on the			

Figure 8.5 Twenty-five most frequently occurring two-word clusters

wild weedy plants	of gene flow	the wild species	the presence of
rapa subsp campestris	of genetic engineering	centers of diversity	the wild weedy
brassica rapa subsp	wild weedy relatives	F. Virginiana plants	transgenic wild weedy
the United States	of F. Virginiana	from the cultivar	a number of
gene flow from	of the wild	its wild relative	and its wild
in the United	the university of	related wild species	as a result
the production of			

Figure 8.6 Twenty-give most frequently occurring three-word clusters

are actually terms and (b) whether any or all of these are actually functioning as larger units. We have decided to postpone this activity until page 150 as we first want to show you another way of identifying the most typical lexical words in our mini-corpus.

Using keyword lists

As we already saw in Chapter 7 (pages 114–15), some corpus processing tools (e.g. WordSmith Tools) have a facility that will identify words that occur with an unusually high frequency in a text or corpus when that text or corpus is compared with another corpus. The advantage of using this type of facility is that it will generally give you an even better indication than frequency lists of what a text is about. We should, however, point out that not all corpus processing tools come with this particular feature.

brassica rapa subsp	genes	rapa subsp campestris	wild weedy plants
centers of diversity	genetic engineering	related wild species	wild weedy relatives
F. Virginiana	plant	transgenic wild weedy	wild
F. Virginiana plants	genetic	the cultivar	wild weedy
gene flow	plants	wild relative	
gene	pollen	wild species	

Figure 8.7 Alphabetically ordered most frequently occurring lexical items (single words and two- and three-word clusters)

wild	crop	gene	weedy	virginiana
plants	plant	flow	strawberry	al
pollen	transgenic	genes	weed	relatives
crops	genetic	populations	transgenes	hybrids

Figure 8.8 Twenty most key single words

We have used the keyword facility to produce a list of the most key single words (Figure 8.8), the most key two-word clusters (Figure 8.9) and the most key three-word clusters (Figure 8.10) in the collection of texts. If you compare Figure 8.4 (most frequently occurring single words) and Figure 8.8 (most key single words), you will see immediately that Figure 8.8 contains far more lexical words than Figure 8.4.

If we then compare Figure 8.5 and Figure 8.9, we see again that there are far more lexical words (and consequently **candidate terms**) in Figure 8.9 than there are in Figure 8.5.

Finally, if we compare Figure 8.6 and Figure 8.10, we can see that although there are far more lexical words in Figure 8.6 than there are in Figures 8.4 and 8.5, there are even more in Figure 8.10.

It is clear, therefore, that keywords are a more efficient way of identifying the words or phrases that are most typical of a particular domain.

You should, however, remember that when we were working with the frequency lists for Figures 8.4, 8.5 and 8.6, we were only working with the twenty or twenty-five most frequently occurring items. If we had

gene flow	of transgenic	wild plants	flow from
et al	the wild	wild populations	weedy plants
genetic engineering	wild relatives	pollen from	to wild
the crop	of genes	oilseed rape	wildweedy plants
wild species	the cultivar	populations of	and wild

Figure 8.9 Twenty most key two-word clusters

brassica rapa subsp	the risk of	the transgenic crop
gene flow from	its wild relative	cultivated and wild
the united states	related wild species	gene flow between
in the united	transgenic wildweedy plants	of wild strawberry
of gene flow	from the cultivar	from crops to
of genetic engineering	centers of diversity	from the crop
the wild species	and its wild	

Figure 8.10 Twenty most key three-word clusters

worked our way down through the frequency lists and looked at all of the potentially relevant words or phrases, we would have come up with similar results to those displayed in Figures 8.8, 8.9 and 8.10. The main difference between using frequency lists and keyword lists to identify candidate terms is that it takes slightly longer to do it using frequency lists alone. One further advantage of using keyword lists is that words that may not appear frequently in a specialized text or corpus may still be unusual (and therefore an indicator of text or domain specific terms) when compared to a reference corpus.

What next? Expanding the list of term candidates

Now that we have a list of the most frequently occurring or most key words and word clusters in our collection of texts, we can move on to the next stage which involves increasing our terminological coverage by adding further candidate terms to our list. We can do this very easily either by continuing to work our way through the frequency and key word lists or by doing the following. We simply take the words or phrases already selected from our frequency or keyword lists, produce concordances for each of them and make a note of all of the term candidates that appear in the concordance lines. With this method, we are likely to find term candidates in the vicinity of our search pattern and term candidates that include the search pattern itself.

Here, we have chosen to work initially with 'wild' as it is the most frequently occurring lexical word and also the most key word in our collection of texts. We produced a concordance of 'wild', sorted it first to the left and then to the right and made a note of all of the multiword term candidates which contain the word 'wild' itself. The results are displayed in Figure 8.11.

The results speak for themselves in the sense that 'wild' is clearly associated with a large number of candidate terms, some of which may be related in some way. An optional next step at this stage involves grouping related terms together so that we can start to think about producing a

'wild' sorted one word to the left	'wild' sorted one word to the right		
transgenic wild/weedy plants	wild beets	wild population(s)	wild turnip
sexually compatible wild/weedy relatives	wild-crop hybrids	wild progeny	wild/weed hybrids
crop-wild progeny	wild crop relatives	wild radish raphanus sativus	wild/weed x crop hybrids
native wild plants	wild flora	wild relative(s)	wild/weed populations
nonhybrid wild plants	wild gene pool	wild rye grass	wild/weedy plants
related wild species	wild h. annuus	wild species	wild/weedy relative(s)
	crop-to-wild hybridization	wild strawberry	wild/weedy parent
	wild plant populations	wild sunflowers	wild/weedy plant populations
	wild plants	wild tomato	
	wild pollen	wild tuberous solanum species	

Figure 8.11 Potential terms containing the word 'wild'

system of concepts or hierarchical structure. Within the list provided in Figure 8.11, you may already be able to see potential groupings, i.e. candidate terms which are likely to have some characteristics in common and which may therefore belong to the same system of concepts or hierarchical structure. Below, we have listed some of the potential groupings. You may not agree with these or you may spot others that we have overlooked. Why not try doing the exercise yourself to see what you find?

We would put 'wild/weedy plants', 'wild/weedy relatives', 'wild/weedy parent', 'wild/weedy plant population(s)' together because we think that these are all related in some way. We note also that 'transgenic wild/weedy plants' belong to the family of 'wild/weedy plants' and that 'sexually compatible wild/weedy relatives' belong to the family of 'wild/weedy relatives'.

We note that 'wild species' functions as a superordinate term for a number of terms. Under the superordinate 'wild species', we would include the following: 'wild beets', 'wild H. Annuus', 'wild radish Raphanus Sativus', 'wild rye grass', 'wild strawberry', 'wild sunflowers', 'wild tomato', 'wild tuberous solanum species', 'wild turnip'. We note that the various wild species are sometimes identified by their botanical name and sometimes by their more commonly known name. If we chose to include all of these different wild species in our glossary, we would probably need to locate both the botanical and common names for each of them.

We think that the following may also be related in some way: 'wild plants', 'wild flora', 'wild populations(s)', 'native wild plants' and 'nonhybrid wild plants'. This would then leave the following items in our groupings unaccounted for: 'wild relatives', 'crop-wild progeny', 'wild-crop hybrids', 'wild gene pool', 'crop-to-wild hybridization', 'wild pollen', 'wild progeny', 'wild/weed hybrids', 'wild/weed x crop hybrids', 'wild/weed populations'. We can guess that some of these may be related in some way (e.g. 'crop-to-wild hybridization', 'crop-wild progeny' and 'wild relatives') but we do not have sufficient clues to support or refute our suspicions. Again, this does not matter for the moment because we are simply trying to trawl our corpus for potential terms.

As 'plants' was the next most key word, we then produced a concordance of 'plants', to establish whether it too functioned more often as part of a larger unit. We could have initiated a search for 'plant*' which would have recovered occurrences of 'plant', 'plants', 'planted', 'planting' but we decided to use 'plants' alone as the search pattern as this was the word which had been identified as key.

As you can see from Figure 8.12, 'plants' usually functions as part of a larger term unit rather than as a term on its own. What is interesting about this list is that we appear to have a lot of contrasting pairs, e.g. 'crop plants' vs 'wild plants', 'genetically engineered plants' vs 'nonengineered plants', 'hybrid plants' vs 'nonhybrid plants', 'transgenic plants' vs 'nontransgenic plants', 'parental plants' vs 'progeny plants'. We find 'wild F. Virginiana plants' and 'potted F. Virginiana plants'.

sexually compatible plants	nonengineered plants	progeny plants
crop plants	nontransgenic plants	squash plants
genetically engineered plants	ornamental plants	transformed plants
flowering plants	parental plants	transgenic plants
hybrid plants	wind-pollinated plants	potted F. Virginiana plants
nonhybrid plants	chlorosulfuron-resistant plants	wild F. Virginiana plants
invading plants	potato plants	wild plants
local plants	potted plants	native wild plants
native plants	insecticide-producing plants	transgenic wild/weedy plants
		wild/weedy plants

Figure 8.12 Words co-occurring with 'plants', sorted to the left

We also find 'native plants' and 'local plants' that appear to be synonymous. We make a note of this for further investigation. We find 'wild plants' and 'native wild plants', 'wild/weedy plants' and 'transgenic wild/weedy plants'. The items not accounted for in our groupings include: 'invading plants', 'ornamental plants', 'chlorosulfuron-resistant plants', 'potato plants', 'insecticide-producing plants', 'transformed plants'. Again, we simply make a note of these for further investigation at a later stage.

Now that we have looked at two keywords in order to see to which larger units they belong, we are going to move on to a different stage. In this next stage, we take another keyword, this time a two-word cluster, namely 'gene flow', and we look at the concordance lines in which it appears to see if we can spot any additional terms in the vicinity of 'gene flow'. The concordance has been sorted to the left (Figure 8.13).

In Figure 8.13, we find, in order of appearance: 'long-distance gene flow', 'horizontal gene flow', 'interpopulation gene flow' and 'crop-weed gene flow'. We make a note of these as being different types of 'gene flow'.

If we then look at the concordance lines to see what other term candidates we can find, we note (concordance line number in brackets) 'biologists', 'plant population' (1), 'genetic material', (2), 'crop plants' (4), 'crop diversity', 'genetic variability' (5), and many more. Why not try working your way through the remainder of the lines in Figure 8.13 to see which candidate terms you would like to include? Bear in mind that there is rarely unanimous agreement about which terms to include or exclude. This is why the advice of subject field experts can come in handy.

```
1.  rial is called gene flow. Among biologists, gene flow into a plant population may
2.  This transfer of genetic material is called gene flow. Among biologists, gene flo
3.    dependent on the amount of long-distance gene flow that there is,' explains
4.  will substantially reduce the potential for gene flow. Many crop plants are outcr
5.    nters of crop diversity. The capacity for gene flow to alter genetic variability
6.    ibuted to mechanisms other than horizontal gene flow. Few other claims of plant
7.      escape. Other factors that may influence gene flow by pollen include pollinato
8.  wild/weedy populations. Factors influencing gene flow. The significance of gene f
9.  lant conservation genetics. Interpopulation gene flow by pollen in wild radish
10. he potential to eliminate or at least limit gene flow from the cultivated to the
11.    arkers in addition to estimating rates of gene flow, we have conducted experime
12.   t where there are repeated high levels of gene flow. Second, genetic drift may
13. s dioecious, further increasing the risk of gene flow from the cultivar to wild
14. ne risk of gene flow by pollen. The rate of gene flow by pollen may be influenced
15. ts, the incidence, rate and consequences of gene flow between the cultivated stra
16.   influencing gene flow The significance of gene flow is determined by the extent
17. ions showed the highest percentage (27%) of gene flow. Gene flow was found to dec
18. States. For these crops, the likelihood of gene flow into wild populations as a
19. niniana in a preliminary test of potential gene flow, potted plants of F.
20. advantage. First, when the migration rate (gene flow) is high, the effect of
21. populations are particularly vulnerable to gene flow from a larger population of
22. importance of population shape on crop-weed gene flow, and  the 4,040 achenes gen
```

Figure 8.13 Extract from the concordance for 'gene flow' sorted one word to the
       left

Building a terminological profile

Once you have drawn up the list of candidate terms you believe to be
typical of a particular domain, you then have a number of options. The
most straightforward one is that you simply provide the list of terms as
it is. This option, while straightforward, is not going to be very useful
for someone who knows nothing about the domain. We suggest therefore that, at the very least, you should provide a definition and some
information about how the terms are used.

Formulating a definition

As we mentioned in our earlier discussion of how terminologists work
(pages 140–3), terminologists rarely find ready-made definitions perfectly

formulated in accordance with terminological standards. Consequently, they often have to formulate their own definitions drawing on a range of existing definitions that they may find in glossaries or dictionaries. In this section, we plan to show you how you can use your corpus to help with this task. We plan to look more closely at the term 'gene flow' and at the concordance for 'gene flow' to see if we can glean any interesting information that we might use in a definition.

If you look again at Figure 8.13 and focus on line 2 of the concordance for 'gene flow', you will notice something interesting going on. You will find the sentence 'this transfer of genetic material is called gene flow'. We can therefore state already that 'gene flow' involves a 'transfer of genetic material'. The use of the demonstrative adjective 'this' suggests that the previous sentence may also contain some clues about the meaning of the term. If we expand the concordance line in order to retrieve more context, we may get some more information. The expanded concordance line is displayed in Figure 8.14.

In the expanded concordance line, we find that the term 'gene flow' is used here to describe the phenomenon whereby transgenes in crops transfer by natural means to other plants. We also find that biologists use the term to describe the introduction of genes by pollen, seed or asexual propagules. We note that the term is being used here to refer specifically to the flow of genes via pollen during sexual reproduction. It seems therefore that, based on the information we have in just this one concordance line, we can already start to formulate a definition, namely,

> **gene flow:** the transfer of genes (including transgenes) from one population to another

We do not include any of the hedged information provided in the concordance line because we wish to have a definition that applies in general to the term 'gene flow'. What is missing from this tentative definition is how gene flow occurs. We could include 'via pollen, seed or asexual propagules' but we are unsure of our ground. This is where it would be

---

The other major category of risk associated with large-scale releases of transgenic crops is that transgenes in crops will be transferred by natural means to other plants, which may then become weeds. This transfer of genetic material is called gene flow. Among biologists, gene flow into a plant population may refer to the introduction of genes by pollen, seed, or asexual propagules. This report considers only the flow of genes via pollen during sexual reproduction; thus, the term gene flow here means only the flow of genetic material from one population to another via pollen. Wild/weedy plants that are recipients of transgenes by gene flow are referred to as transgenic wild/weedy plants.

Figure 8.14 Expanded concordance line for 'gene flow'

> **gene flow:** the exchange of genes between dissimilar but (generally) related populations
>
> **gene flow:** the passage and establishment of genes typical of one breeding population into the gene pool of another by hybridization and backcrossing

Figure 8.15 Definitions for 'gene flow' sourced on the Internet

useful to consult a subject expert who would be able to give a definitive answer.

Now, if we compare our draft definition with definitions sourced in glossaries on the Internet, we find that the draft definition is actually quite accurate. Figure 8.15 contains two definitions sourced from two different web sites. We retrieved them by using the search pattern 'gene flow glossary' on the Internet.

The first one is essentially not very different from our draft definition but the second one contains additional information that may be of interest to us. It tells us that gene flow can occur by hybridization and backcrossing.

Here, we have shown you one indicator of defining information in your corpus but there are many others. Take a look at Figure 8.16 and you will see other indicators of some type of defining information. For example, the use of 'i.e.' will usually indicate that some defining information is about to follow. The use of 'e.g.' usually indicates that examples will follow. Brackets or parentheses can also contain useful defining information. Can you think of other clues you might look out for?

Locating phraseological information

Once definitions for all terms on our list have been created or located, we could decide that we had now done enough, especially as this is all that most specialized dictionaries will provide. We know, however, that students frequently need more information than dictionaries can provide (see pages 139–40). This applies in particular to information about how a term is used. How many times have you found yourself armed with the correct terminology but unable to use it simply because you do not know which word goes with which? In our experience, students are more likely to let themselves down by using incorrect collocates than by using incorrect terms. This is why we think it important to spend some time looking at the environment of terms in order to pick up as many clues as possible about how they are used.

In this section, we propose to look again at the concordance for 'gene flow'. This time, however, instead of looking for information about its *meaning*, we are looking for information about its *usage*. The easiest way

In an initial test of potential gene flow, potted plants of F. Virginiana were introduced into a single strawberry farm . . . most seeds produced by these potted plants were hybrids (i.e., seeds were sired by F. Ananassa pollen).

Brassica rapa subsp. campestris possesses many agronomically important characters (e.g. yellow seed colour, pathogen resistance, cold tolerance) that are demanded in the breeding of B. napus.

The cultivated strawberry (Fragaria Ananassa) and its wild relative (F. Virginiana) represent a particularly suitable system for investigating transgene escape.

Figure 8.16 Indicators of defining information

to do this for any term is to produce a concordance and then play around with the sorting feature in order to see which patterns emerge. We have displayed the concordance sorted one word to the left (Figure 8.13) and one word to the right (Figure 8.17) but we could also have displayed it in many other ways (two words to the left, two words to the right, etc.). As the total number of concordance lines is greater than the number of lines displayed here, you will note that there is some discrepancy between the contents of the two figures.

We start by looking at the concordance that has been sorted one word to the left (Figure 8.13 is reproduced here for your convenience) and look for lines where 'gene flow' is preceded by a preposition.

We find that it is preceded by 'for', 'of' and 'to'. We then look at the words which precede the prepositions and find the following, in order of appearance in the concordance: 'potential for gene flow', 'capacity for gene flow', 'rates of gene flow', 'levels of gene flow', 'risk of gene flow', 'rate of gene flow', 'incidence, rate and consequences of gene flow', 'significance of gene flow', 'percentage of gene flow', 'likelihood of gene flow', 'vulnerable to gene flow'. As some of these have characteristics in common, we group similar ones together, allowing the end users of the glossary to make their own choice (see Figure 8.19 for draft record sheet for 'gene flow').

We then look for verbs and verb phrases to the left of the search pattern and find 'factors influencing gene flow', 'eliminate or at least limit gene flow'. We can also see other verbs such as 'increase' and 'estimate' but these are generally associated with 'risk' and 'rates' rather than with 'gene flow' itself. We do not therefore make a note of them for the moment.

We then look at the concordance which has been sorted one word to the right (Figure 8.17). Here again, we start by looking at prepositions and we find 'at', 'between', 'by', 'from', 'into' and 'via'. We then look at the words which appear to the right of these prepositions and note those displayed in Figure 8.18.

```
1.  rial is called gene flow. Among biologists, gene flow into a plant population may
2.  This transfer of genetic material is called gene flow. Among biologists, gene flo
3.     dependent on the amount of long-distance gene flow that there is,' explains
4.  will substantially reduce the potential for gene flow. Many crop plants are outcr
5.   nters of crop diversity. The capacity for gene flow to alter genetic variability
6.   ibuted to mechanisms other than horizontal gene flow. Few other claims of plant
7.     escape. Other factors that may influence gene flow by pollen include pollinato
8.  wild/weedy populations. Factors influencing gene flow. The significance of gene f
9.  lant conservation genetics. Interpopulation gene flow by pollen in wild radish
10. he potential to eliminate or at least limit gene flow from the cultivated to the
11.   arkers in addition to estimating rates of gene flow, we have conducted experime
12.  t where there are repeated high levels of gene flow. Second, genetic drift may
13. s dioecious, further increasing the risk of gene flow from the cultivar to wild
14. ne risk of gene flow by pollen. The rate of gene flow by pollen may be influenced
15. ts, the incidence, rate and consequences of gene flow between the cultivated stra
16.    influencing gene flow The significance of gene flow is determined by the extent
17. ions showed the highest percentage (27%) of gene flow. Gene flow was found to dec
18. States. For these crops, the likelihood of gene flow into wild populations as a
19. niniana in a preliminary test of potential gene flow, potted plants of F.
20. advantage. First, when the migration rate (gene flow) is high, the effect of
21. populations are particularly vulnerable to gene flow from a larger population of
22. importance of population shape on crop-weed gene flow, and  the 4,040 achenes gen
```

Figure 8.13 reproduced Extract from the concordance for 'gene flow' sorted one
word to the left

We examine the data in Figure 8.18 in order to verify the tentative definition that we drew up previously. It is clear from the data in Figure 8.18 that we should include some reference to the fact that, in the context of transgenic plants, gene flow refers more to the flow of genes 'from' crops or cultivars 'to' wild populations than vice versa. We therefore reformulate our definition so that it now reads as follows:

gene flow: the transfer of genes (including transgenes) from cultivars to related wild populations

We then look to the concordance again to see which verbs appear to the right of the search pattern and find 'gene flow occurred' and 'gene flow was found to decrease'.

```
1.    separated by different distances. Gene flow at different distances wil
2.    s. The first experiment estimated gene flow between wild and cultivate
3.    ith at least one wild species and gene flow between cultivated crops a
4.    cidence, rate and consequences of gene flow between the cultivated str
5.     crops to related wild species is gene flow by pollen (Kareiva et al.,
6.     Other factors that may influence gene flow by pollen include pollinat
7.    here are no barriers to potential gene flow from cultivated to wild st
8.    f my research is to determine how gene flow from a genetically enginee
9.    ns are particularly vulnerable to gene flow from a larger population o
10.   common among bacteria, horizontal gene flow from plant to plant has ne
11.   ), further increasing the risk of gene flow from the cultivar to wild
12.    Transgenes into Wild Populations Gene flow from crops to wild relativ
13.    (1983) surveyed situations where gene flow from nontransgenic crops t
14.   le previous studies on  potential gene flow from crops to wild species
15.   lled gene flow. Among biologists, gene flow into a plant population ma
16.   or these crops, the likelihood of gene flow into wild populations as a
17.    decrease with distance; however, gene flow occurred up to distances o
18.   red crops into the environment is gene flow via pollen from crops to r
19.   at percentage (27%) of gene flow. Gene flow was found to decrease wit
```

Figure 8.17 Extract from one concordance for 'gene flow' sorted one word to the
right

Collating the results

As soon as you start making notes about terms, you should record the
information somewhere in a systematic way. We saw in Figure 8.2 that
terminologists use record sheets to record their terminological data. We
suggest that you devise something similar for yourselves, either on paper
or on computer, and that you then enter data as and when you find it.
Specialized terminology management software is commercially available
and you may be fortunate enough to have access to this. If not, you can
simply use your word processor to create your record sheets. You may
not fill all of the slots all of the time but at least all of the data you have
entered will be easily accessible and transparent for yourself and other
users. We are now going to try and collate the information we have
already collected for 'gene flow'.

Preposition	Co-occurrence
at	gene flow at different distances
between	gene flow between wild and cultivated sunflowers
	gene flow between cultivated crops and their wild relatives
by	gene flow by pollen may be influenced by
from	gene flow from a genetically engineered crookneck squash
	gene flow from a larger population
	gene flow from the crop overwhelms the
from... to...	gene flow from cultivated to wild strawberry
	gene flow from plant to plant
	gene flow from the cultivar to wild populations
	gene flow from crops to wild relatives
	gene flow from nontransgenic crops to weeds
	gene flow from crops to wild species
into	gene flow into wild populations as a result of use in the United States
	gene flow into a plant population may refer to the introduction
via	gene flow via pollen from crops to related wild species
	gene flow via pollen from cultivated strawberry into nearby populations

Figure 8.18 Prepositions to the right of 'gene flow'

You may note that the slots listed in our draft record sheet Figure 8.19 are a little different from those listed in Figure 8.2. We have, for example, omitted the slot for contextual fragments. We have also added slots for corpus-attested collocations and for related terms. The reason we have done this is that, as we already mentioned, one of the biggest problems students encounter is that they do not know how to use a term. We hope that by inserting collocation information and information about related terms, users of the glossary will be better equipped to use the terms in context. In our experience, you can record more contextual information in this way than by providing just one or two contextual fragments.

Domain: biotechnology

Subfield: transgenic plants

Language: English

Term: gene flow (no plural attested)

Grammatical category: noun

Definition: the transfer of genes (including transgenes) from cultivars to related wild populations (incomplete)

Synonym: *gene escape.* Note: only used in negative contexts

Abbreviated form

Short for

Corpus attested collocations

Verbs: *(to the left) factors influencing . . . , eliminate . . . , limit . . . ,(to the right) . . . decrease, . . . occur*

Nouns: *potential for . . . , capacity for . . . , rate(s) of . . . , levels of . . . , risk of . . . , likelihood of . . . , significance of . . . , percentage of . . . , vulnerable to . . . , incidence, rate and consequences of . . .*

Related terms: *long-distance gene flow, horizontal gene flow, interpopulation gene flow, crop-weed gene flow*

Usage notes

Figure 8.19 Draft record sheet for 'gene flow'

Adding another language: Scenario two

You will remember that in our second scenario, you were required to supplement the information already collated with information in another language. To do this, you will need to compile a mini-corpus in another language; this mini-corpus will contain the same types of texts and deal with the same topic as the first mini-corpus. We have chosen to work with French. We compiled a mini-corpus of fifteen articles dealing with the topic of transgenic plants. We then followed the exact same procedures as we had followed for the creation of the English version. In other words, we produced frequency lists, keyword lists and started to build up a hierarchical representation of the terms in French. We collated information about terms, their meaning, their usage, other related terms, etc.

We then needed to identify which French terms related to which English terms. Here, we focus on 'gene flow' as we have already treated it in depth for the English part of the glossary. Judging by the frequency lists and keyword lists for our French mini-corpus, the French term *flux de gènes* appeared to be a very strong candidate as the French equivalent for the English term 'gene flow'. Rather than take the short cut of assuming that this was so, however, we produced a concordance of the search pattern *gène** in order to ensure that we had not missed out on other possible equivalents. We were happy to find that our original hunch was correct. We only found one other possible equivalent (*échange de gènes*) and this occurred only once in our mini-corpus whereas *flux de gènes* occurred twenty-one times. In reality, some of the concordance lines retrieved had already pointed clearly to *flux de gènes* as the appropriate equivalent. As you can see from the following two expanded concordance lines (Figure 8.20), the meaning of *flux de gènes* is very similar, if not identical, to that of 'gene flow'.

Once you have identified the equivalents for the terms in your glossary, you can start to complete terminological record sheets for the second language in much the same way as you did for the first language. You make a note of collocates and related terms. We used an expanded version of the concordance extract displayed in Figure 8.21 to compile our French terminological record sheet.

We then collated this information and recorded it on a bilingual terminological record sheet (Figure 8.22). The bilingual terminological record sheet actually has the same number of possible fields as the monolingual record sheet but, for reasons of space, some of these have been omitted from the figure (the omitted fields are: 'language', 'abbreviated form', 'short for').

Storing your data

As soon as you start collecting information about terms, even if you are only collecting terms and their equivalents in other languages, you should think about how you are going to record this information so that you can retrieve it in the form you need whenever you need it. We recommend that you devise a record sheet on the lines of those presented here and that you carry blank copies of the record sheet with you whenever you are doing language assignments. You can then enter information as you find it. The advantage of using a standardized record sheet is that it will help you to be consistent in the way you do your terminology work.

Nowadays, many translators record their terminological data on computer, either in a word processor or dedicated terminological database. If you have ready access to computers, you should consider doing the same by creating a database. This would mean that you would not

> On sait aujourd'hui que les plantes cultivées échangent, par croisements spontanés, leurs gènes avec les espèces sauvages apparentées, qui sont souvent de mauvaises herbes. On appelle cela le *flux de gènes*.
>
> Le second problème concerne la question des *flux de gènes*, c'est-à-dire le passage du gène inséré à des espèces apparentées ou non à l'organisme modifié.

Figure 8.20 Expanded concordance lines for '*flux de gènes*'

```
ou du risque particulier du flux de gènes si l'on ne peut pas démontrer u
oins en ce qui concerne les flux de gènes, elle dispose d'une base de con
ion horizontale. L'étude de flux de gènes entre plantes cultivées et appa
d chez nous le problème des flux de gènes est réel. Plusieurs plantes lar
lesquelles la question d'un flux de gènes pouvait se poser ont fait l'obj
elles-même ? Les risques de flux de gènes depuis les espèces transgénique
t de limiter les risques de flux de gènes. C'est un sujet complexe, simpl
rogression pour désigner le flux de gènes dans les populations d'hybrides
 au Mexique pour voir si le flux de gènes était à craindre. Il existe
me concerne la question des flux de gènes, c'est-à-dire le passage du gèn
a nécessité de maîtriser le flux de gènes. En effet cette maîtrise est dé
abilité de réalisation d'un flux de gènes dépend des espèces et des écosy
s OGM, - problèmes liés aux flux de gènes (croisements avec des plantes
```

Figure 8.21 Extract from concordance for '*flux de gènes*'

need to worry about losing the original paper copies and that you could easily enter additional information and update your entries as and when you choose.

Summary of glossary compilation

This chapter has shown you how to use a corpus and corpus processing tools for glossary work. While it is true that a corpus-based approach will not always provide all of the answers (because of inadequate corpus size, or because your corpus is inappropriate), you should find that it can be much more efficient to work in this way. A corpus-based approach allows you to identify subject-specific term candidates quickly and easily, and, most importantly for you as a language student, to identify typical collocation patterns.

Name of field	English	French
Domain	biotechnology	
Subfield	transgenic plants	
Term	gene flow (no plural attested)	flux (m) de gènes
Gramm. category	noun	noun, m.
Definition	the transfer of genes (including transgenes) from cultivars to related wild populations (incomplete)	the transfer of genes (including transgenes) from cultivars to related wild populations (incomplete)
Synonym	gene escape. Note: only used in negative contexts.	fuite (f) de gènes. Note: only used in negative contexts.
Collocations	Verbs (to the left) factors influencing…, eliminate…, limit…, (to the right)…decrease, …occur	Verbs (to the left): contrôler, maîtriser, limiter les risques, (to the right) dépendent de, sont à la base de…
	Nouns potential for…, capacity for…, rate(s) of…, levels of…, risk of…, likelihood of…, significance of…, percentage of…,vulnerable to…, incidence, rate and consequences of…	Nouns risque(s) de…, étude de…, problème des…, réalisation d'un… Prepositions: depuis les espèces transgéniques, … entre… et…, … par le pollen
Related terms	long-distance gene flow, horizontal gene flow, interpopulation gene flow, crop-weed gene flow	transmission horizontale, plantes cultivées, plantes sauvages apparentées, espèces transgéniques, introgression, etc.

Figure 8.22 Bilingual record sheet for 'gene flow'

Key points

- A glossary is essentially a list of terms in one or more languages.
- Glossaries allow you to store all information about terms in a systematic manner.
- Traditionally, professional terminologists have worked from paper.
- Nowadays, professional terminologists can use corpus handling tools to speed up the glossary production process.
- Word lists, keyword lists and lists of word clusters allow you to judge which are the most appropriate terms to include in your glossary.
- Concordances allow you to collect information about what terms mean and how they are used.

Further reading

Cabré, M. Teresa (1999) *Terminology: Theory, Methods and Applications*, edited by J. C. Sager, translated by J. A. DeCesaris, Amsterdam/Philadelphia: John Benjamins.

Dubuc, Robert (1997) *Terminology: a Practical Approach*, adapted by Elaine Kennedy, Brossard, Quebec: Linguatech.

Sager, Juan C. (1990) *A Practical Course in Terminology Processing*, Amsterdam/Philadelphia: John Benjamins. See Chapter 5.

Exercise

Create a small specialized corpus in a domain of your choice (see Chapter 3, page 54 for a reminder of criteria to bear in mind).

Produce lists of all two-word and three-word clusters in your small corpus.

Select three term candidates from the list of two-word clusters and three term candidates from the list of three-word clusters, i.e. a total of six term candidates.

Using a concordancer, create a concordance for each of the term candidates. Now work your way through the concordances, making a note of any information which tells you something about the meaning and usage of your term candidates.

On the basis of your findings, which, if any, of your term candidates are likely to be actual terms? Justify your choice.

9 Term extraction

In Chapter 8, you learnt how you could search through a corpus to find information that was useful for producing a glossary. This chapter will introduce you to **term extraction** tools, which are also sometimes known as term recognition or term identification tools. These tools can help you to get a head start on glossary compilation by searching through corpora and extracting lists of potential terms that you might like to include in your glossary. One important thing to note is that although these tools are often referred to as *automatic* term extraction tools, this is actually a bit of a misnomer. Although the initial extraction attempt is performed by a computer, the resulting list of candidate terms contains just that – candidates. As we will see, some of the candidates on the list may not be terms at all, whereas some actual terms in the corpus may be overlooked by the program and do not appear on the list. Therefore, the list of candidates must be verified by a human, and for this reason, the process is best described as being computer-aided or semi-automatic rather than fully automatic.

Term extraction tools have been developed to operate in monolingual and bilingual environments. As the name suggests, monolingual term extraction tools attempt to analyse monolingual LSP corpora in order to identify candidate terms. Meanwhile, bilingual term extraction tools analyse aligned bilingual corpora in an attempt to identify potential terms and their translation equivalents. In addition to extracting terms, some tools also provide the option of extracting the immediate context (e.g. sentence or paragraph) surrounding the term. With this data you already have an embryonic and potentially useful term record at your disposal, which you can then augment through additional research.

Some of these tools can operate as stand-alone products but, more and more often, they are being integrated into packages that contain other types of tools, such as translation memories and terminology management systems. For example, both Logi Term TRADOS 5 and MultiTrans have now integrated term extraction tools into their suites of tools.

A term can consist of a single-word (e.g. 'microprocessor') or of multiple words (e.g. 'central processing unit'). Different tools use different techniques in order to identify potential terms. Some of these techniques, along with their strengths and weaknesses, are described below. At the end of the chapter, you will learn how you can apply some of these techniques using basic corpus analysis tools.

Monolingual term extraction

The following sections describe techniques used to identify single-word and multiword terms in a monolingual corpus.

Single-word terms

The most common way to identify single-word terms is on the basis of their frequency of occurrence, as we saw with word frequency lists in Chapter 7. Essentially, the term extraction tool will begin by going through the corpus and counting how many times each word appears. Keep in mind that computers are not intelligent, and so an unsophisticated term extraction tool might operate on the basis of exact pattern matching. This means that two words must look exactly the same in order to be counted as the same type. For example, even though you can recognize that the tokens 'microprocessor', 'Microprocessor' and 'microprocessors' are all referring to the same concept and should logically be grouped together, a computer cannot do this unless it has been pre-programmed with this knowledge.

As a user, it is generally up to you to set a minimum frequency value, which means that you can decide on the minimum number of times that a lexical item must appear in the corpus in order for it to be presented as a candidate term. If the minimum frequency value is set to five, then a word must appear in the corpus at least five times before the term extraction tool will treat it as a candidate. Once the tool has finished counting all the words in the corpus, it will present you with a list of those words that meet the minimum frequency value.

The basic idea here is that if a term is important in the field, it will appear often in the corpus. This does not, however, mean that terms that do not appear frequently are unimportant. In fact, it may well be the terms that are less commonly used that pose difficulties for LSP users because these are the words that may not be included in dictionaries or other published resources. This is an added incentive for including less common terms in your own personal glossaries.

Even terms that are actually quite common in a corpus may not appear to be so when you begin your initial investigation. For example, a term may have a synonym (e.g. 'main memory' and 'system memory'), an abbreviation (e.g. 'random access memory' and 'RAM'), or a spelling variant (e.g. 'disk' and 'disc'). As mentioned above, it may also be the case that the tool does not recognize when words belong to the same lemma. A lemma is used to group together related forms of a word, such as the singular and plural forms of a noun, or the different conjugations of a verb. For instance, if you consider the terms 'computer' and 'computers', you will note that the first is singular while the second is plural, but both refer to the same concept and should be grouped together in a single lemma. Similarly, the different forms of the verb 'to process' include 'process', 'processes', 'processed' and 'processing', but if you want to know how common this verb is in the LSP of computing, it makes more sense to count all the different verb forms together (i.e. as one group or lemma) rather than counting each form separately.

If you set the minimum frequency value too high, terms that actually do appear frequently, but in slightly different forms, may not make the cut-off mark. Consider the case of the term 'megabyte'. Imagine that each of the following forms of the term appeared in the corpus the number of times indicated in parentheses:

- megabyte (12)
- megabytes (9)
- mega byte (7)
- mega bytes (7)
- mega-byte (4)
- mega-bytes (8)
- MB (14)
- Mb (9)

Now imagine that you have set fifteen as the minimum frequency value for the number of times that a term must appear in the corpus before it is considered a candidate term. None of the individual patterns in the list would qualify because they each appear less than fifteen times; however, they all refer to the same concept and, taken as a group, this concept appears seventy times, which might be an indicator that it is a relevant concept and should be included in your glossary.

Another technique for identifying single-word terms is to compare the LSP corpus against a general reference corpus. This strategy is similar to the method of generating keywords described in Chapter 7. Keywords are words that do not necessarily appear a great many times in your corpus in terms of absolute numbers; however, they do appear with an unusually high frequency in your corpus when this corpus is compared with another corpus. For example, if your LSP corpus has 1000 tokens and the lexical item 'scanner' appears five times in this corpus, it would not appear very high up on the frequency list, which may seem to indicate that it is not a very important term. However, if that same term 'scanner' appears only once in a general reference corpus consisting of 10,000 tokens, then it would be identified as a keyword for your LSP corpus.

Multiword terms

Although it is possible for a term to consist of a single word, terms are frequently composed of multiple words. Most techniques for term extraction take advantage of this fact, using linguistic or statistical techniques, or a combination of both, to identify a series of words that might make up a term.

There are two main approaches to multiword term extraction: linguistic and statistical. For clarity, these approaches will be explained in separate sections; however, aspects of both approaches can be combined in a single term extraction tool.

Linguistic approach

Term extraction tools that use a linguistic approach typically attempt to identify word combinations that match particular part-of-speech patterns. For example, in English, many multiword terms consist of noun + noun or adjective + noun combinations. In order to implement a linguistic approach, you must first tag each word in the corpus with its appropriate part of speech. This can be done using a tagger, as described in Chapter 5. Once the corpus has been correctly tagged, the term extraction tool simply goes through the corpus and identifies all the occurrences that match the specified part-of-speech patterns. For instance, a tool that has been programmed to identify noun + noun and adjective + noun combinations as potential terms would identify all lexical combinations matching those patterns from a given corpus, as illustrated in Figure 9.1.

After this extract has been processed, the term extraction tool would present the following list of term candidates that follow the noun + noun or adjective + noun patterns:

- expansion slots
- peripheral devices
- network adapters

Unfortunately, not all texts can be processed this neatly. If the text is modified slightly, as illustrated in Figure 9.2, problems such as noise and

---

This computer has seven <u>expansion slots</u>, which have a peer-to-peer design that allows all

<u>peripheral devices</u> to get attention from the processor. In this system, <u>network adapters</u>

occupy four of the slots.

Figure 9.1 A sample that has been processed using a linguistic approach to term extraction

This <u>new computer</u> has seven <u>expansion slots</u>, which have a peer-to-peer design that allows all <u>peripheral devices</u> to get <u>equal attention</u> from the <u>busy processor</u>. In this system, <u>network adapters</u> occupy four of the slots.

Figure 9.2 A modified version that has been processed using a linguistic approach to term extraction

silence begin to appear. Noise refers to unwanted items that are erroneously retrieved (i.e. patterns that are *not* terms), while silence refers to cases where patterns that *are* terms do not get retrieved.

First, not all of the combinations that follow the specified patterns will qualify as terms. Of the noun + noun and adjective + noun candidates that were identified in Figure 9.2, some qualify as terms ('expansion slots', 'peripheral devices', 'network adapters'), whereas others do not ('new computer', 'equal attention', 'busy processor'). The latter set constitutes noise and would need to be eliminated from the list of candidates by a human.

Another potential problem is that some legitimate terms may be formed according to patterns that have not been pre-programmed into the tool. This can result in silence – a situation where relevant information is not retrieved. For example, the term 'peer-to-peer design' has been formed using the pattern noun + preposition + noun + noun; however, this pattern is not all that common, and so it may not be recognized by many term extraction tools.

Another problem that may arise concerns the phenomenon known as ellipsis. Ellipsis occurs when a word is implied but not explicitly stated. For example, in the sentence 'This process applies to both multimedia and text files', the word 'files' is only used once, but as a human reader, you understand that there are in fact two kinds of files being referred to: 'multimedia [files]' and 'text files'. You would therefore like to include both terms in your glossary; however, because of the ellipsis in the text, the term extraction tool would not identify 'multimedia [files]' as a candidate.

An additional drawback associated with the linguistic approach is that it is heavily language dependent. Term formation patterns differ from language to language. For instance term formation patterns that are typical in English (e.g. adjective + noun, noun + noun) are not the same as term formation patterns that are common in French (e.g. noun + adjective, noun + preposition + noun). This means that term extraction tools that use a linguistic approach are generally designed to work in a single language (or closely related languages) and cannot easily be extended to work with other languages. Similarly, certain patterns may be typical for a given subject field but not at all for other subject fields.

Operating systems based on I2O technology are now more cost-effective and less difficult to implement. Such operating systems have evolved to capitalize on the features offered by I2O technology. Intelligent scheduling of processes to use local CPUs and an awareness of the relatively slow times associated with remote memory access are just two of the factors that have been addressed.

Figure 9.3 A sample that has been processed by a statistical term extraction tool using a minimum frequency value of two

Statistical approach

Using a statistical approach, a term extraction tool basically looks for repeated series of lexical items. The minimum frequency value, which refers to the number of times that a series of items must be repeated, can often be specified by the user. For example, as illustrated in Figure 9.3, if the minimum frequency value is set to two, then a given series of lexical items must appear at least twice in the text in order to be recognized as a candidate term by the term extraction tool.

Based on a minimum frequency value of two, the text in Figure 9.3 yielded two potential terms: 'operating systems' and 'I2O technology'. Unfortunately, this simple strategy often leads to problems because language is full of repetition, but not all repeated series of lexical items qualify as terms. For instance, consider the slightly modified version of the text shown in Figure 9.4.

Working solely on the basis of identifying repeated series of lexical items, the term extraction software has identified 'the features offered' as an additional candidate. Unfortunately, this candidate constitutes noise rather than a legitimate term, and as such it would need to be eliminated from the list of potential terms by a human. Stop lists, as described in Chapter 7, can be used to reduce the number of unlikely terms that may otherwise be identified as candidates. For instance, a stop list could be implemented to instruct the term extraction tool to ignore those series that begin or end with function words, such as articles, conjunctions or prepositions, since these rarely constitute terms. Of course, there are always exceptions, such as 'off line processing', which is a term that begins with a preposition!

Another drawback to the statistical approach is that not all of the terms that appear in a given text will be repeated, which may lead to silence. For instance, in Figure 9.4, the terms 'intelligent scheduling' and 'remote memory access' were not identified as candidates because they only

Operating systems based on I2O technology are now more cost-effective and less difficult to implement. Such operating systems have evolved to capitalize on the features offered by I2O technology. Intelligent scheduling of processes to use local CPUs and an awareness of the relatively slow times associated with remote memory access are just two of the features offered.

Figure 9.4 A slightly modified version that has been processed by a statistical term extraction tool using a minimum frequency value of two

appeared once in the text and the minimum frequency value was set to two.

A similar problem may occur if abbreviations are used. For example, the term 'operating system' is often shortened to simply 'OS'. In Figure 9.4, if the second occurrence of 'operating system' had been replaced by 'OS', then this term would not have been identified as a candidate because, from the point of view of the tool, the pattern 'operating system' occurred only once and this is below the minimum frequency value. It is important to remember that these tools are not intelligent. Although you, as a human reader, can quite easily make the connection between 'operating system' and 'OS', these tools work strictly on the basis of pattern matching.

Nevertheless, a statistical approach to term extraction does have one clear strength: because it works by identifying repeated patterns, it is not language dependent. This means that a term extraction tool employing this approach can, in principle, be used to process texts in multiple languages.

Bilingual term extraction

Bilingual term extraction is carried out on aligned corpora. Typically, such corpora have been pre-aligned at sentence level, and it is the job of the bilingual term extraction tool to try to identify corresponding equivalents within the aligned sentence pairs. This is most often done using statistics. For example, when a term is identified in the source text (e.g. using one of the statistical techniques described above for single-term or multiword term extraction), the tool consults all the source text segments in which that term occurs, and it then analyses each of the corresponding target text segments. As part of this analysis, the tool tries to identify which element(s) in the target text segment occur with a similar frequency to that of the source text term. The tool may also rely on other clues, such as formatting. For example, if the term is in bold or italics in the source text, then it is probable that the corresponding equivalent will also appear in bold or italics in the target text.

As with monolingual term extraction tools, bilingual term extraction tools aim to present a list of candidates. It is up to you to make the final decision about which, if any, equivalent(s) should be included in your glossary. For example, the tool may propose the following French candidate terms as potential equivalents for the English term 'browser': '*navigateur*', '*navigation*', and '*fureteur*'. These suggestions may inspire you to do some further research into the terms, and you may decide to include both '*navigateur*' (standard French term) and '*fureteur*' (Canadian French term) on your term record.

One phenomenon to be aware of when using a bilingual term extraction tool is homonymy, which refers to a case where a word has more than one meaning. For example, the system may propose the following equivalents for the English term 'key': '*touche*', '*clé*' and '*clef*'. Further inspection of the contexts indicates that these are three different concepts: (1) '*touche*' = a key on a keyboard, (2) '*clé*' = an important item, such as a 'key word', and (3) '*clef*' = a device used to lock a door (e.g. an icon that appears on some buttons for 'locking' documents, etc.). In such cases, you may wish to retain all the equivalents for inclusion in your glossary, but remember to create a separate term record for each different concept.

Using term extraction techniques with basic corpus analysis tools

Even if you do not have access to a term extraction tool, you can still use some of the techniques used by these tools in order to try to automate your own research to some degree when using basic corpus analysis tools, such as word listers and concordancers.

For example, as explained in Chapter 7, you can produce word lists and word clusters to help you identify those lexical items that appear most frequently in your corpus. Such data can be refined by using stop lists; these are lists of items that you would like the computer to ignore. This means, for instance, that you could tell the computer not to include function words, such as prepositions, conjunctions or articles, in the frequency lists since these items rarely form terms. Some corpus analysis tools also allow you to generate a list of keywords by comparing the contents of an LSP corpus against those of a general reference corpus to see which words appear to be important in the LSP as compared to LGP. To refresh your memory on how word lists, word clusters and key words can be generated and interpreted, turn back to Chapter 7 and re-read the relevant sections.

In addition, if you have access to a tagged corpus (see Chapter 5), you can conduct corpus searches using term formation patterns. For instance,

```
across_IN across  a_DT a  network_NN network  server._NN server.  Until_IN

based_VBN client-based  antivirus_NN antivirus  protection_NN protection

                      Virus_NN virus  protection_NN protection  rece

 nt.  Server_NN server  antivirus_NN antivirus  protection_NN protection

ontagious_JJ contagious  computer_NN computer  virus_NN virus,  called_VBN

ows_NP window  NT._NP nt.  Server_NN server  antivirus_NN antivirus  prote
```

Figure 9.5 Concordance retrieved using the search pattern '*NN *NN'

as mentioned above, many multiword terms in English are composed of noun + noun or adjective + noun, but these patterns may vary depending on the subject field and language in question. To identify patterns that are relevant for your work, you may need to begin by doing some manual analysis. Find a few texts that are typical of the LSP that you wish to investigate. Read through these texts and underline any multiword terms that you find. Now look at these terms and try to determine the part of speech that should be attached to each element of the term. For example, if your text contains the terms 'virus checker' and 'serial port', you can identify the following term formation patterns: 'virus' (noun) + 'checker' (noun) and 'serial' (adjective) + 'port' (noun). Now instead of using the actual lexical items as search patterns, you can search a tagged corpus using just the part of speech tags (i.e. noun + noun and adjective + noun). Keep in mind that to do this, you must use the appropriate tags that correspond to the tagset used to tag your corpus. For example, in Figure 9.5 the tag _NN is used to represent singular nouns and the tag _JJ to represent adjectives. Therefore, your search patterns would be '*NN *NN' and '*JJ *NN'. Figure 9.5 shows a concordance that was generated using the search pattern '*NN *NN'. As you can see, some of the retrieved patterns are indeed terms, such as 'network server' and 'computer virus', while others, such as 'server antivirus' are not.

Keep in mind that terms do not always appear in their canonical form (i.e. singular for nouns, infinitive for verbs, etc.). Therefore, it might be useful for you to expand on the basic patterns you have identified to search for variations such as plural nouns. For example, if plural nouns are marked with the tag NNS, your new search patterns would be '*NN *NNS' and '*JJ *NNS'. Now you will also find any instances of terms appearing in the plural, such as 'virus checkers' and 'serial ports'.

Key points

• Term extraction tools can be used to help you get a head start in building up your glossaries.

- Although they are sometimes referred to as automatic term extraction tools, these tools only suggest possible terms, and the list of proposed candidates must be verified by a human.
- Term extraction tools can be either monolingual (extracting terms from a monolingual corpus) or bilingual (extracting terms and their equivalents from an aligned corpus).
- Different techniques for extracting terms include counting the frequency of individual lexical items or series of lexical items, and identifying lexical items that match particular part-of-speech patterns (e.g. noun + noun).
- Even if you do not have access to a term extraction tool, you can implement some of the same basic techniques used by these tools. For example, you can generate word frequency lists and keyword lists to help you identify single-word terms, and you can generate word clusters or use term formation patterns as search patterns in order to identify multiword terms.

Further reading

Ahmad, Khurshid and Margaret Rogers (2001) 'Corpus linguistics and terminology extraction', in Sue Ellen Wright and Gerhard Budin (eds) *Handbook of Terminology Management* (Vol. 2), Amsterdam/Philadelphia: John Benjamins, 725–60.

Cabré, M. Teresa, Rosa Estopà Bagot and Jordi Vivaldi Palatresi (2001) 'Automatic term detection: a review of current systems', in Didier Bourigault, Christian Jacquemin and Marie-Claude L'Homme (eds) *Recent Advances in Computational Terminology*, Amsterdam/Philadelphia: John Benjamins, 53–87.

Gaussier, Eric (2001) 'General considerations on bilingual terminology extraction', in Didier Bourigault, Christian Jacquemin and Marie-Claude L'Homme (eds) *Recent Advances in Computational Terminology*, Amsterdam/Philadelphia: John Benjamins, 167–83.

Kageura, Kyo and Bin Umino (1996) 'Methods of automatic term recognition: a review', *Terminology* 3(2): 259–90.

Pearson, Jennifer (1998) *Terms in Context*, Amsterdam/Philadelphia: John Benjamins.

Some products containing term extraction tools

Ferret: http://www.computing.surrey.ac.uk/SystemQ/
Logi Term: http://www.terminotix.com
MultiTrans: http://www.multicorpora.ca
Nomino: http://www.ling.uqam.ca/nomino/
Trados: http://www.trados.com
Xerox TermFinder: http://www.mkms.xerox.com/

Exercises

Exercise 1

In the following text, which lexical items would you identify as:

- single-word terms
- multiword terms

Express yourself sideways

Emoticons (a word created by combining 'emotion' and 'icons') are ASCII glyphs originally designed to show an emotional state in plain text messages. In other words, they are used to compensate for the inability to convey voice inflections, facial expressions and bodily gestures in written communication such as electronic mail messages, Internet Relay Chats, or other forms of computer communications. The use of an emoticon in an e-mail message or IRC can help a reader to avoid misinterpreting the writer's intentions. Over time emoticons have turned into an art form as well.

Emoticons generally represent facial expressions and are produced using a sequence of ordinary characters you can find on your computer keyboard. Most of the common ones involve some form of smile or frown, which explains why emoticons are also referred to as 'smilies' or 'smileys'. When viewed sideways, most emoticons will look like a face (eyes, nose and mouth). While there are no standard definitions for the following emoticons, we have supplied their most usual meanings.

> :-) basic smiley face, used for humour
> :-(basic frowney face, used for sadness or anger
> ;-) winky face, used for sarcasm
> :-O used to indicate surprise

Originally inserted into Email messages to denote 'said with a cynical smile', smileys now run rampant throughout the email culture.

Are emoticons a creative expression of the high-tech culture? Or are they an aberration that reduces written communication to a shorthand of silly symbols? Who really cares? ;-)

Exercise 2

Looking at the same text again, which items do you think would be identified by term extraction tools (using either linguistic or statistical approaches)? There will probably be some discrepancies in your lists. How do you account for these differences?

Exercise 3

Look back to the list of multiword terms that you identified in the text. What term formation patterns do they follow? Try using these term formation patterns to search for candidate terms in other corpora. How successful was your search?

10 Using LSP corpora as a writing guide

This chapter explores the potential of LSP corpora as a resource for technical writing. Most of you, whether as a student, teacher or professional, will be required at some stage in your lives to write in different styles for different occasions. You may need to learn how to write business letters, how to present an annual report, how to write up a scientific experiment, how to write a product review. In other words, you may need to learn how to produce different text types. We believe that small **specialized corpora** containing texts of a particular style can be a useful resource when you are learning to write in a particular style or produce a particular text type. In this chapter, we will take a couple of small corpora, each representative of different writing styles, and we will show you how to exploit them. The first corpus we will examine contains articles from a scientific journal, while the second contains reviews of computer hardware. You may be interested in very different types of texts from those under discussion in this chapter, but you should be able to apply the same type of methodology to the text type that interests you.

Creating a small corpus

If you want to work on a particular text type, you will first have to create a small corpus. As we are going to discuss writing science and writing product reviews in this chapter, we need to create a small corpus for each of these text types. For the corpus of science writing, we selected twelve full text science articles from a journal available via ScienceDirect (http://www.sciencedirect.com), an electronic information source for scientific, technical and medical information on the Internet. For the product reviews, we selected forty-six short product reviews of printers from the CD-ROM *Computer Select*. As we wished to focus on the introduction and discussion sections in science articles, we had to break our science corpus up further. In order to focus on the language of introductions, we needed to copy the introduction from each science article and paste it into a new document, thereby giving us a mini-corpus of introductions. We repeated the procedure for the discussion section and copied all twelve discussions into a separate file. This resulted in a mini-corpus of all of the discussion sections.

Writing science

If you are a science student, you may on occasion be required to write up laboratory experiments. If you are a research student or are planning to become a research scientist you will need to know how to write a scientific article. Whether you are required to write up a laboratory experiment or to write a scientific article, the structure of your presentation will be broadly similar in both cases. The report or article will include the following sections: introduction, materials and methods, measurements, results, discussion, conclusions, with discussion and conclusions being conflated on occasion. If you were to analyse and compare the typical language content of the different sections in either the laboratory report or the scientific article, you would find a number of differences between the different sections in the same document and a number of similarities between the same sections in different documents. You would find that each section has its own idiom, its own set of syntactic patterns which mark it out as being different from other sections. In other words, the introduction, for example, will have different patterns from the conclusion in the same article, and the patterns of introductions and conclusions are likely to be broadly similar across scientific articles or laboratory reports. We propose to look in some detail at the patterns of two different sections in a scientific article, namely the introduction and the discussion sections, in order to demonstrate that you can learn how to write science by basing your initial attempts on the patterns you have identified.

Introducing a topic

In this section, we propose to use a corpus-based approach to show you how to introduce a topic in a scientific article or laboratory report. Let us look first of all at what you need to include in an introduction. You need to state the problem, describe it and provide a synopsis of relevant research so that readers can understand the experiment. Once you have stated the problem, you have to state why it is important to research this particular topic. You then need to propose a solution. The solution will be your experiment. You should describe your experiment, outline your hypothesis, your research questions and your general methodology. As it is not possible for us to cover all of these areas here, we propose to look at patterns for stating the purpose of an experiment and patterns for reviewing relevant literature.

When you provide a statement of objectives or a hypothesis, you need to state what you think is going to happen during your investigation. If you are using a corpus-based approach to identify the appropriate way

```
possible. The goal of the present study was to quantitatively validate th
g, 1999b). The aim of the present study was to identify intermuscular myo
1995). The purpose of the present study was to gain an understanding of h
The underlying hypothesis of this study was that under normal hip anatomy
f the hip. The objectives of this study were: (1) to determine the normal
m EDL muscle. The purpose of this study is to investigate length effects
aily profile. The purpose of this study was to develop and apply a system
 published soon. The goal of this study was to create an unique data base
inical tests. The purpose of this study was to determine which muscle for
```

Figure 10.1 Edited concordance of search pattern 'study'

of doing this, the first thing you will need to do is to select a number of words which you can use as search patterns to access the statements of objectives in your mini-corpus. We have chosen two search words, namely 'study' and 'hypothesis' because we believe that they should allow us to access expressions of aims and objectives. Perhaps you can think of others that could be used. In Figure 10.1, you will find an edited concordance for the search pattern 'study'.

The concordance in Figure 10.1 was sorted first one word to the left and then two words to the left. When you look at the concordance, what patterns can you spot straight away? Given that you know that the concordance has been sorted to the left, you should first look to the left of 'study' to see if there are any words which occur in more than one concordance line. What you will find is that the two recurring words are 'present' and 'this'. If you then look further to the left, you will see that 'the' and 'of' co-occur with 'present' and 'this' respectively. If you look further to the left again, you will see that the range of words which can precede 'of the present study' and 'of this study' is more varied and includes 'goal', 'aim', 'purpose' and 'objectives'. It is interesting to note, in passing, that 'objectives' is in plural form while the other three are in singular. This may or may not be significant and you will only be able to check this by looking at a larger corpus of introductions. Finally, if we look one word further to the left again, we find the word 'the' in all cases. We can therefore suggest the following pattern for the words which precede 'study': 'the (aim, goal, purpose, objectives) of (this, the present) study . . .'. If we now look to the right of the search pattern 'study' we find 'was to' or 'were to' in all but one case (Figure 10.2). This suggests that it is preferable to use the past tense when outlining the objectives of a study, probably not something you would have done intuitively. After 'was to' and 'were to', we find verbs that introduce the purpose of the study, i.e. 'gain an understanding of', 'quantitatively validate', 'identify', 'determine', 'develop

```
1995). The purpose of the present study was to gain an understanding of ho
possible. The goal of the present study was to quantitatively validate the
g, 1999b). The aim of the present study was to identify intermuscular myof
inical tests. The purpose of this study was to determine which muscle forc
aily profile. The purpose of this study was to develop and apply a system
 published soon. The goal of this study was to create a unique data base
f the hip. The objectives of this study were: (1) to determine the normal
```

Figure 10.2 Edited concordance of search pattern 'study' sorted to the right

```
is study was designed to test the hypothesis that the yield strains of hum
one depend on anatomic site. This hypothesis was tested on samples of bone
tive procedure.   The underlying hypothesis of this study was that under
```

Figure 10.3 Concordance of search pattern 'hypothesis'

and apply', 'create', 'determine'. As you can see, the syntactic pattern 'the * of * study was to *' is quite productive, and it would be worth your while to make a note of the possible fillers for the various slots in the pattern so that you can use them when writing an introduction yourself.

If we now look at the concordance for 'hypothesis' in Figure 10.3 we find a small number of examples of the use of 'hypothesis' rather than actual patterns. This is in part due to the small size of the corpus. As we mentioned earlier, we only selected twelve articles. It would appear that a larger corpus might be more useful when you are only interested in very specific subsections of that corpus, as is the case here where we are only looking at introductions.

Reviewing previous work

In your introduction, you will need to review relevant research to provide a rationale for the experiment or study you are proposing to carry out. When reviewing relevant literature, you will tell readers what has already been achieved by others and what remains to be achieved. In other words, the statement of objectives or hypothesis for your experiment will be supported by evidence from previous experiments or articles. The most common method of reviewing relevant research is by referring to existing publications. In order to establish how writers refer to earlier work, we used the search pattern '(*)'. We used this search pattern because we guessed that the authors would include a reference to the year in which

```
s more accurate results. Bell et al.   (1990), for example, found that the p
tional method, while Leardini et al.    (1999) found the opposite to be true,
 trabecular bone. Brown and Ferguson    (1980) found a strong linear correlat
n of the cells. Bassett and Herrmann    (1961) hypothesized that mechanical s
ristofolini (1997) and Colgan et al.    (1994) listed a large number of numer
operative procedures. Morlock et al.    (2001) measured the activity levels o
d by Taylor and Taylor. Hodge et al.    (1986) measured the joint pressure in
uct; the subjects of Leardini et al.    (1999) performed the same motions and
ter and Hayes (1977) and Rice et al.    (1988) reported single ultimate stres
; Wyse et al., 1984). Marx and Allen    (1986) reported that inclusion of the
ermittent hydrostatic pressure. Hall    (1968) showed that intermittent compr
```

Figure 10.4 References to earlier work

a particular piece of work was published and would probably provide the year in brackets or parentheses. By using the search pattern '(*)', we were in fact hoping to access all references to dates.

As you can see from Figure 10.4, our guess was a good one as we find that whenever a date is provided within brackets, this signals that there is some reference to previous work. The concordance is sorted one word to the right and you can see that the verbs used in conjunction with the names of researchers are 'found', 'hypothesized', 'listed', 'measured', 'performed', 'reported', 'showed'.

When you review relevant work, you need not only refer to work already completed but you also need to explain why more needs to be done. It is perhaps more difficult to identify how this is achieved when you are using a corpus-based approach. We decided to use the search pattern 'not' to see if this would help us in our search for ways to comment on earlier work. The results are shown in Figure 10.5.

As you can see, 'not' is actually quite a useful search pattern in this instance. We find that results from previous research 'are not as predictable', that earlier researchers 'did not investigate', that previous 'techniques' or 'methods' do 'not allow' for quantification, that 'it is not clear', etc. These instances provide you with the basic wherewithal for formulating your own opinions on previous research related to your work.

Passive or active voice in the introduction?

As science students, you have probably been told more than once to avoid marking your own presence in your assignments. This usually translates into advice to avoid using the first person ('I' or 'we'). While it is generally

```
6; Mitchell, 1974) their results are not as predictable as those managed w

emoral prosthesis. However, they did not investigate the loading condition

adiographically. This technique does not allow quantification of callus ma

phy (EMG). However, this method does not allow quantitative validation of

1991; Silva et al., 1998) and it is not clear if site-specific relations
```

Figure 10.5 Edited concordance for search pattern 'not'

believed that scientists avoid using the first person, the reality is in fact quite different, and research scientists do actually use the first person surprisingly frequently. It is, however, possible that the use of the first person may be confined to certain sections of an article and may not be present throughout. In this very small mini-corpus of introductions, we found the following occurrences of 'we' (Figure 10.6). There were no occurrences of 'I' but this is hardly surprising as most of the articles are by multiple authors. We also found ample evidence of use of the passive voice (using searches such as 'is/are *ed'), and this is what we expected.

If you look at the concordance in Figure 10.6, you can find some really useful patterns, not just in what follows the search pattern 'we' but also in what precedes it. Lines 7 and 8, for example, show you how to express statement of purpose, followed by action. With regard to what follows the search pattern 'we', we find 'studied', 'constructed', 'developed', 'focused', 'use', 'hypothesized', 'intend to use', 'investigated', 'subjected', 'review data from'. Again, you can use these patterns to help you formulate your own introduction.

The discussion section

Once you have carried out your experiment and collated your results, you then move on to presenting and discussing your findings. You need to consider for each finding what conclusions you can draw, whether the goal of your study was reached, how the results relate to your initial expectations. If your findings are negative, you need to identify possible explanations. You also need to try and put your results into a broader context, spelling out possible future research, practical applications, etc. We do not plan to cover all of these areas in this section. Rather, we are going to focus on how findings, results and conclusions can be expressed. Earlier in this chapter, we looked at how one can express the aim or purpose of a study; in this section, we are going to look at the outcome of the study. You will remember that in the introduction, the aim or purpose of a study was, with only one exception, expressed in the past tense. You can see from Figure 10.7 that the outcome of a study can be expressed in past, perfect or present tense. We can see that a study 'has

```
1.  ppler-derived pressure differences. We also studied (both in patients
ove  chondrocyte  culture conditions.  We constructed an oxygen/IHP chamb
2.  hem contains detailed gait data.   We developed two types of instrume
3.  . Regarding biosynthetic activities we focused on collagen synthesis a
4.  aured arm⁻leg pressure differences. We further use a hydraulic pulsati
5.  rlier described theoretical models, we hypothesized that persistent in
6.   performed using 2D AP radiographs. We intend to use these results as
7.  tructions. To address this purpose, we investigated which muscle group
8.  e.    In order to investigate this, we subjected the ingrown mesenchym
9.  ost-operative coarctation patients. We therefore first review data fro
10. gical for articular chondrocytes.   We therefore hypothesized that a c
```

Figure 10.6 Concordance of search pattern 'we'

```
complex and EDL muscle  The present study has demonstrated intermuscular
uscles or muscle fibers. The present study indicates that neighboring musc
ytical methodology", but the present study showed that variation in the ty
TA+EHL complex.         The present study shows also that proximal EDL fo
summary, the results of the present study suggest that the accuracy of th
ing of smaller errors in the present study supports the idea that the link
al., 1991).  5. Discussion    This study demonstrates, that an implant e
```

Figure 10.7 Edited concordance for search pattern 'study'

demonstrated', 'indicates', 'showed', 'shows', 'supports the idea that', 'demonstrates' and that the results of the study 'suggest'.

In Figure 10.8, we find that the findings of a study can 'emphasize', 'establish' and 'help to explain'. If we expand the concordance lines one to four in Figure 10.8, we find even more interesting patterns, as illustrated in Figure 10.9. We discover, for example, that a finding 'leads us to conclude', 'supports the idea that', 'indicates that', 'is consistent with'.

We now propose to look at 'results'. In many respects, 'results' and 'findings' are synonymous and we could have treated them together. We thought it more useful, however, to deal with them separately as the concordances are easier to read. In Figure 10.10 you will see that 'results' can 'suggest', 'confirm', 'imply', 'indicate', 'provide strong arguments', 'show', and 'suggest' and 'indicate' are the most frequently co-occurring verbs.

We mentioned earlier that the use of the first person seemed to be quite common in the introductions we had looked at. We thought it would be

```
becula at the lower end.          The finding of less bone in the loaded sp
ted mean errors of 37.9±19.0 mm. The finding of smaller errors in the pres
rease if fewer points were used. The finding that HJC errors were consiste
ior can depend on anatomic site. Our finding that the relationship between
rs to the bony skeleton. The present findings emphasize that neighboring m
racteristics of trabecular bone. Our findings establish that the yield str
rease with patient activities. These findings may thus help to explain rep
```

Figure 10.8 Edited concordance for search pattern 'finding*'

```
The finding of less bone in the loaded specimens…leads us to conclude that
The finding of smaller errors in the present study supports the idea that
The finding that HJC errors were consistent…indicates that errors associat
Our finding that…depends on…is consistent with the results of previous stu
```

Figure 10.9 Concordance for search pattern 'finding' expanded to the right

```
tion (Perren and Baupre, 1984).  Our results also suggest that loading of
ar bone depend on anatomic site. The results confirmed this hypothesis and
ng, fibrous tissue was found.    Our results imply that cartilage induced
Van Soest et al., 1995). Our present results indicate that in vivo muscle
s of accuracy. Taken together, these results indicate that yield criteria
of HJC location.    In summary, the results of the present study suggest
shold levels ( An et al., 1989). The results of this study indicate that l
., 2000).    Most importantly, these results provide strong arguments for
torsional loading ( Fig. 10). These results show that interlocking does n
in the diaphysis at 10% gait. These results suggest that for pre-clinical
```

Figure 10.10 Edited concordance for search pattern 'results'

interesting to see whether or not this was also the case in the discussion section. We found that it was indeed, as evidenced by the concordance in Figure 10.11. You can see that, more often than not, 'we' co-occurs with 'found' when it is used in the discussion section.

At the end of your discussion section, you will need to present your conclusions. You can do this in a number of ways, as you can see from Figure 10.12. You can use impersonal forms such as 'in conclusion', 'it is reasonable to conclude that', 'it is concluded that', 'lead to the conclusion that', 'the conclusions drawn in this study', or you can be more involved and use phrases such as 'leads us to conclude that', 'we conclude that'. There does not appear to be any preference for one form over the other.

In this section, we have tried to give you a taste of how you can use a corpus-based approach to help you learn how to write science. We have not been able to cover all of the different types of information which you might be able to glean from a mini-corpus but we hope that we have given you some ideas for your own work.

Writing a product review

We now propose to look at how to write a product review. We have chosen this particular text type because it is in sufficient contrast to the preceding text type and should therefore appeal to a very different audience. A product review is the type of document that you may be asked to write if you are a student of communications or marketing. As the name suggests, a product review involves using prose to describe and evaluate something; that something may be a concrete product (e.g. a printer, a washing machine, a car) or it may be an event (e.g. a music festival, a sports event, a garden festival, a film or play). Here, we have chosen to look at how to write a product review for a printer. We believe, however, that the same techniques can be used to review any product of your choice. All you need is sufficient material to create a mini-corpus for the product of your choice. In this case, we used forty-six short product reviews of printers from the CD-ROM *Computer Select*.

Assessing performance

When writing a product review, an important aspect of the review will be how you rate the product's performance. With a printer, performance is usually measured in terms of the quality of its output. We chose therefore to produce a concordance for 'quality' and 'output' and to see what type of language was used to describe quality and output. As you will see from the edited concordances in Figures 10.13 and 10.14, we have only included concordance lines followed immediately to the right by *is, was, were*. In other words, we excluded concordance lines where 'quality' and 'output' co-occurred with different verbs, for the simple reason that there were too many of them.

We can see that some of the evaluative language used is quite informal when compared with the language used in the science articles in the previous section. For example, 'quality' is described as being 'impressive' (line 1), 'outclassed by the competition' (line 2), 'a mixed bag' (line 3), 'unimpressive' (line 14), 'on a par with that from other [printers]' (line 11).

of the yield property measurements. **We** are aware of no other single study

nstantaneous pressure difference.   **We** conclude that in the post-operatio

is no strict relation between both. **We** could not relate the occurrence of

e was not quantified in this study, **we** could not directly determine its i

and is important for pH adjustment. **We** found a decrease in media pH of ab

tivity (see Table 3). Interestingly, **we** found a decrease in synthesis of c

ved in obtaining these measurements. **We** found no influence of tissue densi

on-compliant) isthmus zone. However, **we** found no clinical important pressu

(Grimshaw and Mason, 2000). However, **we** found significant stimulations in

or for chondrocyte dedifferentiation **we** found that reduced PO2 and additio

layer cultures. In contrast to this, **we** found that IHP 2/30 min increases

gage length (Keaveny et al., 1997). **We** propose this as the most plausible

1987; van der Rest and Mayne, 1988). **We** show for the first time that reduc

Figure 10.11 Edited concordance for the search pattern 'we'

this may not be the case. Hence, the **conclusions** as drawn in this study ar

alking parameters, even so no direct **conclusion** can be drawn towards cause

sions closest to average. Hence, the **conclusions** drawn in this study may n

rces remained fairly constant.   In **conclusion**, length and force changes

tresses that induce cartilage.   In **conclusion**, mechanically induced cart

educed under these conditions.   In **conclusion**, our data demonstrate that

n some of the specimens, leads us to **conclude** that the loading parameters,

riod. Therefore, it is reasonable to **conclude** that the peak contact pressu

bone loading. This would lead to the **conclusion** that a loading configurati

antaneous pressure difference.   We **conclude** that in the post-operation c

e is innervated independently, it is **concluded** that the concept of morphol

hin this time frame. Thus, it can be **concluded** that a combination of reduc

ive motions of muscle bellies. It is **concluded** that the functional relevan

Figure 10.12 Drawing a conclusion

Figure 10.14 (*facing*) Edited concordance of search pattern 'output'

1. onds to print.The 740's print **quality** is impressive. Text and mixed te
2.   please some users, its print **quality** is outclassed by the competition
3. ately, the OkiPage 20's print **quality** is a mixed bag. It does particul
4. duce knockout documents. Text **quality** is nearly equal, though the Optr
5. c for color correction.Output **quality** was the best on our tests. The H
6. rint and crisp type. Graphics **quality** was good; gradient fills were sm
7. 100 sheets.In our labs, image **quality** was good. The company's patented
8. with your business. Its image **quality** was excellent for both text and
9. ing respectable speeds. Image **quality** was reasonable on our tests; tex
10. and USB connectivity. Output **quality** was the same as the HL-1040. Thr
11. ge for an 8-ppm laser. Output **quality** was on a par with that from othe
12. ints. The older model's print **quality** was generally adequate, but the
13.   Print Shop.The OkiJet's text **quality** was acceptable but not up to tha
14. data's performance and output **quality** were unimpressive. This printer

Figure 10.13 Edited concordance of search pattern 'quality'

DeskJet 600 ink jet series, but the **output** is not as crisp as that of a
. And as our jury found, much of the **output** is stunning.This roundup gave
oFantasy, and PhotoStudio.The XJ6C's **output** is unremarkable. Text was goo
best on our tests. The HP 4500 DN's **output** was slightly better in one te
nd gray-scale images on the fly.Text **output** was slightly better and appro
 images were acceptable; in general, **output** was virtually identical to th
er-feed mechanism. Text and graphics **output** was very similar to that of t
ess throughout. This printer's photo **output** was rated fair on our jury te
eavy, perhaps, but still good. Photo **output** was not quite as good as that
lights and shadows; the unit's photo **output** was judged fair by our jury.
howing only as graininess.Even photo **output** was remarkably consistent --
the same network management software.**Output** was similar in quality to out
 to offer such connectivity.Our test **output** was very good. The Stylus Col
ike the HP printer, its default text **output** was excellent, with crisp, cl
usy/alarm.In our labs, the P8's text **output** was excellent, with solid bla
and HP units; in best mode, its text **output** was roughly equal to that of
 Lite.On our tests, plain-paper text **output** was good for an entry-level u
ic output on our tests, but its text **output** was substandard. Close examin
ark hallmark -- to be excellent. The **output** was indistinguishable from la
ttings. At high quality, the Xerox's **output** was more consistent than the

```
1. text was dense and well-formed but would not be mistaken for laser print. On the
2. consistent than the Okidata's, but still not first-rate. The photographic output
3. es dithering and added luster, but still not good enough to rate better than fair
4.  was acceptable for a $100 printer, but not great. Text on plain paper (using th
5. output showed only minor banding but did not have the depth and sizzle of output
6. fonts. Speed was better than the 6e, but not quite up to the 8-ppm competition. A
7. impressive. Graphics were acceptable but not stellar; our gray-scale photo image
8. OkiJet's text quality was acceptable but not up to that of others in its class. I
```

Figure 10.15 Edited concordance of search pattern 'not'

When we look at the edited concordance for the search pattern 'output', we find, on the positive side, that 'output' can be 'good', 'very good', 'excellent' and even 'stunning'. On the negative side, we find that 'output' can be 'not as crisp' as that of others, 'substandard', 'unremarkable' or simply 'fair'. We also find that 'output' can be 'slightly better', 'more consistent' or 'roughly equal' when compared with output from other printers.

Comparison with other products is an important element of any product review. We have seen some examples in Figure 10.14. Another way of expressing comparison is to say something about the product under review and then to claim that it is 'not' as good as another one. In other words, you may wish to state that the product under review is better or worse than other models. Figure 10.15 gives you some indication of how you can do this. We used the search pattern 'not', and specified that 'but' had to appear as a context word within three words to the left of the search pattern. In line 1, you can see that the text output from a particular printer is good but 'would not be mistaken for laser print'. In line 2, the output is 'more consistent' than another printer 'but still not first rate'. Can you spot what the patterns are in the remaining lines? Are there any lines where the language appears to you to be unusually informal? Can you explain why?

Assessing performance using tagged output

We decided to tag our mini-corpus with part-of-speech tags (see Chapter 5 for a discussion of POS tags) in order to be able to carry out investigations which did not rely exclusively on using word or parts of words as our search patterns. We did this because we wanted to examine classes of words rather than individual words. We thought it would be useful, for example, to look at which adjectives were used to describe or evaluate printers, to see which, if any, adverbs were used, which verbs

big printer	large printer	personal printer	serious printer
cheap printer	lightweight printer	portable printer	solid, plucky, little printer
colour inkjet printer	monochrome printer	quick printer	sporty little printer
highly usable printer	new useful printer	robust printer	

Figure 10.16 Adjectives co-occurring with 'printer'

were used, etc. It is much easier to carry out this type of investigation using a tagged corpus.

We started by looking at all of the adjectives which co-occurred with 'printer'. We retrieved these by looking for 'printer' as our search pattern and specified 'JJ' (the tag for adjective) as the context word immediately to the left of 'printer'. The list of adjectives retrieved in this manner is provided in Figure 10.16.

As you can see from the adjectives in Figure 10.16, some of the adjectives are simply descriptive and others are evaluative. A descriptive adjective is one which simply states what the product is (e.g. 'colour inkjet printer'). An evaluative adjective gives you some indication of the reviewer's opinion of the printer (e.g. 'robust printer' suggests that the reviewer believes that it will not break down easily). Which of the adjectives would you classify as descriptive and which would you classify as evaluative? Are there any adjectives you yourself would be reluctant to use? Can you explain why?

When we produced a word frequency list for the tagged corpus, we found that the tag for verbs in the third person singular (VBZ) was one of the highest ranked tags on the frequency list. We decided therefore to carry out a search using this part-of-speech tag and found that the following verbs occurred most frequently: 'delivers', 'offers', 'comes in/with', 'includes', 'provides', 'uses', 'supports'. Figures 10.17 and 10.18 contain edited concordances for the search patterns 'delivers' and 'offers' respectively.

If you look closely at Figure 10.17 you will see that 'delivers' is almost invariably associated with positive features (e.g. 'good output', 'good images', 'great quality'). Make a note of all of the positive features that can be delivered. Do you notice any lines which are not entirely positive? There is one definite case; can you spot which line it is? There is also one less definite case; can you spot it?

As with 'delivers', 'offers' is generally associated with positive things, e.g. 'a good balance of features', 'a decent feature set', 'a rich feature set', 'a winning combination'. 'Offers' and 'delivers' are both used for descriptive and evaluative purposes, i.e. to specify particular features of printers and to make comments about printers respectively.

Let us look at one last example, this time using a combination of words and part-of-speech tags as the search pattern. We entered 'performance'

```
oC-4400 from Canon Computer Systems delivers a nice bundle of home-orien
ge IJ700 is a four-color model that delivers a good balance of features,
g. This easy-to-use ink jet printer delivers acceptable black-text outpu
paper at top settings. But the 712C delivers better print quality for te
s Lexmark's Optra Color 1200 (left) delivers blazingly fast color laser
r laser printer.The HP DeskJet 722C delivers excellent output. ---------
t highly usable inkjet printer that delivers excellent value despite its
fordable and dependable inkjet that delivers excellent printing costs, t
as well.The affordable Lexmark 3200 delivers fine text.-----------------
or 440 ($150). This Editors' Choice delivers good output and respectable
40. This home-user-oriented printer delivers good images and moderate sp
5700 Color Jetprinter, for example, delivers great quality and strong sm
. Its latest entry, the OkiPage 20, delivers impressive performance for
 generous warranty, the OkiJet 2500 delivers relatively slow performance
h HP and Epson for market share and delivers respectable products at ver
 The 650C is not a standout, but it delivers speed and image quality equ
o goes to the Canon BJC-5000, which delivers tabloid output for an unbel
625 is a much better deal. The 1625 delivers text documents at 11.7 ppm,
d the Lexmark 3200 Color Jetprinter delivers the best text output at its
```

Figure 10.17 Edited concordance of search pattern 'delivers'

```
s 8L.The more heavy-duty OkiPage 10i offers a good balance of features, p
home users, the NEC SuperScript 650C offers a decent feature set for an a
 home office.Like the 697C, the 712C offers a full range of capabilities
s a Fast Ethernet connector. HP also offers a third version, the 8500 DN
it is easy, and its intuitive driver offers a range of printing options,
ter as well. The 712C's photo output offers a bit more contrast than that
 8-ppm units. The Xerox DocuPrint P8 offers a rich feature set and good p
an excellent all-around printer that offers a winning combination of pric
's the only one at this writing that offers duplexing at tabloid size.HP
s Brother MFC-7150C ($500). The unit offers good color ink jet output and
et 3100se ($700), a 6-ppm laser that offers great monochrome printing, sc
was simple, and the PrintGear driver offers lots of handy features, inclu
o photo printing. But while the 712C offers somewhat better color graphic
```

Figure 10.18 Edited concordance of search pattern 'offers'

```
International yields above-average performance and strong everyday text
ares some of the same below-average performance and output ratings. Its
face to yield across-the-board fast performance, and delivering excellen
et series has a reputation for good performance and ease of use, and the
the OkiPage 20, delivers impressive performance for the price, cranking
kiJet 2500 delivers relatively slow performance and below-average output
rice of $239, yet produced sluggish performance and spotty quality. Furt
SuperScript 870, demonstrated solid performance throughout the tests, ex
ssed text quality and the speediest performance on our Word document in
ice. Unmatched connectivity, strong performance, and very good quality o
emonstrated solid but unspectacular performance and quality. The same ca
```

Figure 10.19 Edited concordance of 'performance' preceded by an adjective

as the search pattern and specified that we wanted to retrieve all occurrences where 'performance' was preceded by the part-of-speech tag for
adjective (-JJ) within three words to the left of 'performance'. The results
are displayed in Figure 10.19.

We have edited the output to include only one example of each adjective. As you can see, good performance can be described using 'above-
average', 'fast', 'good', 'impressive', 'solid' and 'strong'. Poor performance
can be described using 'below-average', 'slow', 'sluggish', 'unspectacular'.
Can you identify which verbs are associated with these adjectives in the
concordance lines above?

Key points

- You can use a corpus-based approach to learn how to produce a
  particular text type or to write in a particular style.
- Different text types have their own syntactic and lexical patterns.
- Within each text type, different sections may have their own syntactic
  and lexical patterns.
- It may be worth your while to break down a specialized corpus into
  smaller components, i.e. to create a mini-corpus for each important
  section (introduction, discussion, etc.) in the corpus.
- Style patterns can be identified using both raw and tagged text.
- A tagged corpus is more beneficial if you are more interested in
  syntactic rather than lexical patterns.

Further reading

Aston, Guy (ed.) (2001) *Learning with Corpora*, Houston: Athelstan; Bologna: CLUEB.

Thomson, Paul and Tribble, Chris (2001) 'Looking at citations: using corpora in English for academic purposes', *Language Learning and Technology*, 5(3): 91–105. http://llt.msu.edu/vol5num3/thompson/default.html

Exercise

Create a small corpus of texts of a particular type, preferably texts of interest to you. If your texts have different sections, open each of the texts in your corpus and decide which sections you wish to investigate. Create a mini-corpus for each of the types of section you wish to look at (e.g. a mini-corpus of introductions, a mini-corpus of abstracts in the case of science articles, a mini-corpus of lists of ingredients, a mini-corpus of preparation instructions in the case of recipes). Using a wordlist tool, identify which are the most common two-, three- and four-word clusters in your mini-corpora.

Choose the most frequent of each of these, produce a concordance and try to describe what you have found. Are there different patterns for different sections of your texts?

11 Using LSP corpora as a translation resource

Translation is the act of taking a text in one language, known as the **source language**, and re-creating it in another language, referred to as the target language. This transfer must be done in such a way that the meaning of the source text is accurately rendered using the terminology and style that are appropriate in the target language. When expressed in this simple fashion, it may sound as if translation is a relatively straightforward task, but those of you who have had even a small amount of experience of trying to translate a specialized text will be aware that there are many challenges involved. For instance, you may have difficulty locating an equivalent, or you may be faced with choosing between several possible equivalents. And, if you are lucky enough to find the terms you need, you may still have trouble knowing how to put the whole text together in a style that is appropriate to the LSP.

Many of the corpus-based techniques that can be useful for translation have already been discussed elsewhere in this book. In Chapter 6 you learnt how to exploit bilingual parallel corpora to find translation equivalents; in Chapter 8 you learnt how to conduct terminological research with the help of a corpus and in Chapter 10 you discovered how a corpus could be used as a writing guide. The purpose of this chapter is to review some of these strategies and to bring them together to demonstrate how corpora can be useful to translators. We will begin by considering how you can use a parallel corpus and we will then move on to explore the potential of a monolingual corpus for providing valuable translation information.

Using a parallel corpus as a translation resource

In this section, you will see how a parallel corpus can be exploited to help you with some of your translation-related tasks. As explained in Chapter 6, a parallel corpus contains texts in one language that are aligned with their translations in another language. The corpus we will be referring to is a French–English parallel corpus that consists of a collective agreement for employees of a bilingual institution in Canada. A collective agreement is a document that outlines the workloads, compensation and benefits for employees, as well as the procedures that should be followed if there are any labour disputes. This particular collective agreement contains 226,601 tokens and it has been aligned at the sentence level. The working conditions at most companies are re-negotiated every few years, which means that changes will be made to the collective agreement. Imagine that you have been hired to translate some new amendments that will be added to the collective agreement. Let us see how the existing agreement, which has been aligned and stored as a parallel corpus, can help you to translate these additions.

Identifying terminological equivalents

You are likely to find that there are some terms in the text of the amendments for which you will need to identify an appropriate target language equivalent. For example, imagine that you need to find an English-language equivalent for the French term '*plaignant*'. Your first instinct might be to look up the term in a dictionary, and upon doing so, you are faced with three suggestions: 'litigant', 'plaintiff' and 'complainant'. The dictionary indicates that all three terms are commonly used in the legal field, but there are no contexts provided and no indication as to which, if any, might be most appropriate in a collective agreement. Rather than simply trying to guess which term to use, you can choose instead to treat your parallel corpus as a sort of bilingual dictionary. You can enter '*plaignant*' as the search term in a bilingual concordancer, which will retrieve all the French sentences containing that term along with the corresponding English sentences. A selection of concordances from the collective agreement corpus is shown in Figure 11.1.

By examining the corresponding English sentences, you can determine that none of the terms suggested by the dictionary (i.e. 'litigant', 'plaintiff', 'complainant') appear in the collective agreement. Rather, in this LSP in Canada the appropriate equivalent for '*plaignant*' is 'grievor'. As this example demonstrates, a suitable parallel corpus can in fact sometimes be a better option than a dictionary. In this instance, there is an additional benefit for your client: because you are using the collective agreement as your corpus, the terms you use in your translations of the amendment texts will be consistent with the terms used in the original collective agreement.

Investigating usage

In addition to providing useful terminological equivalents, a parallel corpus can also provide examples that can help you to phrase things in a way that sounds natural or idiomatic in the LSP. For example, you might already know that in the context of a collective agreement, the French

Toutefois, il est entendu que l'Association ne poursuivra pas le grief d'un membre qu'elle a assumé lorsque le <u>plaignant</u> désire le régler ou le retirer, et ce sans préjudice quant à la position de l'Association en cas de griefs subséquents de nature semblable.	It is understood, however, that the Association shall not pursue a member's grievance which it has assumed where the grievor wishes to settle or withdraw the grievance, but this shall be without prejudice to the position of the Association in dealing with subsequent grievances of a similar nature.
13.2.4 Lorsqu'un mémoire tel qu'il est décrit à 13.3.6 ou 14.4.5, n'est pas signé dans les délais prescrits au présent article, le <u>plaignant</u> peut soumettre son cas à la prochaine étape, comme si il avait reçu une réponse négative ou un refus.	13.2.4 If a memorandum under either 13.3.6 or 14.4.5 is not executed within the time limits prescribed in this article, the grievor may submit the matter to the next step as if a negative reply or denial had been received.
13.2.5 Lorsqu'aucune démarche n'est prise pour soumettre la question à la prochaine étape, ou lorsque le <u>plaignant</u>, sans motif valable, n'assiste pas à une réunion pré-grief ou à une réunion de première étape, le désaccord ou le grief est réputé être retiré ou réglé, selon le cas.	13.2.5 Where no action is taken to submit the matter to the next step, or where the grievor, without good reason, fails to attend a pre-grievance or Step 1 meeting, the disagreement or grievance shall be deemed to have been withdrawn or settled, as the case may be.
(c) dans le cas d'un grief présenté par l'Association, le président de l'Association ou son délégué assiste à la réunion à titre de <u>plaignant</u>.	(c) in the case of a grievance initiated by the Association, the president of the Association or her delegate shall attend as the grievor.

Figure 11.1 A selection of bilingual concordances retrieved using the search term '*plaignant*'

term '*grief*' can be translated into English as 'grievance', but you may not know the collocates of this term or how to use it in a sentence. For instance, if you have a grievance, what do you actually do in order to bring it to your employer's attention? This type of usage information is easily accessible in a parallel corpus because the terms are shown in context. By examining the context surrounding the term 'grievance', as shown in Figure 11.2, you can discover some of the typical things that you can do with a grievance.

Étape 1 – Présentation d'un grief	STEP 1 – Initiating a grievance
Un grief amorcé par un membre ou des membres constitue un grief privé avant et pendant la réunion de première étape, et le demeure jusqu'à ce que et à moins qu'il ait été assumé par l'Association.	A grievance which is initiated by a member or members is a private grievance prior to and throughout the Step 1 meeting, and remains so thereafter unless and until assumed by the Association.
13.2.1 Tout grief présenté contre l'employeur par un membre ou des membres peut être assumé par l'Association, auquel cas l'Association remplace le membre ou les membres comme partie.	13.2.1 Any grievance initiated by a member or members against the employer may be assumed by the Association, at which point the Association replaces the member(s) as a party.
13.2.3 Les délais pour la soumission d'avis de désaccord aux termes de 13.3.1 et pour la soumission, aux termes de 13.4.1, des types de griefs énumérés à 13.4.6 sont obligatoires.	13.2.3 The time limits for filing letters of disagreement under 13.3.1 and for initiating grievances under 13.4.1 for the types listed in 13.4.6 are mandatory.
13.2.10 Lorsqu'un grief est déposé contre une décision de l'employeur, ladite décision demeure valable et exécutoire jusqu'à ce que et à moins que l'employeur révoque sa décision.	13.2.10 Where a grievance is filed against an employer's decision, the employer's decision shall stand and remain effective until and unless the employer reverses its decision.
(c) dans le cas d'un grief présenté par l'Association, le président de l'Association ou son délégué assiste à la réunion à titre de plaignant.	(c) in the case of a grievance initiated by the Association, the president of the Association or her delegate shall attend as the grievor.

Figure 11.2 A selection of bilingual concordances retrieved for '*grief*' and 'grievance'

These contexts reveal that in English, a grievance is typically 'initiated' (five occurrences), but may also be 'filed' (one occurrence), whereas in French, there is a greater variety of possibilities, including '*amorcer*' (one occurrence), '*présenter*' (three occurrences), '*déposer*' (one occurrence), and '*soumission*' (one occurrence). As specialized dictionaries rarely provide much information about collocates, a parallel corpus is an invaluable resource for this type of investigation.

Investigating style

Identifying appropriate terms and their collocates is certainly important, but it is not the only type of information that you need in order to produce a good translation. People who are not familiar with the discipline of translation are often under the false impression that all translation problems can be resolved by turning to a dictionary; however, as you have no doubt experienced for yourselves, a dictionary can sometimes be helpful, but it rarely answers all your questions. What people tend to forget is that translators do not work with isolated words but rather with complete texts. In order to produce a natural sounding translation, it is not enough to use accurate terminology and correct grammatical structures. You also have to write in an appropriate style. In other words, in order to be accepted by other LSP readers, your translation should resemble other texts produced within that particular LSP. Chapter 10 suggested a number of ways in which a corpus could be used to investigate writing style, but let us consider another example here.

If you look back to Figure 11.2, you can see that most of the references to 'grievances' have been constructed using the passive voice (e.g. 'grievance initiated by a member') and not the active voice (e.g. 'a member initiates a grievance'). Moreover, the contexts in Figures 11.1 and 11.2 also reveal that the text is written in the third person, as evidenced by references to 'members', 'employers', 'grievors', etc. There are no examples where the employer is referred to in the first person (e.g. 'we') or where the employees are referred to in the second person (e.g. 'you').

We confirmed these observations by searching the entire corpus to find examples of the active constructions 'initiate/initiates' and of the first and second person pronouns 'we'/'you'. There were no instances of any of these patterns in the whole corpus. Based on this evidence, we can surmise that collective agreements are typically written in a style that uses passive constructions and the third person. This means that if you were to translate the text in the active voice using second person pronouns (e.g. 'if you initiate a grievance'), your translation would not be suitable even though you may have used the correct terms and collocates. In order for it to be a good translation, it must be stylistically appropriate as well as terminologically accurate and, in the case of collective agreements, this means using the passive voice and third person.

Another stylistic observation that can be made by examining the concordances in Figures 11.1 and 11.2 is that the sentences in the collective agreement are typically very long and complex. It would not, therefore, be stylistically appropriate to translate this text using short simple sentences.

Using a monolingual corpus as a translation resource

The value of using a parallel corpus as a translation resource is clear, but the problem is that suitable parallel corpora are not always readily available. Chapter 6 explains how you can go about creating a parallel corpus yourself, but even this may not always be feasible because in order to create a useful parallel corpus, you need to have access to a collection of previously translated texts. What is more, these texts need to be about the specialized field you are studying, be of the same text type as the text you are translating and be in the two languages that you are working with – a tall order to say the least! If you cannot easily find or build a parallel corpus to meet your translation needs, you might consider turning to a monolingual corpus since this type of corpus is easier to find or construct (see Chapters 3 and 4). Although it might seem strange to think of using a monolingual corpus as a translation resource, we assure you that it can be done – you just have to be a little more enterprising to get relevant information out of it. In the following sections, we will provide some ideas for strategies that can be used to extract relevant translation data from a monolingual corpus, but we are sure that as you continue to work with specialized corpora, you will come up with many more techniques that are suited to your particular LSP needs. Creativity, flexibility and patience are some of the most important qualities needed by anyone who wants to use a computer to explore and analyse language. As an LSP learner, you have these qualities in abundance – all you need to do is apply them!

In the following sections, we will be referring to a monolingual English-language corpus that we extracted from the *Computer Select* CD-ROM. The corpus totals 29,589 tokens and consists of popularized articles about computer viruses (e.g. articles explaining what viruses are and how you can protect your computer against them). These articles are aimed at people who are computer users, but who are not computer experts. Imagine that you have been hired to translate such an article from French into English, and that you are going to use this corpus to help you.

Verifying your intuition

One of the simplest, and yet most valuable, ways you can use a corpus is to investigate a hunch. If you have ever translated a text, you have probably had the experience of thinking that you know the correct term, but wanting to double-check your hunch in another resource just to be safe. Most translators will use a dictionary for this purpose, and a corpus can also be used in this way.

For example, imagine that one of the terms in your French source text is the term *'cheval de Troie'*. You suspect that the correct equivalent is probably 'Trojan horse', since this is the appropriate LGP translation, but

```
cognize several viruses and Trojan horses picked up by our client

tasks for which viruses and Trojan horses (similar to viruses but

are increasingly turning to Trojan Horses to steal passwords and

a virus and the picture.exe Trojan horse, which has been propagat

e a hacker might sneak in a Trojan horse-like picture.exe by doub

sion, false positive scans, Trojan horses, hostile applets, opera

, but beware of the growing Trojan horse threat and ever-smarter

ir non-reproducing cousins, Trojan horses, are increasingly being

a virus and the picture.exe Trojan horse, both of which emerged e
```

Figure 11.3 Concordance for the search pattern 'Trojan horse*'

you decide to generate a concordance just to be sure that this term is also used in the LSP of computer viruses. As shown in Figure 11.3, your intuition is correct and you can now confidently use this term in your translation.

You decide to check another term in the corpus. You need a translation for the term *'virus dans la nature'*, and this time your instincts tell you that the equivalent might something along the lines of 'natural virus' or 'a virus found in nature'. There are almost 600 occurrences of the term 'virus' in your corpus and it would take a long time to sort through them all, so you decide to search using the pattern 'natur*' instead. The results of this search are shown in Figure 11.4.

The concordancer retrieved five occurrences of the pattern 'natur*' in your corpus, but a closer inspection reveals that each of these occurrences are LGP uses of the word, and none of them is part of a term describing a type of computer virus. This time your intuition was not quite right, but by conducting a corpus search you have learnt something valuable – you have learnt that 'natural virus' is probably not the correct term, and you therefore need to do some more research. Try not to be too discouraged if

```
d politicians see this as the natural way; just as we all carry

n of an information-gathering nature. The March 2nd issue of th

s of wholesale changes to the nature of business itself. VPN ma

cause of the mission-critical nature of electronic messaging, e

are reveals your 'instinctive nature' by analyzing your answers
```

Figure 11.4 Concordance for the search pattern 'natur*'

your corpus does not support all your hypotheses. After all, ruling out an incorrect equivalent is a step in the right direction. However, you now find yourself faced with a more challenging problem: how can you find the correct term in a monolingual corpus when you do not really know what you are looking for? Keep reading to find some suggestions.

Searching for unknown equivalents

Since you cannot normally use the complete source term as a search pattern, you must come up with more creative techniques for trying to locate equivalents. Let us turn back to our problem expression from the previous section: *'virus dans la nature'*. We have already seen that a search using the pattern 'natur*' did not turn up any useful concordances. A search using the pattern 'virus*' produces almost 600 concordance lines, while a search using the pattern 'in the' retrieves seventy-seven concordance lines. It will take you a long time to search through all those concordance lines manually, but what if you were to combine these two search patterns by carrying out what we refer to as a **context search?** A context search is a type of search that allows you to look for a specific pattern that is in the vicinity of another pattern. This means that you can instruct the concordancer to retrieve all instances of the pattern 'in the' when it is found within five words of the pattern 'virus*'. By narrowing down your search in this manner, you retrieve nineteen concordance lines – a number that you can analyse much more easily. In order to make your analysis even more straightforward, you can sort the data to the right of the search term so that multiple occurrences of the same pattern will appear together. The resulting concordance is shown in Figure 11.5. Can you spot the pattern that looks most promising as a translation of *'virus dans la nature'*?

Another possible strategy that you could use to try to find an equivalent for *'virus dans la nature'* is to produce a list of word clusters. As described in Chapter 7, the clustering facility enables you to identify multiword units. For example, if you ask the corpus analysis tool to generate all the three-word clusters containing the words 'in the' which appear in the corpus at least three times, you get the list shown in Figure 11.6.

Let us look at another example. Suppose that you need to translate the phrase *'les virus furtifs et semi-furtifs'*. Your first instinct is to do a concordance search using a search pattern such as 'furtive', but this does not produce any results. What else can you try? Why not conduct a search using just the pattern 'semi*', as shown in Figure 11.7.

Among the contexts that were retrieved are a number for the term 'semi-stealth virus', which looks like a promising equivalent for the French term *'virus semi-furtif'*. Now that you have a clue, you can try conducting a search using the pattern 'stealth', which reveals eight concordances for the term 'stealth virus'. You have your solution!

```
strategies are all you need in the battle against computer viruses
e Michelangelo virus, hides in the boot sector and only pops up on
this year, a wake-up call - in the form of a virus called Melissa
d Web-based virus scanning. In the Melissa and ExplorerZip outbrea
d of viruses are out there? In the past, virus experts classified
ater today than it has been in the past. Previously, most viruses
of viruses-a useful feature in the right setting. For pure Windows
-based systems are deployed in the same manner as virus scanners o
a macro virus were reported in the United States. By the end of th
uses are the switch-hitters in the virus lineup. They originate as
 was informed of the latest in the virus case by the Carnegie Mell
viruses currently reported "in the wild" are Microsoft Word macro
n to be in circulation, or "in the wild," in virus-speak. Viruses
ate and size.  Many viruses in the wild are not programmed to eras
 viruses, some of which are in the wild and some that are very rar
d," in virus-speak. Viruses in the wild are the ones you're most l
iruses that currently exist in the wild. Norton AntiVirus 2.0, our
three  most common viruses in the world, said Carey Nachenberg, c
files. The new development in the Worm.ExploreZip virus saga was
```

Figure 11.5 Sorted results of a context search for the pattern 'in the' when it appears within five words of the pattern 'virus*'

in the wild	8
in the early	4
in the future	4
in the past	3
viruses in the	3

Figure 11.6 Three-word clusters containing the words 'in the'

```
products revealed at the semi-annual trade show in Los Angeles. N

uter. The main task for a semi-stealth virus is to hide the size i

rus is a memory resident, semi-stealth virus which infects .EXE an

lime is a memory resident semi-stealth virus that infects .COM pro

categorizes The Rat as a semi-stealth virus. The Rat goes memory

s largest manufacturer of semiconductors and other essential compo
```

Figure 11.7 Concordance for the search pattern 'semi*'

Can you think of other techniques for identifying unknown equivalents? What about using your knowledge of the structural patterns of a language? Suppose that you need to find a translation for the term *'réseau poste à poste'*. You know that the translation for *'réseau'* is 'network', but a search using this pattern produces over eighty concordance lines. You do not want to examine all of these concordances manually, so you try a search using the pattern 'post*', but unfortunately this produces no results. What other strategies can you try in order to narrow down your search?

If you know something about the structures of French and how these correspond to structures in English, you might be able to guess that a structure in the form of 'X *à* X' (e.g. *tête à tête*) is usually translated into English with a structure such as 'X-to-X' (e.g. head-to-head). You can use this knowledge to formulate a search pattern such as '*-to-*'. Then, you can carry out a context search where '*-to-*' must appear within five words of 'network'. The resulting concordance is shown in Figure 11.8.

Since you know that the pattern you are looking for takes the form X-to-X and not X-to-Y, you can quickly rule out occurrences such as 'easy-to-create', 'easy-to-install', 'PC-to-Mac' and 'up-to-date'. Now you are left with 'host-to-host', 'peer-to-peer' and 'Point-to-Point'. Of these three, you can see that 'peer-to-peer' seems to be used to modify 'network' directly, which looks promising. Now that you have a potential equivalent, you can conduct further research (e.g. by examining extended contexts) in order to verify that 'peer-to-peer network' is indeed the correct translation for *'réseau poste à poste'*.

Choosing between multiple options

We have seen that a corpus can be useful when you are trying to find an equivalent, but it can also be useful in cases where you have too many equivalents to choose from. For instance, you may need to make a decision such as whether or not to hyphenate a term (e.g. 'anti-virus' or 'antivirus'). A simple frequency calculation using a word list reveals that

```
ing on the network where easy-to-create macro viruses proliferate.

g for the big event, the easy-to-install network version, in much

d typically support only host-to-host VPN and Class A networks. It

ompany's network where the PC-to-Mac conversion software that includ

intended to be used as a peer-to-peer network; however, with the s

iginally envisioned as a peer-to-peer network, but with the advent

technique. The following peer-to-peer network software packages ar

ndows 2000, and as with Point-to-Point Protocol and other network

   ould get the benefits of up-to-date virus lists on the network whe
```

Figure 11.8 Concordance for the search pattern '*-to-*' within five words of
         'network'

'anti-virus' appears twenty-one times in the computer virus corpus, whereas
'antivirus' occurs 209 times. It would therefore seem that the majority of
the authors whose texts are part of this LSP corpus prefer not to use a
hyphen.

   A similar technique can be used to investigate synonymy. Imagine that
you need to translate the French term *'se propager'*. A quick check in the
dictionary reveals that this can be translated by either 'propagate' or
'spread', but there is no indication given as to which might be more appropriate in the LSP of computer viruses. A concordance search reveals that
both terms appear in your corpus; however, the frequency statistics show
that 'spread' appears forty-six times, while 'propagate' occurs only four
times. Of course, frequency should not be your only consideration when
choosing an equivalent, but it may help you to make your decision, and
it is much easier to establish frequency by consulting a corpus than by
consulting a dictionary or a printed text.

Investigating usage

Sometimes when you are translating, you may know the equivalent for a
specialized term, but you may not be sure of how to use this term in an
idiomatic way in the LSP. For example, you may have established that
the English-language equivalent for the French term *'logiciel antivirus'* is
'antivirus software'; however, you may not know what words collocate
with this term. One way to learn what words typically accompany
'antivirus software' in a sentence is to generate a concordance, such as
that shown in Figure 11.9. By sorting the concordance one place to the
right of the search pattern, you can easily identify the verbs that commonly
collocate with the term 'antivirus software'.

```
 e-mail, make sure your antivirus software checks sent and received
file back? Because the antivirus software detected a virus on it,
 virus protection. The antivirus software detected the XYZ virus.
 on the network. If the antivirus software detects a problem, MIMEs
? Don't panic! If your antivirus software detects a virus, it will
ixty thousand. Popular antivirus software detects known viruses ju
  are help against DoS? Antivirus software detects viruses, it does
t received via e-mail? Antivirus software protects a computer syst
   update. Trend Micro's antivirus software protects against the Mel
  how Symantec's Norton Antivirus software protects organizations f
for Notes. Multi-layer antivirus software protects PCs, servers an
uter viruses. Luckily, antivirus software protects you from the na
d the message to them. Antivirus software protects you from the te
s protection software. Antivirus software protects your computer a
gram on your computer. Antivirus software protects your computer f
are all items that the antivirus software scanned. Try looking for
make certain that your antivirus software scans all files, not jus
  onto a user's system. Antivirus software scans files, but typical
t viruses. Traditional antivirus software scans files for maliciou
California. Typically, antivirus software scans servers for any si
```

Figure 11.9 Concordance for the search pattern 'antivirus software'

As you can see, the verb in this corpus that collocates most often with 'antivirus software' is 'protect' (eight occurrences), followed by 'detect' (six occurrences), 'scan' (five occurrences) and 'check' (one occurrence). It is also interesting to note that while 'detect' and 'scan' occur in both the present and the past tense, 'protect' occurs only in the present tense.

If you look to the right of the verbs, you can also see what types of things are usually acted on by antivirus software. For instance, if the verb is 'detect', then the thing that is most often detected is a 'virus', whereas if the verb is 'scan', then the thing that is most often scanned is a 'file'. In the case of 'protect', the thing that is protected is either a 'computer' or the user of the computer (i.e. 'you', 'organization').

By studying a term in context, you learn what other words typically collocate with that term. This information can help you to use the term in a way that sounds idiomatic or natural in the LSP.

Investigating style

As we have already noted, it is not enough for a translator to simply identify the correct terminology. The entire text must be written in such a way that it resembles the style of other texts in the LSP. In this case, you are translating a text that is a popularized article about viruses that is aimed at non-experts. One of the passages that you need to translate is as follows: '*Si l'on ne supprime pas le virus, le virus effacera les fichiers*'. A fairly literal translation of this passage would be something along the following lines: 'If one does not eliminate the virus, the virus will erase the files.' All of the terms used in this literal translation are accurate, and the sentence is grammatically correct, but does it correspond to the style of other texts of this type?

Let us begin by investigating the pronoun '*on*', which is an impersonal pronoun that is very common in French, and which can be translated in a variety of ways including 'one', 'you' or by a passive construction. A search in the computer virus corpus using the pattern 'one' reveals that while this word appears in the corpus sixty-nine times, the vast majority of occurrences are not examples where 'one' is being used as a personal pronoun. Instead, we see mainly examples where 'one' is being used in more of a numerical sense, such as 'one popular misconception' and 'the hackers are one step ahead'. There were also several instances of 'no one', but there was only a single occurrence of 'one' being used as a personal pronoun: 'representing the diversity one might find on a typical corporate file server'. This would seem to indicate that it might not be appropriate to translate '*on*' by 'one' in this particular type of text.

Next, you try a search using the pattern 'you*', which reveals 312 occurrences. A selection of these is shown in Figure 11.10. It certainly appears as though the use of second person pronouns to address the reader directly is very common in this type of text.

Based on this evidence, you might decide to alter the literal translation slightly by using the second person pronoun 'you' instead of the impersonal pronoun 'one'. Your new translation now reads: 'If you do not eliminate the virus, the virus will erase your files.' But are there other stylistic changes you should make?

Looking at the concordance lines in Figure 11.10, you may notice that contractions (e.g. can't, don't, haven't, you're) seem to be a common feature in this type of text. You decide to investigate further by using search patterns such as '*n't', '*'re' and '*'ll'' and you discover that there are over 300 contracted forms in the corpus. This might inspire you to consider using the contraction 'don't' in your translation instead of the expanded form 'do not'. With regard to this specific choice, the corpus reveals twenty-nine occurrences of 'don't' and only three of 'do not'.

The concordance lines in Figure 11.10 provide evidence that the style used in this particular text type is relatively informal. This is demonstrated

```
1.  a macro in a document. When you open the infected document, th
2.  PC in your organization. If you can' t do this, you should at l
3.  ost infected files, leaving your data intact. Some antivirus u
4.  ble. Put it near the top of your 'must have' list if you' re do
5.  t more advanced attacks. If you don' t keep up with current ale
6.  ance or even destroy all of your disk files. There are even vi
7.   any antivirus strategy. If you haven' t backed up your critica
8.  aid. "If everyone connects, you can cycle the virus around the
9.  ity 2000 - Our experts give you the skinny on firewalls, antiv
10. company advised "Make sure you know what type of licensing me
11. den virus is fiddling with your favourite programs or deletin
12. nes asked me "What else do you need besides a firewall?" but
13. s in the wild are the ones you' re most likely to pick up from
14. g experts are here to help you if you' re a Johnny-come-lately
15. o clean infected files. If you can' t repair quarantined files
```

Figure 11.10 A selection of concordance lines for the search pattern 'you*'

through the use of the second person pronoun 'you' to address the reader directly, and also through the use of contractions. Do you see any other evidence of informal style? Some of the expressions that appear in the corpus, such as 'your "must have" list' (line 4), 'give you the skinny on' (line 9), 'Johnny-come-lately' (line 14) and even 'fiddling' (line 11) are quite colloquial. Another indicator of informality is the use of direct speech as demonstrated through the use of quotation marks on lines 8, 10 and 12. If you consider all this information together, it appears as though the style that is typical of this type of text is one that is very relaxed and almost conversational in tone. Being aware of these features will help you to make appropriate stylistic decisions when you are faced with choices in your own translation.

Searching for explanatory contexts

Up to this point, we have been focusing on how you can use a corpus to investigate linguistic features such as terms and style. But as we explained in Chapter 2, LSP learners also need to have a good understanding of the concepts that make up the specialized subject field. As a translator, you probably have a background in language and linguistics, but you may not have received any formal training in specialized fields such as law, medicine or computing. Therefore, when you set out to translate a text in one of these fields, you need to learn about the important concepts in the field so that you can be sure your translation is conceptually accurate. A corpus that consists of texts about the specialized subject in question can be a valuable source of knowledge about the concepts in the field.

Since you are translating a text about computer viruses, it is important that you understand what a computer virus is. If you do a concordance search in the computer virus corpus for the pattern 'virus*', you will retrieve almost 600 occurrences. Some of these contexts will undoubtedly contain useful explanations of the concept, but it will take you a long time to read and sort through all of these occurrences. What you need is a method for narrowing down your search so that only those contexts that are rich in explanatory information will be retrieved. But what is it that signals that a context will be knowledge-rich? As you will learn in Chapter 12, researchers are currently looking for ways in which corpus analysis tools can be made to automatically retrieve knowledge-rich contexts by looking for specific lexical patterns, but until such time as these tools are commercially available, you can still make use of the same basic strategy by identifying and formulating the relevant search patterns yourself.

If you are looking for contexts that explain or define what a virus is, then you are essentially looking for contexts that answer the question 'What is a virus?' The answer to this type of question generally takes the following form: 'A virus is an X ...' Therefore, we can use this basic information to conduct a search using the pattern 'virus is a'. As illustrated in Figure 11.11, using this search pattern you are able to narrow down the number of concordance lines to ten, which is much more manageable.

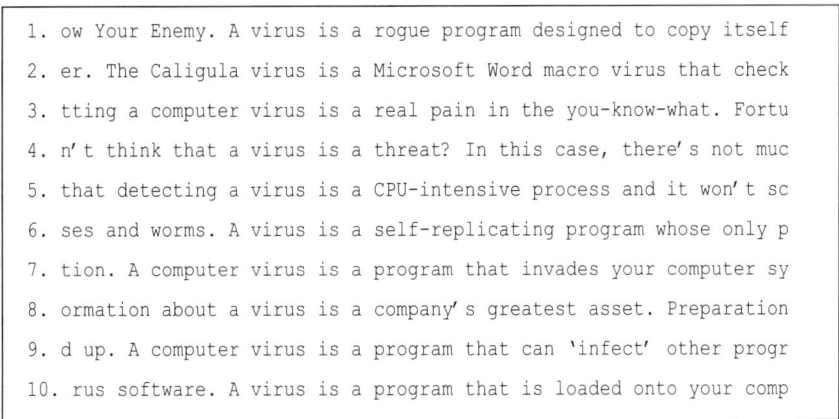

```
1. ow Your Enemy. A virus is a rogue program designed to copy itself

2. er. The Caligula virus is a Microsoft Word macro virus that check

3. tting a computer virus is a real pain in the you-know-what. Fortu

4. n't think that a virus is a threat? In this case, there's not muc

5. that detecting a virus is a CPU-intensive process and it won't sc

6. ses and worms. A virus is a self-replicating program whose only p

7. tion. A computer virus is a program that invades your computer sy

8. ormation about a virus is a company's greatest asset. Preparation

9. d up. A computer virus is a program that can 'infect' other progr

10. rus software. A virus is a program that is loaded onto your comp
```

Figure 11.11 Concordance for the search pattern 'virus is a'

1 A virus is a rogue program designed to copy itself into your PC's memory and onto your hard disk. Once in active memory, a virus can interfere with the operating system, corrupt program or data files, or simply post intrusive messages on the screen.

6 A virus is a self-replicating program whose only purpose is to distribute itself. It is distributed by changing another program's code to include the virus code itself. The only way for a computer virus to be distributed is for the user to activate the program that contains the virus code.

7 A computer virus is a program that invades your computer system, hides there, and makes copies of (replicates) itself. You might, for example, download a program that includes a destructive computer virus that replicates itself until you have no space left on your hard disk or in memory.

9 A computer virus is a program that can 'infect' other programs by modifying them to include a version of itself. All computer viruses copy themselves, and may also try to escape detection by mutating slightly or encrypting themselves each time they replicate.

10 A virus is a program that is loaded onto your computer without your knowledge and runs against your wishes. Most viruses can also replicate themselves. All computer viruses are manmade.

Figure 11.12 Expanded contexts for concordances

Looking at the concordance lines that have been retrieved, you will notice that the pattern 'is a' is not used exclusively to indicate knowledge-rich contexts. Lines 3, 4, 5 and 8 do not look very promising as knowledge-rich contexts, while line 2 appears to be giving information about one specific virus, rather than about viruses in general. However, the remaining lines (1, 6, 7, 9 and 10) look to be worthy of further investigation. If you expand the context surrounding these lines, you will find some valuable explanatory material, as shown in Figure 11.12.

By looking at these expanded contexts, you can learn quite a lot about what a computer virus is and what it does. For instance, you learn that viruses are a type of program, that they are self-replicating, and that they may damage your computer or data. In addition, by using a corpus analysis tool to focus in on these knowledge-rich contexts, you have probably saved yourself quite a bit of time. Just imagine how many pages of printed text you might have had to read before coming across a relevant explanatory context.

The pattern 'is a' is just one example of a type of pattern that might indicate a knowledge-rich context. Keep in mind, however, that concordancers will only retrieve the specific patterns that you ask them to retrieve, so in order to find useful information, you may need to search for variations of this pattern, such as 'is an', 'is the', or 'is one'. You might also consider searching for patterns that take into account plural forms (e.g. 'viruses are'), or patterns such as 'kind of', 'sort of' or 'type of', which are also commonly found in explanatory phrases (e.g. 'a virus is a kind of computer program . . .').

There is a lot of work still to be done in order to identify all the lexical patterns that might indicate different kinds of knowledge-rich contexts. For instance, it might be easier to explain some concepts in terms of their parts (e.g. 'a disk drive has a read/write head'), which means that patterns such as 'has a', 'part of', 'made up of' or 'consists of' might be good search patterns. Similarly, other concepts can be explained in terms of their function (e.g. 'a keyboard is used to enter data into a computer'), in which case patterns such as 'used to', 'used for' or 'employed as' could be helpful. Can you think of other patterns that may be good indicators of explanatory contexts?

Key points

- A corpus can provide you with both linguistic and conceptual information.
- You can consult a parallel corpus in much the same way as you consult a bilingual dictionary, but a corpus will provide more collocational and stylistic information than a dictionary.
- A monolingual corpus can also be used as a translation resource, but you have to be more creative in devising strategies to find equivalents.
- You can also use monolingual corpora to help you choose between synonyms, identify usage information and determine what style is appropriate for your translation.
- Certain types of lexical patterns, such as 'is a' or 'kind of' may be good indicators of explanatory contexts, which can provide you with the information you need to understand specialized concepts.

Further reading

Bowker, Lynne (2000) 'Towards a methodology for exploiting specialized target language corpora as translation resources', *International Journal of Corpus Linguistics* 5(1): 17–52.

Lindquist, Hans (1999) 'Electronic corpora as tools for translation', in Gunilla Anderman and Margaret Rogers (eds) *Word, Text, Translation*, Clevedon: Multilingual Matters.

Meyer, Ingrid (2001) 'Extracting knowledge-rich contexts for terminography: a conceptual and methodological framework', in Didier Bourigault, Christian Jacquemin and Marie-Claude L'Homme (eds) *Recent Advances in Computational Terminology*, Amsterdam/Philadelphia: John Benjamins: 279–302.

Pearson, Jennifer (1996) 'Electronic texts and concordances in the translation classroom', *Teanga* 16: 85–95.

Pearson, Jennifer (1998) *Terms in Context*, Amsterdam/Philadelphia: John Benjamins.
Zanettin, Federico (2001) 'Swimming in words: corpora, translation and language learning', in Guy Aston (ed.) *Learning with Corpora*, Houston: Athelstan; Bologna, CLUEB, 177–97.

Exercise

Choose a short text (or an extract from a text) that you would like to translate. Create a small monolingual corpus of texts in your target language. Make sure that the texts in your corpus are of the same type as your source text. Identify three terms in your source text for which you need to find a translation and try to devise techniques for identifying appropriate equivalents. These techniques could include using wildcards, using context searches, using structural clues, etc.

Once you have identified the equivalents, explore the contexts in which they appear. Can you see any collocates or other patterns of usage? Keep in mind that different types of patterns might emerge if you sort the concordances in different ways (e.g. first sort according to the word before the search term and then sort according to the word following the search term). As you examine the contexts, keep your eyes open for any stylistic features that seem to be in evidence.

Finally, choose a concept in your text that you would like to learn more about and see if you can locate some explanatory contexts for this concept. What lexical patterns can you use to in order focus your search and reveal knowledge-rich contexts?

12 Other applications and future directions

Throughout this book, you have learnt how to create different types of LSP corpora and how to use these resources to help with tasks such as glossary building, translation and writing. The aim of this final chapter is to briefly outline some additional ways in which LSP learners can use corpora and to consider how corpus analysis tools for LSP users are evolving. As you continue to work with corpora, we are sure that you will come up with innovative ways of using them to meet your own LSP needs but, in the meantime, some of the applications described here might provide you with inspiration. We begin by describing LSP learner corpora and then move on to discuss ways in which corpora can be used to study neologisms, which are new words in a language, as well as metaphor, which is a common feature of many LSPs. Finally, we consider some ways in which corpus analysis tools are being refined to meet the specific needs of LSP learners.

Creating LSP learner corpora

As its name suggests, a learner corpus is a corpus made up of texts that have been produced by learners of a foreign language. One of the earliest and best known projects involving learner corpora is the International Corpus of Learner English (ICLE) project which began in 1990. The ICLE corpus currently contains over 2 million words of student essays written by advanced learners of English from fourteen different mother-tongue backgrounds. The existence of such a corpus makes it possible to take a new, more concrete approach to studying the features of learner English. Many people have offered opinions about how learner language actually differs from native-speaker language, but these have not always been substantiated by hard evidence from larger collections of texts. The ICLE corpus can be used to investigate questions such as whether there is a general advanced learner language that shows consistent differences from equivalent native-speaker language, and to what extent influence of the different native languages is manifested when writing in English as a foreign language.

Although the ICLE project deals with LGP and is restricted to one text type, namely essays, the basic idea can be applied to the construction of LSP learner corpora. This can be done on an individual basis (e.g. a student building up a corpus of his or her own work), or on a larger scale (e.g. a teacher compiling a corpus of texts produced by all the students in the class).

For example, if you are a science student learning to write up experiments, you can collect together all the experiments that you have written up over the course of your studies and put them into a corpus. If you annotate the corpus (see Chapter 5), for example, by labelling each text with the date on which it was written, you could compare your early work against your most recent work. You could study your early texts to see what types of decisions you made and what terms or constructions you used, and then trace the development of your language skills to see how your knowledge of the LSP has changed and improved. For example, by generating a word list of one of your early texts, you can see what type of vocabulary you commonly used. You can then compare this to a word list generated from one of your more recent texts to see whether you are using the same type of vocabulary, or whether your command of the LSP has improved. An improvement in your command of the LSP may be evidenced by the fact that you are now using a wider range of vocabulary which includes words that are longer or more complex in meaning than those you used to use previously. In a similar way, you can generate concordances for the two texts to investigate whether you are still using the same types of structures or whether your writing is becoming more idiomatic and fluent as your knowledge of the LSP improves.

If you are a teacher, you can use a corpus of learner texts to help you identify those areas of LSP learning that are causing difficulties for the students in your class. Imagine that you are a translator trainer teaching a course on legal translation. You could ask all the students in your class to submit electronic copies of their translations and you could then put these into a corpus of learner translations. By studying different versions of the same text that have been produced by different class members, a teacher can identify areas where the class as a whole is having difficulty, as distinct from problems that may have beset only one or two students. This type of information can help a teacher to decide what to focus on in class discussions, for example. Of course, many teachers already conduct this type of investigation using the printed copies of work handed in by students, but imagine how much easier it would be to investigate an electronic corpus with the help of corpus analysis tools!

To find out more about learner corpora, consult Granger (1998), which contains a collection of papers that cover issues such as designing, compiling, annotating and investigating learner corpora. Bowker (forthcoming) contains some ideas for constructing and applying learner corpora in a translator training context.

Using LSP corpora to identify and study neologisms

The world around us is evolving and in many specialized fields – particularly in science and technology – inventions are created and new discoveries are made all the time. In order to talk about these new ideas and things, we need to come up with terms to designate them, and these new terms that come into a language are called neologisms. Corpora are a very important resource for LSP learners wishing to study neologisms because, as mentioned in Chapter 1, it takes a long time to compile and publish a printed resource such as a dictionary, which means that by the time a dictionary is published, it may no longer reflect the current state of knowledge or language in an LSP.

Neologisms can be formed in a number of different ways. They can be completely new words that have never been used before, such as 'byte', which is the term that was coined to describe a unit of computer storage. Completely new words are somewhat rare, and it is more common to find neologisms that are formed by combining existing words (e.g. 'upload'), by combining parts of words (e.g. 'Internaut', formed from the first part of 'Internet' and the last part of 'astronaut'), or by adding prefixes or suffixes to existing words to create novel terms (e.g. 'laptop-less', formed by adding the suffix '-less' to the noun 'laptop'). You may have noticed, for example, that the increasing popularity of the Internet has resulted in the creation of a whole new set of neologisms beginning with the prefix 'e-' (which stands for 'electronic'), including 'e-mail', 'e-commerce', and 'e-business'. Can you think of other 'e-' neologisms? How about neologisms beginning with 'cyber-'?

When neologisms are formed by arranging letters or words into new combinations, a tool that is similar to a spell checker can be used to try to identify these neologisms automatically in a corpus. A spell checker works by comparing every word that you type against a stored dictionary of correct words. If any word in your text does not match a dictionary entry, then the spell checker will mark this word as being incorrect. A number of different researchers, such as those working on the AVIATOR/APRIL projects (Baayen and Renouf 1996), have developed similar tools that try to identify neologisms in a corpus. These tools compare all the different words in your corpus against a stored database of existing words. Neologism finder tools work on the principle of pattern matching. If a word in the corpus does not match the pattern of one of the words stored in the database, then it is identified as a potential neologism. The potential neologism is stored in a separate file to be further investigated by a human. Of course, not every term identified by a neologism finder is actually a neologism. For example, many proper names will not be found in the database, but this does not necessarily mean that they should be identified as neologisms. Similarly, if a word in the corpus is spelt incorrectly it might be mistakenly identified as a neologism. Nevertheless, neologism finders can still be useful to people such as dictionary makers, who are always on the lookout for new words entering a language, because these tools can search through vast amounts of text in a much shorter time than it would take a person to read through a corpus.

Neologisms can also be formed in another way, however, by assigning a new meaning to an existing word. This type of neologism is very common in LSP. For example, an existing word that has a particular meaning in LGP may be assigned a new meaning when it is used in an LSP, or a word from one LSP can be given a new meaning in a different LSP. In many cases, the new meaning has some kind of metaphorical relation to the existing meaning. For example, the LGP word 'port' typically refers to a harbour where ships load or unload cargo, but in the LSP of computing, the term 'port' has been given a new meaning and is used to designate a pathway into and out of a computer for transmitting or receiving data. Meanwhile, the term 'virus' originated in the LSP of medicine, where it is used to refer to an infectious agent that spreads illness or disease, but it has now been brought into the LSP of computing, where its definition has been modified to refer specifically to computer programs that spread themselves to other computers and often destroy or distort data.

A similar way of forming a neologism is to give an existing word a new part of speech without necessarily changing its written form. For example, when a computer that is running a Windows operating system crashes, it may display a 'blue screen'. The term 'blue screen' was originally made up of a noun + adjective, but it can now be used as a verb, as in the sentence 'If I press that key, my computer will blue screen.'

When a neologism is formed by assigning a new meaning to an existing word, or by changing a word's part of speech without changing its form, this neologism cannot be easily identified in an automated way. The pattern matching techniques used by the neologism finder tools described above do not work for neologisms formed through meaning extension or change in part of speech because new terms created in this way have the same form (i.e. are spelt in the same way) as an existing word. Nevertheless, a corpus can still be a useful resource for investigating such neologisms because corpora allow you to study words in context, and you can thus learn about a term's new usage, which can then be compared with the original usage. For example, the meaning and usage of the term 'spam' in the LSP of computing can be compared with the LGP word 'spam' as illustrated in Figures 12.1 and 12.2. What can you learn about the meaning and use of 'spam' from studying these concordance lines? Note also how 'spam' can be used as both a noun and a verb in the LSP of computing, whereas it was only used as a noun in LGP.

```
he then Queen Elizabeth eating spam from a gold plate during the S
might as well have been eating spam.
            For others they evoke spam sandwiches, fake-fur rugs and
rty Russian breakfast -- fried spam with sour cream and tinned pea
late held a curious mixture of Spam, jelly, iced buns and lettuce
with Thermos flask of coffee, spam sandwiches, bulging notebooks,
es spread with butter and jam, spam sandwiches, marmalade sandwich
by the contents of two tins of Spam, equally wafer-like, drew crie
meats of vague origins branded Spam, Prem and Tang somebody's grin
ersuading busy young mums that Spam makes an easy meal in minutes.
```

Figure 12.1 Concordance demonstrating the LGP usage of 'spam' taken from the British National Corpus

Using corpora to investigate metaphor in LSP

Metaphors are an important part of language. When we use a metaphor, we describe a thing (e.g. person, object, idea) by referring to something else that has similar characteristics to the thing we are trying to describe. Shakespeare's observation that 'All the world's a stage' is part of a metaphor that compares life to a theatre performance. Metaphors are often considered to be literary devices that make a text more interesting to read, but Lakoff and Johnson (1980) have demonstrated that metaphor goes beyond language and is in fact an important basis for conceptual understanding.

As we learnt in Chapter 2, conceptual understanding is fundamental to LSP. Experts must be able to communicate information about specialized concepts, and metaphors have an important role to play in LSP communication. In LSP, metaphors are often borrowed from domains that are not related in topic but may be related in some other way. Thus, you will find a lot of 'war' language in medicine because medicine is perceived to be a battle against illness, and so you will find descriptions of cancer cells 'invading' healthy tissue and viruses 'attacking' cells.

A corpus can be a useful tool for investigating metaphor. A corpus allows you to see a search term in context, and you can study these contexts to identify other terms and expressions that can be used to construct a metaphor. The concordance for 'disease/diseases' shown in Figure 12.3 contains a number of expressions that help to construct the metaphor 'medicine is war'. Can you spot them?

To find out more about using corpora to investigate metaphor, consult Meyer *et al.* (1997), who have conducted a corpus-based investigation of

th direct mail messages. Email spam lists are often created by sca
ive their address away. Usenet spam robs users of the utility of t
he group after he attempted to spam our main discussion list. Clic
' messages per day? Hardly. If spam grows, it will crowd our mailb
per day spent discarding their spam, just on AOL. By contrast, the
tworks and disks with unwanted spam messages, takes up their manag
ing with all the undeliverable spam messages, and subjects them to
s. Many of the people fighting spam are already conducting commerc
to distribute their materials. Spam is the equivalent of third-cla
ontact methods as an excuse to spam us with offers for your compan

Figure 12.2 Concordance demonstrating the use of 'spam' in the LSP of
computing

e : The latest weapon against disease. A radical new type of va
esidents to help battle heart disease and stroke by participati
ion over five years to combat diseases in the tropics such as t
ese infections. Common fungal diseases invade the superficial l
ir arsenal for treating heart disease, Alzheimer's, kidney ston
rt attacks and cardiovascular disease kill almost 1,000,000 Ame
s not effective in preventing disease once invasion of tissue h
first line of defense against disease, a healthy body has a num
irms donate vaccines to fight disease in developing countries.
hey might even participate in diseases that attack muscles. The
ular markers, we can outflank disease threats and market challe
ember 1996. People with heart disease can arm themselves agains
d the Pierces to confront the disease. The denial was a terribl
to pronounce victory over the disease, not only for electoral r
lied. When the enemy is heart disease, the strategy is no diffe
's counter-attack against the disease. In Australia and New Zea

Figure 12.3 Concordance for 'disease/diseases' containing expressions that create
the metaphor 'medicine is war'

metaphors in the LSP of the Internet, and Partington (1998: 107–20), who has conducted a corpus-based study of metaphors in the LSP of business.

Customizing tools to meet LSP needs

Throughout this book, we have investigated a number of ways in which corpora can be applied to LSP learning. More and more LSP learners are beginning to see the value of adopting a corpus-based approach to language study and, as this number continues to grow, there will also be an increased demand for tools that have been customized to meet the needs of LSP learners. A number of specialized tools are already being actively developed, including tools that use conceptual search patterns and tools that can extract equivalents from bilingual comparable corpora.

Searching for conceptual information

Chapter 2 explained that in order to become a proficient user of an LSP, you will need to acquire not only linguistic knowledge, but also conceptual knowledge. In other words, it is not enough to simply learn the terms used in an LSP. It is essential that you understand the concepts that these terms designate. One way to do this is to look for those contexts in a corpus that are rich in knowledge about the concept, such as contexts that contain definitions or explanations, rather than contexts which simply contain an example of the term in use. This was explored briefly in Chapter 11, but let us now examine this issue more closely.

When you use a corpus analysis tool to produce a concordance for a specific search term, you will retrieve all the occurrences of that string that are found in your corpus. Some of these will contain conceptual information, while others will be less informative. If there are a lot of occurrences of the search term in your corpus, then you will have to spend time looking through all these contexts in order to find the ones that are most useful (i.e. the ones that are rich in conceptual knowledge). For example, Figure 12.4 contains a selection of contexts that were retrieved for the search term 'bagpipe/bagpipes'. Which of these contexts would you describe as being knowledge-rich?

After reading through each of these contexts carefully, you have probably decided that contexts 4, 7, and 10 are quite informative, contexts 1, 5 and 6 are reasonably informative, while contexts 2, 3, 8 and 9 do not contribute much to your understanding of the concept 'bagpipe'. Just think how nice it would be if the corpus analysis tool could do this work for you!

In order to reduce the amount of work involved in manually sorting through concordance lines, LSP researchers are now looking for ways in which they can help corpus analysis tools to focus in on knowledge-rich contexts directly. As we have learnt, corpus analysis tools work on the

1 The Great Highland Bagpipe is a complex instrument that can be difficult to learn to play.
2 Bagpipes are relatively uncommon, and most people either love the sound or hate the sound, regardless of the ability of the piper.
3 The bagpipe is slowly becoming more popular.
4 Main bagpipe components include a bag, a blowstick, a number of single-reed drone pipes (usually three), and a double-reed chanter.
5 The bagpipe is a loud instrument that is meant to be played outdoors.
6 To this day the bagpipes are used to express strong emotions in passages of popular music, orchestral music and background music for TV and motion pictures.
7 The Great Highland Bagpipe consists of a bag made from elk hide with three drones, a blowpipe, and a chanter.
8 Bagpipes can be played at weddings to the enjoyment of all.
9 Purchasing your first set of bagpipes can be quite a chore.
10 In the bagpipe, sound is produced by inflating the bag and then applying pressure to the bag with the arm.

Figure 12.4 Contexts retrieved for the term 'bagpipe/bagpipes'

principle of pattern matching, so researchers are in the process of identifying and enumerating those lexical patterns that might indicate knowledge-rich contexts. We saw in Chapter 8 that 'i.e.', 'e.g.' and even parentheses can be indicators of some type of defining information, and we learnt in Chapter 11 that 'is a' can often signal an explanatory context. There are some additional patterns shown in Figure 12.5, although this list is not exhaustive. Can you think of other lexical patterns that might be good indicators of knowledge-rich contexts?

If you look back to Figure 12.4, you will notice that the contexts that we identified as being most informative contain lexical patterns that tend to indicate the presence of conceptual information (i.e. 'include', 'consists of', 'produced by', 'is a', 'used to'). In contrast, the contexts that provide the least amount of conceptual information do not contain the type of lexical patterns that point to knowledge-rich contexts. If corpus analysis tools are programmed to look for these lexical patterns and to sort the concordances so that the knowledge-rich contexts are displayed first, then you will be able to spend more time learning about the concepts and less time sorting through the data.

Of course, the identification of useful lexical patterns is not completely straightforward. For example, there will be instances when a pattern such

Lexical patterns	Type of conceptual knowledge provided	Example
is a, kind of, type of, includes	Describes generic-specific relations	The tabor is a type of drum.
has a, contains, consists of, includes	Describes part–whole relations	A snare drum has a batter head and a snare head.
used for, used to, employed to	Describes the function of an item	A wooden stick is used to strike the drum head.
causes, produces, produced by, results from	Describes relations of cause and effect	Striking the drum head causes the snares to vibrate.
also called, also known as, sometimes referred to as	Indicates possible synonymy	The tambourin, also known as the tambourin provençale, is the largest of all the tabors.

Figure 12.5 Lexical patterns that can point to knowledge-rich contexts

as 'is a' may be found in a context such as 'A drum is a good birthday present.' Although this context contains the 'is a' pattern, it is not actually a knowledge-rich context because it does not provide us with any information about the concept 'drum'. Nevertheless, the approach of identifying lexical patterns that indicate knowledge-rich contexts is a promising one, and more information on research in extracting knowledge-rich contexts from corpora can be found in Pearson (1998) and Meyer (2001).

Searching for information in bilingual comparable corpora

Chapters 9 and 11 described how parallel corpora, which consist of texts aligned with translations, can be used to identify terminological equivalents. There is no doubt that parallel corpora can be very valuable resources for finding such equivalents, but it may not always be easy to locate or create a parallel corpus that meets your needs in terms of subject matter, text type, langue combination, etc. We saw in Chapter 11 that mono-lingual corpora can also be used as a translation resource. Monolingual corpora are certainly easier to create than parallel corpora, but searching in a monolingual corpus for an unknown equivalent can be tricky, and you may not always find what you are looking for. What you need is a tool that can help you to find terminological equivalents in bilingual comparable corpora.

A bilingual comparable corpus essentially consists of two monolingual corpora that are similar in terms of subject matter, text type and publication date. Both parts of the corpus contain original language material and, since the texts are not translations of one another, they cannot be aligned. Therefore, a tool for processing bilingual comparable corpora must be able to identify translation equivalents in two corpora that are non-aligned and non-translated. How can this be done?

One technique is to look for words that have the same spelling or similar stems in both languages. For example, the spelling of the term 'virus' is the same in both English and French, and the English term 'encryption' and the French term *'encryptage'* both share the stem 'encrypt'. Of course, this simple strategy will not work in all cases since false cognates, also known as false friends, may be retrieved by mistake. False cognates are words that look similar in two different languages but which do not refer to the same concept. For example, although the word 'sensible' exists in both French and English, it does not have the same meaning, and the French word *'sensible'* should actually be translated into English as 'sensitive'. Similarly, while the English word 'library' looks a bit like the Spanish word *'librería'*, the meaning of the Spanish term is 'book-shop' and not 'library'. It is possible to prevent some of these false cognates from being retrieved by using a stop list, which is a list of words that should be ignored by the computer; however, another problem with this simple technique is that it only works for language pairs that are related. It would not work, for example, on language pairs such as English and Korean or French and Chinese.

More sophisticated techniques include using combinations of statistical frequencies and collocational information to try to identify possible equivalents. Research in this area is still relatively new, but when such tools are available, they will be very helpful for LSP learners and also for other language applications such as machine translation. To learn more about techniques for processing bilingual comparable corpora, consult Bennison and Bowker (2000).

Key points

*   LSP learner corpora consist of texts that have been produced by LSP learners and they can be used to chart improvements and to identify areas of difficulty.

- Neologisms are new words that come into a language. Corpora are a useful resource for studying LSP neologisms because they can be kept up to date more easily than printed resources.
- Neologisms that have been formed by arranging letters or words into new combinations can be identified using automatic tools; however, neologisms that have been formed by assigning a new meaning or part of speech to an existing word must be identified manually.
- In LSP, metaphors are often used to explain difficult or unfamiliar concepts by comparing them to concepts that can be readily understood. Corpora are valuable resources for investigating metaphor because they allow you to see the different contexts in which a term appears.
- As more LSP learners begin using corpora, there will be an increased demand for tools that have been customized to meet their particular needs. Specialized tools that can search for conceptual information and identify equivalents in bilingual comparable corpora are already being developed.

Further reading

AVIATOR/APRIL: http://www.rdues.liv.ac.uk/april.shtml

Baayen, Harald and Renouf, Antoinette (1996) 'Chronicling the times: productive lexical innovations in an English newspaper', *Language* 72(1): 69–96.

Bennison, Peter and Bowker, Lynne (2000) 'Designing a tool for exploiting bilingual comparable corpora', *Proceedings of the Second International Conference on Language Resources and Evaluation* (Vol 1), Paris: ELRA, 513–16.

Bowker, Lynne (forthcoming) 'Corpus-based applications for translator training: exploring the possibilities', in Sylviane Granger, Jacques Lerot and Stephanie Petch-Tyson (eds) *Corpus-Based Approaches to Contrastive Linguistics and Translation Studies*, Amsterdam: Rodopi.

Granger, Sylviane (ed.) (1998) *Learner English on Computer*, London/New York: Addison-Wesley-Longman.

ICLE: http://www.bricle.f2s.com/icle.htm

Meyer, Ingrid (2001) 'Extracting knowledge-rich contexts for terminography: a conceptual and methodological framework', in Didier Bourigault, Christian Jacquemin and Marie-Claude L'Homme (eds) *Recent Advances in Computational Terminology*, Amsterdam/Philadelphia: John Benjamins, 279–302.

Meyer, Ingrid, Zaluski, Victoria and Mackintosh, Kristen (1997) 'Metaphorical Internet terms: a conceptual and structural analysis', *Terminology* 4(1): 1–33.

Partington, Alan (1998) *Patterns and Meanings: Using Corpora for English Language Research and Teaching*, Amsterdam/Philadelphia: John Benjamins.

Pearson, Jennifer (1998) *Terms in Context*, Amsterdam/Philadelphia: John Benjamins.

Exercises

Exercise 1

Create a learner corpus of some of your own work (i.e. LSP texts that you have written or translated during the last year). Store the texts in separate files so that you will be able to analyse them separately. Compare your early work with your more recent work by generating separate word lists and concordances for the two files. Do you notice any differences between the two sets of texts? Are your LSP skills improving? What differences do you notice between your early work and your more recent work (e.g. in terms of vocabulary or sentence structure)?

Exercise 2

The term 'flame' is a neologism that is used in the LSP of the Internet. The first concordance shown below contains examples of how 'flame' is conventionally used in LGP, while the second illustrates the usage of 'flame' in the LSP of the Internet. Study these two concordances and try to determine how the meaning of 'flame' has changed. Why do you think that the term 'flame' was chosen to designate this new LSP concept? Apart

```
          was held in the tip of the flame it became white hot and glowed
             The study, which includes flame retardants, antioxidants, heat
                        The candle flame threw shadows, like paper-ash,
          embling fingers around the flame, lit it and inhaled deeply.
          the momentary blue veil of flame on the pudding, been what she
          t alive -- probably with a flame thrower.
          ove the slenderly tapering flame of the candle for a moment.
           Triomphe with the eternal flame burning beneath it could not b
          kly but did not burst into flame, the temperature was judged to
          g the scroll over a candle flame and threatening to destroy it.
          e of fire decay behind the flame front depends to a large exten
          ated in a sheet of searing flame and chunks of contorted metal
          ckled and spurted heatless flame up the chimney.
          y fingers they burned like flame in what was left of the winter
             I quenched the candle flame with my fingers and slid into
```

Figure 12.6 Concordance for 'flame' in LGP

```
, THEN has the audacity to flame me about my page. She obviousl
you become the target of a flame, avoid responding or you might
n an email list -- they'll flame back or worse. It seems to be
unsolicited advertising. A flame is an abusive message. Mailing
forbid the perpetuation of flame wars -- series of angry letter
  turned off if you want to flame with abandon, and even when it
  Resist the temptation to "flame" others on the list. Remember
  think before prolonging a flame war and if you absolutely have
resulting in arguments and flame wars.
y a new system that offers flame retardant email. Have you even
  If, however, you feel the flame is definitely worth a response
r are angry. Rather than a flame mail response, talk to the per
in. Hence the frequency of flame wars on the internet and in em
Now you can flag offensive flame-mail with MoodWatch, which is
e spared "junk" email and "flame" mail. The way an email group
```

Figure 12.7 Concordance for 'flame' in the LSP of the Internet

from the difference in meaning, can you observe any other differences between the LGP and LSP usage of 'flame'?

Exercise 3

Can you identify the metaphor that is being used in Figure 12.8?

```
        Dynamis receives seed investment. Fox Chase spinoff will g
igh returns quickly. A $25 investment can yield an exponential
rs have watched Inter-Arab investments grow by 4.3% in 2000. Re
mature within one year. As investments mature, the cash is then
n late 1998 and watched my investment wither up and blow away.
 Solutions to reap a $1.5M investment. Harvard Instruments, the
f the first private sector investments to sprout up along the c
s, on Wednesday defied the investment drought in the telecoms s
. Among its latest crop of investments are Chromotis Networks,
s have led to worries that investments in Kansas may shrivel, a
llion won. Some government investments went into sterile ground
28 years ago, has seen his investment bloom to $100 million. Sa
 in such a manner that the investments mature prior to the due
businesses have seen their investment blossom and welcome the n
ative environment in which investments can take root. Turkey ca
e state wants to help that investment bear fruit, said Bill Bax
continue to fertilize this investment after the service was up
 because we cultivate your investments with the greatest of car
or a legitimate high yield investment program? You will not fin
opes to see its aggressive investments ripen into improved prof
```

Figure 12.8 Concordance for 'investment/investments'

Appendix

This appendix contains a list of the tools and resources indicated at the end of each chapter in this book. They are assembled here for easy reference.

Tools

Concordancing software

KWiCFinder (Keyword in Context Finder): a stand-alone search agent which retrieves and excerpts relevant documents identified by AltaVista's search engine. More information at http://miniappolis.com/KwiCFinder/KwiCFinderHome/html

Logi Term: a bilingual concordancer and terminology manager. More information at http://www.terminotix.com

MonoConc: a concordancing program available for sale from http://www.athel.com/mono/html

MultiConcord: a multilingual concordancing program for parallel texts developed by David Woolls and others in the Lingua project. More information at http://www.copycatch.freeserve.co.uk

ParaConc: a bilingual/multilingual concordancing program designed to be used for contrastive corpus-based language research and for training and analysis related to translation studies. More information at http://www.ruf.rice.edu/~barlow/parac.html

TransSearch: RALI (Laboratoire de Recherche Appliquée en Linguistique Informatique) at the University of Montreal has developed a number of tools, including TransSearch, the concordancer used for accessing the Canadian Hansard online. More information about RALI at http://www-rali.iro.umontreal.ca/Accueil.en.html. You can try using TransSearch at http://www.tsrali.com where you can download a five-day trial for free, but after that it is a subscription service.

WordSmith Tools: a suite of corpus processing tools available for sale, and in demo mode, from Oxford University Press at http://www.oup.com/elt/global/isbn/6890/. Some more information about WordSmith, as well as some sample corpora, are available from the site of WordSmith developer Mike Scott: http://www.liv.ac.uk/~ms2928/index.htm

Some products containing term extraction tools

Ferret: http://www.computing.surrey.ac.uk/SystemQ/
Logi Term: http://www.terminotix.com
MultiTrans: http://www.multicorpora.ca
Nomino: http://www.ling.uqam.ca/nomino/
Trados: http://www.trados.com
Xerox TermFinder: http://www.mkms.xerox.com/

Search engines and meta-search engines

AltaVista: http://www.altavista.com
C4: http://www.c4.com
Dogpile: http://www.dogpile.com
Google: http://www.google.com
MetaCrawler: http://www.metacrawler.com
Northern Light: http://www.northernlight.com
ProFusion: http://www.profusion.com
Yahoo: http://www.yahoo.com

Resources

Tutorials for effective web searching

The Internet Search Tutorial for Translators: http://www.mabercom.com/
websearch/index.html
   The Complete Planet Guide to Effective Searching of the Internet: http://
www.completeplanet.com/Tutorials.Search/index.asp
   Finding Information on the Internet: A Tutorial: http://www.lib.
berkeley.edu/TeachingLib/Guides/Internet/FindInfo.html
   Web Search Strategies: http://home.sprintmail.com/~debflanagan/main/
html

Some potential LSP resources for corpus building

Business/Economics

Business Week Online: http://www.businessweek.com/
The Economist: http://www.economist.com/
Forbes: http://www.forbes.com/
Fortune: http://www.pathfinder.com/fortune/

Computing/Technology

CNet: http://www.cnet.com
Computer Select: http://www.gale.com/business/wb_intro.htm (also available on CD-ROM and as an online database)

TechWeb: http://www.techweb.com
ZDNet: http://www.zdnet.com

General Science

Nature: http://www.nature.com/
New Scientist: http://www.newscientist.com/ (also available on CD-ROM)
Science Direct: http://www.sciencedirect.com/
Science Magazine: http://www.sciencemag.org/
Scientific American: http://www.sciam.com/

Law

Journal of Online Law: http://www.law.cornell.edu/jol/jol.table.html
Legal journals on the web (site with many links): http://www.usc.edu/
    dept/law-lib/legal/journals.html
Web Journal of Current Legal Issues: http://webjcli.ncl.ac.uk/

Medicine

British Medical Journal: http://www.bmj.com./index.shtml
The Lancet: http://www.thelancet.com/
The New England Journal of Medicine: http://www.nejm.org/content/
    index.asp

Information about multilingual corpora

ELRA (European Language Resources Association) aims to serve as a focal
    point for information related to language resources in Europe. More
    information at http://www.icp.grenet.fr/ELRA/home.html
ELSNET (European Network of Excellence in Human Language Tech-
    nologies), funded by the European Communities' Human Language
    Technologies (HLT) programme. More information at http://www.
    elsnet.org/
European Union laws. By law, all EU legislation must be published in all
    EU languages. The Official Journal, the European Treaties and all
    Community legislation in force are all available and are therefore a
    useful source of parallel texts. More information at http://europa.
    eu.int/eur-lex/en/index/html
LDC (Linguistic Data Consortium), an open consortium of universities,
    companies and government research laboratories which creates,
    collects and distributes speech and text databases, lexicons, and other
    resources for research and development purposes. It has created a
    number of parallel corpora. More information at http://morph.ldc.
    upenn.edu/Catalog/by_type.html#text.parallel

TELRI aims at collecting, promoting, and making available monolingual and multilingual language resources and tools for the extraction of language data and linguistic knowledge; with a special focus on Central and Eastern European languages. More information at http://www.telri.de

INTERSECT: A project involving the creation of parallel aligned corpora (English and French, and English and German) for use in teaching and research. More information at: http://www.bton.ac.uk/edusport/languages/html/intersect.html

Glossary

alignment (see p. 59): a process of creating links between corresponding segments in *source* and *target texts* within a *parallel corpus*, usually carried out automatically. Links may be created between corresponding sections, paragraphs or sentences.

alphabetical list (see p. 117): a *word list* organized in alphabetical order.

annotation (see p. 83): the addition of explicit linguistic information to a document. See *POS tagging, syntactic annotation*.

bilingual concordance (see p. 93): a display showing the results of a search in a *parallel corpus*. Segments containing the search pattern are displayed along with their corresponding translations. Corresponding segments may be displayed either side by side or one above the other.

boolean operators (see p. 61): logical query limiters such as AND, OR, or NOT that can be incorporated into your search pattern to restrict the list of returned results (e.g. search for all occurrences of 'camera' AND 'flash', search for all occurrences of 'camera' NOT 'digital'). Boolean operators can be used with most Web *search engines*.

candidate term (see p. 148): a *term* that has been identified by a *term extraction* tool as one that may potentially be interesting for inclusion in a glossary. Candidate terms should always be verified by a human.

collocates (see p. 124): words that typically occur in the vicinity of your *search pattern* (e.g. 'output', 'quality' and 'text' are likely to be collocates of 'printer').

comparable corpus (see p. 3): a *corpus* containing sets of texts of a comparable *text type* in different languages. The texts are not translations of each other.

concept (see p. 38): a specific thing in a specialized subject field that is usually designated by a *term*. A concept may be a physical object (e.g. organism), but it can also be something more abstract, such as an action (e.g. to catalyse), a process (e.g. photosynthesis) or a quality (e.g. negative).

concordance (see p. 3): a display showing all the occurrences of your *search patterns* in their immediate contexts. See *bilingual concordance, monolingual concordance.*

context search (see p. 200): a type of search that allows you to look for a specific *search pattern* that is in the vicinity of another *search pattern* (e.g. find all occurrences of 'optical' when it is within five words of 'scanner').

corpus (see p. 1): a large collection of authentic texts that have been gathered in electronic form according to a specific set of criteria. See *comparable corpus, parallel corpus.*

corpus linguistics (see p. 3): an *empirical* approach or methodology for studying language use by examining authentic data with the help of computer tools.

de-terminologization (see p. 26): the process whereby *terms* that once belonged exclusively to a specialized domain make their way into the everyday lives of ordinary people, either through the mass media or through direct impact (e.g. 'AIDS', 'BSE', 'Ebola').

DTD (Document Type Definition) (see p. 79): a definition usually expressed in *SGML* which stipulates what the structure of a document is going to be and which elements are necessary.

frequency list (see p. 88): a *word list* ranked according to frequency of occurrence in a *corpus.*

general reference corpus (see p. 3): a *corpus* that can be taken as representative of a given language as a whole and can therefore be used to make generalized observations about that particular language. This type of corpus typically contains written and spoken material, a broad cross-section of *text types* and focuses on *LGP.*

glossary (see p. 4): a list of *terms* in one or more languages, often with definitions, contextual information and other information relevant to the meaning and usage of the terms.

HTML (hypertext markup language) (see p. 16): a *markup* language, based on *SGML*, designed to facilitate storage of documents on the Web.

interference (see p. 18): in a language learning situation, this refers to problems that arise when your knowledge of one language causes you to make mistakes when communicating in another language. For example, you might use English words but organize your sentence according to French grammar (e.g. 'the car red' instead of 'the red car').

key word list (see p. 115): a *word list* of all of the words that occur with an unusually high frequency in one *corpus* compared with another.

knowledge-rich context (see p. 3): a context that contains a definition or explanation of the meaning of a *term* or *concept*.

learner corpus (see p. 13): a *corpus* that contains texts written by learners of a foreign language.

lemma (see p. 116): a word in a corpus that is used to include and represent all related forms. For example, 'be' could be used as the lemma to represent all the forms of this verb, including 'be', 'am', 'is', 'are', 'was', 'were'.

lexicography (see p. 11): the discipline concerned with writing dictionaries. People who write dictionaries are called lexicographers.

LGP (language for general purposes) (see p. 1): the language that we use every day to talk about ordinary things in a variety of common situations.

LSP (language for special purposes) (see p. 1): the language that is used to discuss specialized fields of knowledge.

markup (see p. 3): the automatic insertion of marks, known as tags, to make explicit the appearance and structure of a document.

metaphor (see p. 5): a linguistic device whereby you describe a thing (e.g. person, object, idea) by referring to something else that has similar characteristics to the thing you are trying to describe (e.g. if you say 'Tom is a fox' it means that you think he has the characteristics of a fox, such as being sly or cunning).

monolingual concordance (see p. 120): a display showing the results of a search in a monolingual *corpus*. Typically, all the occurrences of your search pattern are centred vertically on the screen surrounded by their immediate contexts.

neologism (see p. 5): a new word that comes into a language. Neologisms can be formed by combining letters or words in a new way, or by giving a new meaning to an existing word.

noise (see p. 123): unwanted patterns that are retrieved during a *corpus* search.

parallel corpus (see p. 3): a *corpus* containing texts and their translations into one or more languages. These texts are linked through the process of *alignment*.

POS (part-of-speech) tagging (see p. 3): an *annotation* system whereby each word in a *corpus* is automatically assigned a grammatical tag corresponding to the word class (e.g. noun, verb, adjective) to which it belongs.

SGML (Standard Generalized Markup Language, ISO8879) (see p. 78): a *markup* language enabling you to encode documents so that the documents can be recognized by different pieces of software. The emphasis is on formally encoding the structure and type of a document.

search engine (see p. 61): a tool that will search the Web for pages containing your *search pattern*. The results of this search are displayed as a series of links to the corresponding pages.

search pattern (see p. 89): the linguistic pattern that you enter into a concordancer or search engine. This could be a single-word, a group of words or it could be a combination of words and special characters (e.g. wildcard (*), *boolean operators* (AND, OR, NOT)).

semantic annotation (see p. 84): an *annotation* system whereby semantic field tags are added to all words in a corpus in an attempt to facilitate disambiguation.

silence (see p. 169): the case where patterns that you would like to retrieve from a *corpus* are not retrieved. This may be because your search pattern was not well formulated.

source language (see p. 193): in translation, the language in which the original text is written and from which you are translating. See *target language*.

specialized corpus (see p. 177): a *corpus* that focuses on a particular aspect of a language. It could be restricted to the *LSP* of a particular subject field, to a specific *text type*, to a particular language variety or to the language used by members of a certain demographic group (e.g. teenagers).

standardized type/token ratio (see p. 110): the number of different word forms (types) per X number of words (tokens). If X = 1000, the type/token ratio is calculated for the first 1000 words in the text, and then it is calculated again for the next 1000 words and so on. A running average is computed, which means that you get a standardized type/token ratio based on consecutive 1000–word chunks of text.

stop list (see p. 113): a list of items (words, numbers, etc.) which you wish to exclude from your analysis.

subject directory (see p. 61): a catalogue of web sites that have been organized according to subject fields. Each field is broken down into subfields, which are further broken down so that your search is progressively narrowed.

syntactic annotation (see p. 84): an *annotation* system whereby information about the syntactic structure of sentences is added to a *corpus* that has been previously tagged with word class information (see *POS tagging*).

target language (see p. 138): in translation, the language into which you are translating. See *source language*.

term (see p. 3): a word (single word or multiword unit) used in a specialized domain with a clearly defined meaning.

term extraction (see p. 165): a process whereby a computer program searches through a *corpus* and identifies candidate *terms*. The resulting list must later be verified by a human.

terminologist (see p. 26): a person who specializes in the collection and description of *terms*, often producing *glossaries* of specialized domains.

text type (see p. 50): a group of texts that have shared stylistic features. For example, user manuals belong to one text type, advertisements to another and legal contracts to another.

token (see p. 3): each word in a corpus. The total number of words in a corpus is referred to as the number of tokens, so if a corpus contains 1 million words, then it has 1 million tokens.

type (see p. 3): each different word in a corpus. Language is repetitive, which means that some words will appear in the corpus more than once. When calculating the number of types in the corpus, you do not count each word (*tokens*), you only count each different word. So, in a sentence such as 'the cat sat on the mat' you have six tokens but only five types.

XML (extensible markup language) (see p. 83): a *markup* language based on *SGML* designed to facilitate storage and exchange of documents on the Web. Unlike *HTML*, it is capable of handling highly complex documents.

word list (see p. 3): a list of all of the words in a *corpus*, usually produced automatically. See *alphabetical list, frequency list, keyword list*.

Bibliography

Ahmad, Khurshid and Margaret Rogers (2001) 'Corpus linguistics and terminology extraction', in Sue Ellen Wright and Gerhard Budin (eds) *Handbook of Terminology Management* (Vol. 2), Amsterdam/Philadelphia: John Benjamins, 725–60.

Aston, Guy (ed.) (2001) *Learning with Corpora*, Houston: Athelstan; Bologna: CLUEB.

Aston, Guy and Burnard, Lou (1998) *The BNC Handbook: Exploring the British National Corpus with SARA*, Edinburgh: Edinburgh University Press.

Atkins, B. T. S., Clear, Jeremy and Ostler, Nicholas (1992) 'Corpus design criteria', *Literary and Linguistic Computing* 7(1): 1–16.

Austermühl, Frank (2001) *Electronic Tools for Translators*, Manchester: St Jerome Publishing.

AVIATOR/APRIL: http://www.rdues.liv.ac.uk/april.shtml

Baayen, Harald and Renouf, Antoinette (1996) 'Chronicling the times: productive lexical innovations in an English newspaper', *Language* 72(1): 69–96.

Barlow, Michael (1996) 'Parallel texts in language teaching', in S. Botley, J. Glass, T. McEnery and A. Wilson (eds) *Proceedings of Teaching and Language Corpora 1996*, Vol. 9, special issue, Lancaster: UCREL, 45–56.

Barnbrook, Geoff (1996) *Language and Computers*, Edinburgh: Edinburgh University Press.

Bennison, Peter and Bowker, Lynne (2000) 'Designing a tool for exploiting bilingual comparable corpora', *Proceedings of the Second International Conference on Language Resources and Evaluation* (Vol. 1), Paris: ELRA, 513–16.

Biber, Douglas, Conrad, Susan and Reppen, Randi (1998) *Corpus Linguistics: Investigating Language Structure and Use*, Cambridge: Cambridge University Press.

Botley, Simon P., McEnery, Anthony and Wilson, Andrew (eds) (2000) *Multilingual Corpora in Teaching and Research*, Amsterdam: Rodopi.

Bowker, Lynne (2000) 'Towards a methodology for exploiting specialized target language corpora as translation resources', *International Journal of Corpus Linguistics* 5(1): 17–52.

—— (forthcoming) 'Corpus-based applications for translator training: exploring the possibilities', in Sylviane Granger, Jacques Lerot and Stephanie Petch-Tyson (eds) *Corpus-Based Approaches to Contrastive Linguistics and Translation Studies*, Amsterdam: Rodopi.

Cabré, M. Teresa (1999) *Terminology: Theory, Methods and Applications*, edited by J. C. Sager, translated by J. A. DeCesaris, Amsterdam/Philadelphia: John Benjamins.

Cabré, M. Teresa, Estopà Bagot, Rosa and Vivaldi Palatresi, Jordi (2001) 'Automatic term detection: a review of current systems', in Didier Bourigault, Christian Jacquemin and Marie-Claude L'Homme (eds) *Recent Advances in Computational Terminology*, Amsterdam/Philadelphia: John Benjamins, 53–87.

Corpus Encoding Standard: http://www.cs.vassar.edu/CES/

Douglas, Dan (1999) *Assessing Language for Specific Purposes*, Cambridge: Cambridge University Press.

Dubuc, Robert (1997) *Terminology: A Practical Approach*, adapted by Elaine Kennedy, Brossard, Quebec: Linguatech.

Dudley-Evans, Tony and St John, Maggie Jo (1998) *Developments in English for Specific Purposes*, Cambridge: Cambridge University Press.

Engwall, Gunnel (1994) 'Not chance but choice: criteria in corpus creation', in B. T. S. Atkins and A. Zampolli (eds) *Computational Approaches to the Lexicon*, Oxford: Oxford University Press, 49–82.

Gale, William A. and Church, Kenneth W. (1993) 'A program for aligning sentences in bilingual corpora', *Computational Linguistics*, 19(1): 75–90.

Galinski, Christian and Budin, Gerhard (1996) 'Terminology', in Ronald Cole *et al.* (eds) *Survey of the State of the Art in Human Language Technology*. http://cslu.cse.ogi.edu/HLTsurvey/ch12node7.html#SECTION125

Garside, Roger, Leech, Geoffrey and McEnery, Anthony (eds) (1997) *Corpus Annotation: Linguistic Information From Computer Text Corpora*, London/New York: Longman.

Gaussier, Eric (2001) 'General considerations on bilingual terminology extraction', in Didier Bourigault, Christian Jacquemin and Marie-Claude L'Homme (eds) *Recent Advances in Computational Terminology*, Amsterdam/Philadelphia: John Benjamins, 167–83.

Granger, Sylviane (ed.) (1998) *Learner English on Computer*, London/New York: Addison-Wesley-Longman.

ICLE: http://www.bricle.f2s.com/icle.htm

Johansson, Stig, Ebeling, Jarle and Hofland, Knut (1996) 'Coding and aligning the English–Norwegian parallel corpus' in Karin Aijmer and Bengt Altenberg (eds) *Languages in Contrast: Papers from a Symposium on Text-based Cross-Linguistic Studies, Lund 4–5 March 1994*, Lund: Lund University Press, 87–112.

Kageura, Kyo and Bin Umino (1996) 'Methods of automatic term recognition: a review', *Terminology* 3(2): 259–90.

Kennedy, Graeme (1998) *An Introduction to Corpus Linguistics*, London/New York: Longman.

Kittredge, Richard and Lehberger, John (eds) (1982) *Sublanguage: Studies of Language in Restricted Semantic Domains*, Berlin: Walter de Gruyter.

Kytö, Merja, Rissanen, Matti and Wright, Susan (eds) (1994) *Corpora Across the Centuries: Proceedings of the First International Colloquium on English Diachronic Corpora*, Amsterdam: Rodopi.

Lakoff, George and Johnson, Mark (1980) *Metaphors We Live By*, Chicago: University of Chicago Press.

Laviosa, Sara (ed.) (1998) *The Corpus-based Approach*, special issue of *Meta* 43(4).

Leech, Geoffrey, Myers, Greg and Thomas, Jenny (eds) (1995) *Spoken English on Computer: Transcription, Mark-up and Application*, New York: Longman.

Leech, Geoffrey and Smith, Nicholas: The British National Corpus (Version 2) with Improved Word-class Tagging. UCREL, Lancaster University: http://www.comp.lancs.ac.uk/ucrel/bnc2/bnc2postag_manuel.htm

Lindquist, Hans (1999) 'Electronic corpora as tools for translation', in Gunilla Anderman and Margaret Rogers (eds) *Word, Text, Translation*, Clevedon: Multi-lingual Matters.

Malmkjær, Kirsten (1998) 'Love thy Neighbour: will parallel corpora endear linguists to translators?', *Meta* 43(4): 534–41.

McEnery, Tony and Wilson, Andrew (1996) *Corpus Linguistics*, Edinburgh: Edinburgh University Press.

Meyer, Ingrid (2001) 'Extracting knowledge-rich contexts for terminography: a conceptual and methodological framework', in Didier Bourigault, Christian Jacquemin and Marie-Claude L'Homme (eds) *Recent Advances in Computational Terminology*, Amsterdam/Philadelphia: John Benjamins: 279–302.

Meyer, Ingrid and Mackintosh, Kristen (2000) 'When terms move into our every-day lives: an overview of de-terminologization', *Terminology* 6(1): 111–38.

Meyer Ingrid, Zaluski, Victoria and Mackintosh, Kristen (1997) 'Metaphorical Internet terms: a conceptual and structural analysis', *Terminology* 4(1): 1–33.

Mok, Olivia (1995) 'Accessibility of specialized lexicon as criterion for quality assessment of legal translations', *Babel* 41(4): 193–208.

Monachini, Monica, Peters, Carol, and Picchi, Eugenio (1993) 'The PISA tools: a survey of computational tools for corpus-based lexicon building', DELIS Working Paper for TR01/1–2.

Partington, Alan (1998) *Patterns and Meanings: Using Corpora for English Language Research and Teaching*, Amsterdam/Philadelphia: John Benjamins.

Pearson, Jennifer (1996) 'Electronic texts and concordances in the translation class-room', *Teanga* 16: 85–95.

—— (1998) *Terms in Context*, Amsterdam/Philadelphia: John Benjamins.

—— (2000) 'Une tentative d'exploitation bi-directionnelle d'un corpus bilingue', *Cahiers de Grammaire* 25, 53–69.

Peters, Carol, Picchi, Eugenio, and Biagini, Lisa (1996) 'Parallel and comparable bilingual corpora in language teaching and learning', in S. Botley, J. Glass, T. McEnery and A. Wilson (eds) *Proceedings of Teaching and Language Corpora 1996*, Vol. 9 – special issue, Lancaster: UCREL: 68–82.

Sager, Juan C. (1990) *A Practical Course in Terminology Processing*, Amsterdam/Philadelphia: John Benjamins.

Sager, Juan C., Dungworth, David and McDonald, Peter F. (1980) *English Special Languages*, Wiesbaden: Oscar Brandstetter Verlag.

SGML: An Introduction: http://www.incontext.com/SGMLinfo.html

Sinclair, John (1991) *Corpus, Concordance, Collocation*, Oxford: Oxford University Press.

Stubbs, Michael (1996) *Text and Corpus Analysis*, Oxford: Blackwell.

TEI Guidelines for Electronic Text Encoding and Interchange: http://etext/virginia.edu/bin/tei-tocs?div=DIV1&id=HD

Thomson, Paul, and Tribble, Chris (2001) 'Looking at citations: using corpora in English for academic purposes', *Language Learning and Technology* 5(3): 91–105. http://llt.msu.edu/vol5num3/thompson/default/html

Tognini-Bonelli, Elena (2001) *Corpus Linguistics at Work*, Amsterdam/Philadelphia: John Benjamins.

Tribble, Chris and Jones, Glyn (1997) *Concordances in the Classroom*, Houston: Athelstan.

Ulrych, Margherita (1997) 'The impact of multilingual parallel concordancing on translation', in Barbara Lewandowska-Tomaszczyk and Patrick James Melia (eds) *PALC'97: Practical Applications in Language Corpora*, Lodz: University of Lodz, 421–35.

Van Guilder, Linda (1995) Automated Part of Speech Tagging: A Brief Overview http://www.georgetown.edu/cball/ling361/tagging_overview.html

Wynne, Martin (1996) *A Post-Editor's Guide to CLAWS Tagging.* http://www.comp.lancs.ac.uk/computing/users/eiamjw/claws/claws7.html#_Toc334868023

Zanettin, Federico (2001) 'Swimming in words: corpora, translation and language learning', in Guy Aston (ed.) *Learning with Corpora*, Houston: Athelstan; Bologna: CLUEB, 177–97.

Index